1995

This major collection of essays on the Marquis de Sade encompasses a wide range of critical approaches to his *œuvre*, including some of the most celebrated texts in Sade scholarship. It focuses on several distinctly contemporary areas of interest: the explicitly libidinal components of Sade's work and the effects they engender; the textual and narrative apparatus which supports these operations; the ethical and political concerns which arise from them, and the problematic issues surrounding the conceptual closure of representation. Sade is placed at the centre of current debates in literary and philosophical criticism, feminist and gender theory, aesthetics, rhetoric, and eighteenth-century French cultural history, and this volume will be of interest to a wide range of readers across these disciplines.

CAMBRIDGE STUDIES IN FRENCH 52

SADE AND THE NARRATIVE
OF TRANSGRESSION

CAMBRIDGE STUDIES IN FRENCH

Recent titles in this series include

A complete list of books in the series is given at the end of the volume.

SADE AND THE
NARRATIVE OF
TRANSGRESSION

EDITED BY

DAVID B. ALLISON
MARK S. ROBERTS

State University of New York at Stony Brook

ALLEN S. WEISS

New York University

CAMBRIDGE
UNIVERSITY PRESS

Published by the Press Syndicate of the University of Cambridge
The Pitt Building, Trumpington Street, Cambridge CB2 1RP
40 West 20th Street, New York, NY 10011–4211, USA
10 Stamford Road, Oakleigh, Melbourne 3166, Australia

First published 1995

Printed in Great Britain at the University Press, Cambridge

A catalogue record for this book is available from the British Library

Library of Congress cataloguing in publication data

Sade and the narrative of transgression / edited by David B. Allison,
Mark S. Roberts, Allen S. Weiss.
p.   cm.
Includes bibliographical references and index.
ISBN 0 521 44415 2 (hardback)
1. Sade, marquis de, 1740–1814 – Criticism and interpretation.
2. Erotic literature, French – History and criticism. 3. Narration
(Rhetoric) 4. Sex in literature. I. Allison, David B.
II. Roberts, Mark S. III. Weiss, Allen S., 1953– .
PQ2063.S3S153 1995
843'. 6 – dc20 94–20377 CIP

ISBN 0 521 44415 2 hardback

Contents

Contributors

DAVID B. ALLISON teaches philosophy at the State University of New York at Stony Brook, and has written and translated numerous articles on Nietzsche and contemporary French philosophy. He has edited the *New Nietzsche*, and with Roberts and Weiss, edited *Psychosis and Sexuality: Towards a Post-Analytical View of the Schreber Case*, and *Nonsense*.

GEORGES BATAILLE was one of the leading, and one of the most eclectic, intellectual figures of the twentieth century in France, having written fiction, sociology, philosophy, and art and literary criticism. He directed the journals *Documents*, *Acéphale*, and *Critique*, and founded the Collège de Sociologie. His *Oeuvres complètes* have been published by Gallimard.

JANE GALLOP is the author of *The Daughter's Seduction: Feminism and Psychoanalysis*, *Intersections: A Reading of Sade with Bataille, Blanchot, and Klossowski*, and *Reading Lacan*. Professor Gallop teaches in the Department of English and Comparative Literature, the University of Wisconsin, Milwaukee.

MARCEL HÉNAFF is Professor of Literature at the University of California at San Diego. He is the author of *Sade: L'invention du corps libertin*.

DALIA JUDOVITZ is the author of *Subjectivity and Representation: The Origins of Modern Thought in Descartes*, and several articles on traditional and contemporary French literature and philosophy. She is currently completing a book on the work of Marcel Duchamp. Professor Judovitz teaches French at Emory University.

PIERRE KLOSSOWSKI has had a varied and extremely influential career. After his association with Bataille in the Collège de Sociologie, he wrote a seminal work on Sade, *Sade mon prochain*, and a major work on Nietzsche, *Nietzsche et le cercle vicieux*. His novels include *La Vocation suspendue*, *Roberte ce soir*, and *Le Baphomet*, and he has translated Nietzsche, Wittgenstein, Heidegger, and Virgil. He currently devotes himself to painting.

ALPHONSO LINGIS has written numerous articles and books concerning contemporary philosophy and culture. His most recent works include *Libido: The French Existential Theories* and *Excesses: Eros and Culture*, as well as the English translation of Pierre Klossowski's *Sade My Neighbor*. Professor Lingis teaches philosophy at the Pennsylvania State University.

JEAN-FRANÇOIS LYOTARD is one of the founding members of the Collège International de Philosophie, and is Professor Emeritus at the University of Paris VIII. He is the author of numerous books in aesthetics and philosophy, including *The Postmodern Condition*, *Economie libidinale*, *Discours, figure*, and *The Differend*.

NANCY K. MILLER is the author of *Subject to Change: Reading Feminist Writers* and *The Heroine's Text: Readings in the French and English Novel. 1722–1782*, and edited *The Poetics of Gender*. Professor Miller teaches English at the City University of New York.

MARK S. ROBERTS has written extensively on aesthetics and communication theory, and has translated works by Lyotard, Dufrenne, and other contemporary French thinkers. He teaches at Suffolk Community College in New York.

PHILIPPE ROGER is Directeur de Recherche in the Centre National de la Recherche Scientifique in France. He co-edited *Sade, écrire la crise*, and is the author of *Sade: La philosophie dans le pressoir* and *Roland Barthes, roman*.

LAWRENCE SCHEHR is Professor of French at the University of South Alabama. He has published widely on modern

American and European literature; his book *Flaubert and Sons* appeared in 1986, and his recently completed *The Shock of Men* deals with gender-challenged hermeneutics in Proust, Barthes, Renaud, Camus, and Tournier.

CHANTAL THOMAS is Directrice de Recherche in the Centre National de Recherche la Scientifique in France. She is the author of *Sade, l'œil de la lettre, Casanova, un voyage libertin, La Reine scélérate. Marie-Antoinette dans les pamphlets*, and *Thomas Bernhard*. Her most recent book is *Sade* (1994).

ALLEN S. WEISS is the author of *Iconology and Perversion, The Aesthetics of Excess, Miroirs de l'infini: Le jardin à la française et la métaphysique au XVIIe siècle*, and *Shattered Forms: Art Brut. Phantasms, Modernism*. Professor Weiss teaches in the Cinema Studies program at New York University.

Acknowledgments

We would like to thank the following for their permission to use material in the present volume: University of Minnesota Press for permission to use "The use value of D. A. F. Sade," by Georges Bataille. Northwestern University Press for permission to use Pierre Klossowski's "Sade, or the philosopher–villain." Athlone Press for Jean-François Lyotard's "Libidinal economy in Sade and Klossowski." *Enclitic* for permission to use Jane Gallop's "Sade, mothers, and other women." State University of New York Press for Allen S. Weiss's "Structures of exchange, acts of transgression." All other material has been printed by permission of the authors. Nancy K. Miller's "Gender and narrative possibilities" originally appeared in *L'Esprit Créateur* (Winter 1975), under the title "*Juliette* and the posterity of prosperity." Marcel Hēnaff's "The encyclopedia of excess" appeared in different form in the issue on Sade of *Obligues* 12–13, 1977. Chantal Thomas's "Fautanizing Juliette" appeared in *Tel Quel* 74, 1977, a special issue on "Recherches Féminines," edited by Julia Kristeva. Passages quoted from Sade's own works are, unless otherwise noted, drawn from the Richard Seaver and Austryn Wainhouse English-language translations, published by Grove Press.

We would like to acknowledge Stephen Michelman and Brian Schroeder for their assistance in the preparation of the present manuscript. We would also like to thank Hélène Volat for compiling the bibliograpy that appears at the end of the volume, and Kate Brett, of Cambridge University Press, for her support.

Introduction

David B. Allison, Mark S. Roberts, and Allen S. Weiss

The name "Sade," previously the cause of visceral disquietude
and moral panic, now sends us directly to the archives. What
was once scandalous is now part of our literary heritage, a
"classic." To introduce the present volume, we might briefly
consider the conditions by which this drastic change of reception occurred, and the reasons why, despite the entry of Sade
into "acquired knowledge," this philosopher of the bedroom
still claims a decisive role in understanding both the limits
of human possibility and the emerging critique of culture in
postmodernist discourse.

Nineteenth-century belles-lettres abound in references to
Sade by the most diverse group of writers, including such
figures as Michelet, Stendhal, Baudelaire, Flaubert, Fourier,
Huysmans, and Swinburne. These writers demonstrated varied interest in Sade's work, although most, like Swinburne,
admired it from afar. This interest was countered, at the end
of the century, by a vehement disapproval in other quar-
ters: namely, the appropriation of Sade's name by numerous
"scientific" medical authorities, who stigmatized it with a psychological reference of violence and opprobrium – sadism.

It was not until the rediscovery of Sade by Apollinaire and,
later, by the Surrealists in the 1920s, that he came to play a
central role in modern intellectual history. This interest was
in great part made possible by Maurice Heine's efforts to
establish and distribute an accurate contemporary edition
of Sade's works. The Surrealists – most notably Breton,
Aragon, Eluard, Char, and Peret – who celebrated Sade's
work did so with a double intent. There was an activist, even

revolutionary, motivation aimed at overthrowing bourgeois mentality and culture (certainly derived from the Dadaist desire to *"épater le bourgeois"* – hence the Surrealists' thrill at the extremes of Sadean outrageousness). But there was also an aesthetic, psychological motivation, aimed at appropriating Sade's thought as a singular precursor to Surrealism. This was due to its eminence within the broader literary genre of the fantastic, as well as to its preoccupation with limit experiences, especially regarding the relations between death and eros, two favorite Surrealist themes. Yet even here, the name of Sade was often invoked – and apologized for – with regard to the scandalous nature of the allusion, rather than in reference to the content of his discourse. This is apparent, for example, in the classic Surrealist film, Buñuel and Dalí's *L'Age d'or* (1930), where reference to Sade's *The 120 Days of Sodom* in the film's epilogue is made with appropriately shocking and scandalous effect.

The year 1930 saw a rupture in the Surrealist movement, marked by the publication of Breton's *Second Manifesto of Surrealism*, in which Georges Bataille in particular was denounced and expelled from the movement for what Breton (being a somewhat traditional moralist in the guise of a revolutionary) saw as Bataille's baseness and vileness, his interest in what was most unseemly and corrupt. The ensuing polemic centered around the figure of Sade, and Bataille responded to Breton's accusations by claiming that in fact the Surrealists were but apologists for Sade, mere utopian sentimentalists, further accusing them of "pretentious idealist aberrations." In thus parting from the Surrealists, Bataille professed a "heterology" of base materialism, founded on a sociological and literary analysis of the relations between contemporary society and the sacred, excessive, wasteful, and sacrificial aspects of culture. In the context of his critique of Western rationality, Bataille found Sade to be a key figure in the analysis of what he termed sovereign inner experience. It was this debate which marked the beginnings of the modern investigation of Sade's work as an independent and coherent system of thought.

Pierre Klossowski was part of Bataille's entourage during

the period following the break with the Surrealists, which culminated with the founding of the journal *Acéphale* and the Collège de Sociologie. Klossowski, too, found Sade central to every stage of his work, and in 1947 he published a collection of brilliant essays, *Sade mon prochain*, which continues to be one of the seminal texts of Sade scholarship. Here, the relation between the existence of evil, presented by Sade in its hyperbolic and encyclopedic form, and the existence of God is examined. Employing the theme of a destructive theology, where Nature itself is the very principle and source of evil, Klossowski showed how Sade demanded the substitution of radical evil for God. Unlike rationalist forms of atheism – which invert monotheism by replacing God with man – Sade, basing his thinking on a radical materialism acting as a transcendental fatalism, proposed to substitute an omnipotent natural system of causality for the notion of Divine causation.

We find a somewhat different version of this Sadean *amor intellectualis diaboli* in the sections devoted to Sade in Adorno and Horkheimer's *Dialectic of Enlightenment* (1944). In Sade, the manipulation of rational thought is utilized as a critique of rationality itself; Sade's efforts are compared to those of Nietzsche, in the light of the contemporary political implications of Fascism, as an aberration of instrumental reason. Thus, in this modern version of an old moralizing theme (using Sade as a hyperbolic and perhaps ironic example), Adorno and Horkheimer see Sade and Nietzsche as providing a devastating critique of rationalist, Kantian, utopian models – i.e. of the very notion of truth itself – with all of its horrifying political ramifications.

The year 1947 was important in Sade scholarship. Along with the publication of Klossowski's work there appeared Maurice Blanchot's "A la rencontre de Sade" (republished two years later in his *Lautréamont et Sade*), as well as the first volumes of Jean-Jacques Pauvert's edition of Sade's complete works. Blanchot saw Sade as providing the first instance in which philosophy itself is taken as the product of mental aberration, a deviant construction of the passions – in Sade's case, the result of his lengthy incarceration. Thus, Blanchot accounts for the extreme, monstrous forms of sovereignty manifested in Sade as the very apogee of Sade's philosophical system. The effects of aberrant theorization and narration – i.e. the subversion of classical reasoning – in turn serve to liberate the reader's own irrational forces.

Following these key publications, and the appearance of the complete edition of Sade's writings, there were numerous studies of Sade by such notable figures in French intellectual life as Simone de Beauvoir, Maurice Nadeau, Raymond Queneau, Albert Camus, and Jean Paulhan. There also followed, in 1957–58, the infamous trial of Pauvert on charges of distributing pornography (a case which, for that moment at least, he lost). Yet in contradistinction to this notoriety and to the rather negative reconsideration of the ethical elements in Sade's texts both in literary criticism and in the courts, this decade also witnessed the publication of Gilbert Lély's monumental critical biography of Sade, *La Vie du Marquis de Sade* (volume I appeared in 1952, volume II in 1957).

The 1960s saw the efforts which were finally to establish Sade – despite, or perhaps because of, his subversive, revolutionary and perverse attractions – in the literary canon. The highpoints of this re-evaluation and minor canonization were the Colloque d'Aix in 1966, the proceedings of which were published in 1968 as *Le Marquis de Sade*; the republication of Klossowski's *Sade mon prochain* with a major new article, "Le philosophe scélérat" (published in translation in the present volume), in 1967; and in the same year, a special issue of *Tel Quel* (no. 28) on Sade, with articles by Philippe Sollers, Klossowski, Hubert Damisch, Michel Tort, and Roland Barthes (an article which was to be part of his major work, *Sade, Fourier, Loyola*, published in 1971). It was the readings of those associated with the then influential review *Tel Quel* that established Sade as a figure central to the discourse of poststructuralism; a discourse which included the writings of Foucault (on the relations between transgression, politics, and discourse), Deleuze (on the radical difference between sadism and masochism, as a critique of psychoanalytic theory), Barthes (on the rhetorical and poetic rules of the Sadean text), and Lacan (on the subversion of the Kantian ethical imperative by the Sadean imperative of pleasure). The major thrust that connected all of the above works was a concerted, collective attempt to reconcile Marxian dialectic with psychoanalytic metapsychology, in the light of semiotics – thus to establish a theory of subjectivity according to the historical-material conditions of signifying practice. Sade's place in this contemporary project parallels that assigned by *Tel Quel* to Artaud and Bataille, the renegade Surrealists, as models for a new, heterogeneous, revolutionary practice marked by an avant-garde mode of textual production.

Now well established as a "literary" and philosophical figure – yet with little or no loss of his radicalness as a writer – Sade continued to attract interest through the 1970s and 1980s. In 1977 there appeared a special issue of *Obliques* dedicated to Sade. It was edited by Michel Camus, and included documents and articles by most of the major scholars in the field. Numerous books also appeared, notably Françoise Laugaa-Traut's *Lectures de Sade* (1973), Philippe Roger's *Sade: La Philosophie dans le pressoir* (1976), Marcel Hénaff's *Sade: L'Invention du corps libertin* (1978), and Chantal Thomas's *Sade, l'œil de la lettre* (1978). In 1981 a Colloque de Cérisy devoted to Sade was organized by Michel Camus and Philippe Roger, the proceedings of which were published as *Sade, écrire la crise* (1981).

The growth of interest in Sade did not go unnoticed in the arts. The most notable dramatic works were Yukio Mishima's 1965 play *Madame de Sade*, and Peter Weiss's *Marat/Sade* (1965), both of which were widely produced. Sylvano Bussotti wrote a musical composition entitled *La Passion selon Sade* (1965–66), and Pier Paolo Pasolini produced a film, *Salò o le 120 giornate de Sodoma*, worthy of mention not only for its cinematic interest but also for its continued notoriety.

Interest was drawn to Sade in the English-speaking world by such texts as Geoffrey Gorer's *The Life and Ideas of the Marquis de Sade* (1962), but peaked with the Grove Press translations of Sade's major works, accompanied by several of the already classic critical texts by Klossowski, Blanchot, Paulhan, and de Beauvoir. Grove Press later also published a translation of Lély's biography of Sade. Early scholarly attention was focused in the important 1965 issue of *Yale French Studies*, followed by later critical works, such as Angela Carter's *The Sadeian Woman and the Ideology of Pornography* (1978) and Jane Gallop's *Intersections: A Reading of Sade with Bataille, Blanchot, and Klossowski* (1981).

Currently, there is a strong continuation of this interest in Sade, in great part spurred on by Pauvert's republication of Sade's complete works (long out of print), accompanied by a book-length introduction by Annie Le Brun, *Soudain un bloc d'abîme, Sade* (1986), and a new biography in three volumes by Pauvert, *Sade vivant*. This sixteen-volume project will be followed by another major series, edited by Maurice Lever and Sade's descendant, Thibault de Sade, consisting of six volumes of previously unpublished tales, theater, poetry, letters, and essays, as well as an entirely new biography utilizing much previously unknown material, as well as extensive documentation and information from the Sade family archives. Finally, as the ultimate canonization of Sade in the literary hierarchy, the first of a three-volume set has appeared in Gallimard's series La Pléiade, edited by Michel Delon and prefaced by Jean Deprun. With the dramatically increased attention given to Sade recently, there is thus little doubt that this once scandalous and intentionally ignored figure has taken up a central place in current literary and philosophical scholarship – a secure place in the archives.

Despite the burgeoning renewal of interest in Sade's work, his intellectual legacy has hardly been resolved. Nonetheless, in recent years, most significant discussion has tended to focus upon a few areas: the explicitly libidinal components of Sade's work and the effects they engender; the textual apparatus which supports these operations: the ethical and political concerns which mark the effects of the Sadean œuvre; and the problematic issues surrounding the conceptual closure of representation. These general areas of interest have of late been discussed in terms of particular philosophical problems, such as the constitution of subjectivity and gender identity, the question of classical rationality and the moral imperatives it engenders, the limits of practical and intellectual categories and what escapes or precludes these defining sets – the imagination, the excesses of rapture, erotic possession, and violence – in short, what challenges every form of coherency and meaning, transgression itself. It is perhaps under the rubric of transgression that one most dramatically arrives at the "danger" of Sade's enterprise. At issue, for our present concerns, is the radical heterogeneity of libidinal productions, which subtends Sadean transgression and which lends a heretofore unthinkable volatility to the very codes which govern civilized existence.

It was Bataille who first showed the enormous importance of transgression by demonstrating that the composition of the civil subject is effectively that of a fully coded subject. As such, the individual finds his identity, his very interiority, in the interstices of social, economic, ethical, religious, moral, sexual, and linguistic encoding. Sade's extraordinary preoccupation with codes, laws, rules, and classifications of all kinds presented an exemplary terrain for Bataille's investigation. If Sade were thus to have a "use value" as Bataille claims, it might be analogous to the role of Freud's *Civilization and its Discontents*, in that he reveals what subtends the veneer of rational and civil society – the monstrous, uncontrolled, anarchic series of drives and passions. In this sense, what is conventionally termed "sadistic" is but one of the many perversions wrought by civil conformity itself. For Bataille's Sade, on the contrary, it is the enormous set of possibilities tied to the productions of libidinal heterogeneity, unconstrained by limits, bonds, and "good taste," which offer up to us the spectacle of the Sadean individual's "base materiality." As a "trangressive" subject, cast in opposition to these codes, the Sadean figure stands as a veritable indictment of the civil order. All that is most repulsive – revealed in Bataille's concepts of heterological practice, his excremental vision – stands as the emblem or inscription of the otherwise unrepresentable libidinal drives. Exceeding every canon of Western discourse and literature, Sade's texts are thereby empowered, indeed driven, by this set of libidinal forces – hence the disgust they traditionally provoke.

The notions of perversion, anomaly, and integral monstrosity, so central to the Sadean enterprise, are forcefully articulated by Pierre Klossowski in his "Sade, or the philosopher–villain." The terms all refer to those singularities that are excluded from universal reason. Thus these terms contest the laws of utility, conservation, and rationality, in that they are the very reverse of procreation, of what Freud called the "life drive." The height of such libertine perversion is, according to Klossowski, the practice of sodomy. Sodomy is the extreme form of the transgression of norms, a wasteful, unproductive, and useless simulacrum for "normal" reproductive sexuality. As such, it specifically entails the reversal of everyday morality and rationality, not as its simple negation, but rather through a cultivated intellectual apathy and waste, through an "economy" of unproductiveness, one no longer guided by teleology, profit, or even by the "natural" production of pleasure, i.e. orgasm.

The set of monstrous perversions, so excluded from universal reason, is likewise unassimilable to any strictly political economy. Nonetheless, the libertine subjects of the Sadean enterprise have already sublated, through an ironic reversal, the political dimension to the libidinal: hence, each is considered a member of another economy (however fleeting), namely, that of the "Society of the Friends of Crime." In the absence of any natural or political "rights" – indeed, of any transcendental grounding whatsoever – Klossowski argues that Sade's famous injunction, "One more effort, Frenchmen, if you are to become republicans," can only be seen as a hideous derogation of revolutionary idealism.

Exploring the workings of a libidinal economy, as envisioned by Klossowski, Jean-François Lyotard demonstrates how the terms of classical economic exchange are inverted to become mere simulacra of rights – guaranteed by no one, by no thing.

The vaunted egalitarianism of republican ideals is but a set of momentarily agreed-upon fictions to serve as diversion for the Society's members – but only and exclusively within their restrictive enclaves, i.e, in the celebrated "houses of libertinage." In contrast to traditional "social contract" theory, where overarching civil goals condition rational political strategy, for Sade there are only transitory tactics, only improvised rules and alliances, created for strictly temporary reasons, according to a heterogeneous set of motives – desire, boredom, pride, vanity, greed, etc. – motives which, in the end, merely reflect the "passions of the soul." According to Lyotard, Klossowski interprets Sade's model in such a way that, far from being a claim to the equality of the rights of man, it is in fact driven by an insatiable profusion of erotic fantasies and the endless production of libidinal intensities. In this respect, he extends Klossowski's reading, and thus reveals Sade's model to be homologous with the machinations of advanced capitalism, wherein even the minimal constraints of production and exchange value are transcended by the ceaseless profusion of "wild" capital.

Unlike Lyotard, Philippe Roger argues against the very possibility of appropriating Sade politically, characterizing him as "a political minimalist." Due to their fictional nature, a double ambiguity obtains within all political enunciations in Sade's writings. On the level of explicitly political statements, we can never determine whether it is the author or the character who maintains the stated position; on the level of the mode of discourse, we can never determine if the statement is serious or parodic. Thus, the articulations of Sade's political enunciations are determined by the rule of uncertainty and undecidability, without any unequivocal point of view ever emerging. Sade's thought, therefore, proffers a sort of critique of political reason. Neither political nor apolitical, his is an *impolitic* thought founded on the notion of absolute sovereignty: politics is not governed by rationality, but rather by the caprices of sovereign individuals. The effect of this impolitic thought is not social edification, but agitation. Its very articulation constitutes a vacuum. Ultimately, this empty space of "politics" would be metaphorically located somewhere between the ordered law of states and the purely practical arrangements of anarchic bandits.

If the Sadean project imperils the governance of politics, and renders the order of economics risible, it likewise subverts the oedipal "law of the father." In its ostensible role of organizing desire and signification, the phallic law is constantly undermined by the mobility and perpetual transformability of libidinal energy. Erotic objects are not viewed merely as a skein or system of intelligible significations (as was maintained by many proponents of structuralist theory) but rather as a nexus of intensities, of figures, images, and desire-formations – as Lyotard, Deleuze, Guattari, and others would argue. Commensurate with this view, Alphonso Lingis, in "The Society of the Friends of Crime," opposes the phallocentric tendencies of both psychoanalytic and philosophic discourse, arguing within the narrative-fictive structures of his piece that these tendencies forcibly corrupt language for the sake of establishing the insidious, imperative necessity of the universal. Sade moves away from a purely phallic or "centric" eroticism toward a libidinal polymorphism. And yet, Lingis suggests, this expression is in some strange way "rational," insofar as Sade's absolute desire to compile the most convincing empirical evidence of perversion nonetheless creates a "normative" discourse of sexuality. Only the terrifying sovereignty of Sadean libertinage, however, is sufficient to express the intense and multiple formations of this libidinal energy.

The critique of the "phallocentric position" can be more broadly extended to address the status and function of gender in Sade's text, as Jane Gallop does in her "Sade, Mothers, and Other Women." Her critique focuses on Sade's near-obsessional use of the "mother-image," an image he utilizes in a divided and paradoxical way. In the Sadean text, a characteristic hatred toward the mother is invariably affected by a more profound love–hate relation toward "Mother Nature." All libertines aspire to embody the perfect, unencumbered evil of nature, but at the same time they must hate her – as a symbol of the real mother – so as to facilitate their own incestuous desires. The libidinal force of the Sadean text emerges directly from this conflict in the paradoxical form of a "maternal phallus," a paradox that places the libertine in a position in which he or she faces the very impossibility of possessing the mother. In the libertine's attempt to possess her, it turns out that either the mother remains a phallus (i.e., essentially mysterious and incomprehensible) and the libertine becomes a mere player in the oedipal game, or else the libertine possesses the mother, and discovers that her phallus is only symbolic. This, of course, dramatically serves to frustrate the libidinal drives, and leaves the libertine in a state of continual dissatisfaction, constantly seeking the impossible union of all male and female desires, alternating between the two incommensurable positions of the Neronic and oedipal complexes. The libidinal energy which thus gets blocked by this paradox of the "maternal phallus" forcibly disrupts gender specificity, creating both the possibility and the impossibility of the human subject being either simply male or female.

If the libertine character achieves a transgressive overcoming of gender identity and sexual polymorphousness through such explicit psycho-sexual devices as the "maternal phallus" and sodomy, so does the very operation of textuality serve to implement the transgressive movements of the Sadean project. It is in large part the recognition of this agency which has confirmed him as one of the major writers of the eighteenth century. His exact position in the history of eighteenth-century literature is only now beginning to be precisely determined, due to both the radical and the encyclopedic nature of his texts, as well as to the diversity of genres in which he worked: novels, novellas, short stories, theatre, critical essays, letters, etc. Located between the various traditions of eighteenth-century thought (libertine tracts, materialist philosophy, anti-clerical pamphlets, political writings, the nascent *roman noir*, as well as the more traditional French theatrical works), Sade's writing permits that diversity of critical and theoretical response particular to all great writing. His place as

one of the major eighteenth-century literary figures is no longer
seriously in question: the problem, rather, is to determine how
that century must be reread after the rediscovery of Sade, given
his contribution of such distinctively radical textual strategies
– strategies which extend and subvert traditional theories of
both narrative and discourse.

One of Sade's most dramatic and frequently employed strategies is his feigned discourse of totality – Sade's desire "to say
everything," his obsession with excess – whereby he engages
and contests the legitimacy of categorial understanding, the
omnipotence of nature, of universal reason, and of all rule
governance. In this regard, Marcel Hénaff proposes that
Sade's need to say everything is comparable to the basic
psychoanalytic technique of recognizing and arousing desire.
In approaching the text in this manner, Hénaff argues, Sade
knowingly blinds himself to the limits of discourse, which in
the end creates the fundamental aporia of his work, i.e., the
impossibility of having both excess and totality, since excess
by definition always exceeds the strict limits of totality. Such
a knowingly "blind" strategy has the effect of empowering the
dynamism of Sade's texts, each move of which is characterized
by the transgression of totality (excess) – oddly enough, in
the very name of totality. Hence, this necessarily unresolved
discursive strategy maintains the tension and dynamism of
the text, all the while dictating the endless, pointless, wasteful,
and repetitive character of the Sadean narrative. By the same
token, knowing that classical language is itself the very limit
of law and prohibition, Sade perversely induces the reader
to become intensely aware of the possibility of excess. His
narrative strategy is to direct us to the unstated, unarticulated
"place" of the libertine's "inner sanctum" – especially in *The
120 Days of Sodom*, which for Hénaff, serves as a theoretical
limit case – where every unimaginable excess, every unspoken
outrage is alleged to transpire. This classic literary device
of an extended dramatic ellipsis serves as the agency which
establishes the heterogeneity of the Sadean project. Such a
place is, of course, an inverted utopia – a dystopian nowhere
– of unalloyed violence. The occlusion of the libertine's inner

sanctum thus serves to maintain the constant and systematic presence of violence, however unarticulated, as a veritable unconscious register of threat, violation, disaster, holocaust. This is not merely the sacrificial violence which, according to Bataille, Caillois, and Girard, would inaugurate or maintain the dimension of the sacred, and hence would serve to promote civil and societal stability. Even more profoundly, this "other place" is the site of the archaic unconscious violence at the very core of the psyche, where primal impulses engage in perpetual conflict. To open up such a wound in the reader, under the sign of unmitigated desire, is the ultimate and enduring crime of Sade's writing.

One way of critically responding to the tension between excess and totality is to explore its effects on literary representation in Sade's texts. If excess emerges as a dominant and pervasive discursive strategy in Sade, then the representative function of mimesis – which traditionally serves to secure truth-functionality, the adequate depiction of reality, or at least of verisimilitude – becomes markedly altered. According to Dalia Judovitz, mimesis in Sade becomes transformed into an an economy not of the real, but of simulation and simulacrum, and this assumes two distinct configurations. First, Sade employs mimesis to simulate various social and political codes, as well as to augment their dissimulation, in a movement of productive excess. Second, mimesis is transformed through the construction of a distinctly subjectless Sadean hero(ine), i.e. a subject who does not fit any acceptable social definitions, and therefore exceeds traditional forms of literary representation. Thus, Sade produces a discourse and an economy that is no longer involved in the classical production and accumulation of signs, but rather one which concerns their expenditure and waste.

The effacement of the traditional literary subject is also accomplished through the generation of literary tropes, which in turn leads to the figuration of subjectivity as a "play" of textual forms (and not as the representative formation of a real character). One of the many tropes to assume a predominant role in Sade's texts is the chiasmus, a figure which is treated in detail by Allen S. Weiss in his "Structures of exchange, acts of transgression." In the Sadean narrative, the model figure of the chiasmus serves to distort the traditional representation of intersubjective relations. The chiasmic mirror-structure functions not as a model of real, intersubjective reciprocity (where the subject's character is delineated and determined), but as a specific organization of discourse which eliminates subjectivity by eliminating all concern with depth, latency, and auto-figuration. The Sadean hero(ine) no longer retains any real subjective force, but is rather subjugated to the Master through a set of textual strategies. The repeated and effective use of the chiasmus ultimately denies every structure of exchange, precisely because it leaves nothing to be exchanged. Sade effectively transforms the figure of chiasmus by reducing its diacritical function to one of merely sustaining the relations of analogy. In this situation, the case of analogy, the principal term – the Master – must perforce determine all subsequent character relations and formations.

Since Sade's works nonetheless depict a veritable plethora of social relations, other, more comprehensive ways of determining these character relations obviously present themselves. Certainly, one broad area of current interest, in this respect, is the concern to determine the gender and narrative possibilities of these relations. For example, to articulate the sexual-syntactic structures of Sadean libertine relations in *Juliette*, Nancy Miller turns to the work of Lévi-Strauss and Greimas. In so doing, she reveals textual and cultural parallels and oppositions, which in turn determine the limits of "social" relations in Sade's text. Likewise, one can articulate, and extend, the social and moral dimensions of discursive constraints upon the Sadean character to locate the subjective space of literary enunciation. By stressing the opposition between the phatic and apophatic aspects of Sade's texts, for instance, Lawrence Schehr reveals some major differences between Sade's and his literary contemporaries' approaches to the genre of eighteenth-century French erotic literature. By revealing a broad variety of Sadean textual strategies, both approaches allow for the study of Sade's narrative structures, either with respect to literary genre or with regard to the positioning of the subject.

In the end, the phatic dimension of Sade's text – including the performative, libidinal, erotic, passionate, and violent registers of his writing, etc. – inclines the reader to an enormous range of affective responses. If the issues we have attempted to address in the present volume in broad measure derive from the reflections of Bataille, and are developed by way of subsequent psychological, philosophic, and literary theory, the ultimate judgement upon the Sadean text remains determinately personal. Yet what remains at issue, following our reflections on Sade, in large part concerns his transformation of the audience in turn. Should the reading subject suffer the massive "decoding" that Bataille and subsequent thinkers in his orbit proclaim, then such a subject may well emerge transformed by an intensified eroticized state of ecstatic pleasure, *jouissance*. As Chantal Thomas proposes – and in fact *performs*, in the genre of an auto-erotic, fictional "confession" – in "Fantasizing Juliette," all neophyte readers of Sade must confront the concrete pleasure of his discourse, and therefore, of their own secret attachments to his books. These attachments may range from visceral disgust and moral outrage to unglossed delight with one's "clandestine companion." But whatever that individual's response may be, no interpretation, no reading, no category or genre will ever fully circumscribe the meaning of the name "Sade," since this name is a sign of what we dare not speak, but must nevertheless be spoken.

*

CHAPTER I

The use value of D. A. F. Sade
(an open letter to my current comrades)

Georges Bataille
(Translated by Allan Stoekl)

If I think it good to address this letter to my comrades, it is not because the propositions that it contains concern them. It will probably even appear to them that such propositions do not concern anyone in particular at all. But in this case I need to have at least a few people as witnesses to establish so complete a defection. There are, perhaps, declarations which, for lack of anything better, ridiculously need an Attic chorus, because they suppose, as their effect, in spite of everything, a minimum of astonishment, of misunderstanding, or of repugnance. But one does not address a chorus in order to convince it or rally it, and certainly one does not submit to the judgment of destiny without revolting, when it condemns the speaker to the saddest isolation.

This isolation, as far as I am concerned, is moreover in part voluntary, since I would agree to come out of it only on certain hard-to-meet conditions.

In fact even the gesture of writing, which alone permits one to envisage slightly less conventional human relations, a little less tricky than those of so-called intimate friendships – even this gesture of writing does not leave me with an appreciable hope. I doubt that it is possible to reach the few people for whom this letter is no doubt intended, over the heads of my present comrades. For – my resolution is all the more intransigent in that it is absurd to defend – it would have been necessary to deal not with individuals like those I already know, but only with men (and above all with masses) who are comparatively fragmented, amorphous, and even violently expelled from every form. But it is likely that such men do not yet exist (and the masses certainly do not exist).

All I can state is that, some day or other, they certainly will not fail to exist, given that current social bonds will inevitably be undone, and that these bonds cannot much longer maintain the habitual enslavement of people and customs. The masses will in turn be fragmented as soon as they see the prestige of industrial reality, to which they find themselves attached, disappear; in other words, when the process of material progress and rapid transformation in which they have had to participate (passively as well as in revolt) leads to a disagreeable and terminal stagnation.

My resolution thus cannot be defended only in that it eliminates – not without bitterness – every immediate satisfaction.

Outside of propositions that can only take on meaning through very general consequences, it so happens that it is high time for me to quell – at little cost – a part of this bitterness: it is possible at the very least to clear the narrow terrain – where from now on the debate will be carried out – of the intellectual bartering that usually goes on there. In fact it is obvious that if men incapable of histrionics succeed those of today, they will not be able to better represent the tacky phraseology now in circulation than by recalling the fate reserved, by a certain number of writers, for the memory of D. A. F. Sade (moreover it will, perhaps, appear fairly quickly, in a very general way, that the fact of needlessly resorting to literary or poetic verbiage, the inability to express oneself in a simple and categorical way, not only are the result of a vulgar impotence, but always betray a pretentious hypocrisy).

Of course, I do not allude in this way to the various people who are scandalized by the writings of Sade, but only to his most open apologists. It has seemed fitting today to place these writings (and with them the figure of their author) above everything (or almost everything) that can be opposed to them, but it is out of the question to allow them the least place in private or public life, in theory or in practice. The behavior of Sade's admirers resembles that of primitive subjects in relation to their king, whom they adore and loathe, and whom they cover with honors and narrowly confine. In the most favorable cases, the author of *Justine* is in fact thus treated like any given *foreign body*; in other words, he is only an object of transports of exaltation to the extent that these transports facilitate his excretion (his peremptory expulsion).

The life and works of D. A. F. Sade would thus have no other use value than the common use value of excrement; in other words, for the most part, one most often only loves the rapid (and violent) pleasure of voiding this matter and no longer seeing it.

I am thus led to indicate how, in a way completely different from this usage, the sadism which is not *completely different* from that which existed before Sade appears positively, on the one hand, as an irruption of excremental forces (the excessive violation of modesty, positive algolagnia, the violent excretion of the sexual object coinciding with a powerful or tortured ejaculation, the libidinal interest in cadavers, vomiting, defecation . . .) – and on the other as a corresponding limitation, a narrow enslavement of everything that is opposed to this irruption. It is only in these concrete conditions that sad social necessity, human dignity, fatherland, and family, as well as poetic sentiments, appear without a mask and without any play of light and shadow; it is finally impossible to see in those things anything other than subordinate forces: so many slaves working like cowards to prepare the beautiful blustering eruptions that alone are capable of answering the needs that torment the bowels of most men.

But, given that Sade revealed his conception of terrestrial life in the most outrageous form (even given that it is not possible immediately to reveal such a conception other than in a terrifying and inadmissible form), it is perhaps not surprising that people have believed it possible to get beyond its reach. Literary men apparently have the best reason for not confirming a brilliant verbal and low-cost apology through practice. They could even pretend that Sade was the first to take the trouble to situate the domain he described outside of and above all reality. They could easily affirm that the brilliant and suffocating value he wanted to give human existence is inconceivable outside of fiction; that only poetry, exempt from all practical applications, permits one to have at his disposal, to a certain extent, the brilliance and suffocation that the Marquis de Sade tried so indecently to provoke.

It is right to recognize that, even practiced in the extremely implicit form it has retained up to this point, such a diversion discredits its authors (at the very least among those – even if, moreover, they are horrified by sadism – who refuse to become interested, for bad as well as for good reasons, in simple verbal prestidigitation).

The fact remains, unfortunately, that this diversion has been practiced for so long without denunciation, under cover of a fairly poor phraseology, simply because it takes place in an area where, it seems, everything slips away ... It is no doubt almost useless at the present time to set forth rational propositions, since they could only be taken up for the profit of some convenient and – even in an apocalyptic guise – thoroughly literary enterprise: in other words, on the condition that they be useful for ambitions moderated by the impotence of present-day man. The slightest hope, in fact, involves the destruction (the disappearance) of a society that has so ridiculously allowed the one who conceives that hope to exist.

The time has no less come, it seems to me – under the indifferent eyes of my comrades – to bet on a future that has, it is true, only an unfortunate, hallucinatory existence. At the very least the plan I think possible to sketch *intellectually* today of what will really exist later is the only thing that links the various preliminary propositions that follow to a still-sickly will to *agitation*.

For the moment, an abrupt statement not followed by explanations seems to me to respond sufficiently to the intellectual disorientation of those who could have the opportunity to become aware of it. And (even though I am capable to a large extent of doing it now) I put off until later difficult and interminable explications, analogous to those of any other elaborated theory. At this point I will set forth the propositions that, among other things, allow one to introduce the values established by the Marquis de Sade, obviously not in the domain of gratuitous impertinence, but rather directly in the very market in which, each day, the credit that individuals and even communities can give to their own lives is, in a way, registered.

APPROPRIATION AND EXCRETION

1. The division of social facts into religious facts (prohibitions, obligations, and the realization of sacred action) on the one hand and profane facts (civil, political, juridical, industrial, and commercial organization) on the other, even though it is not easily applied to primitive societies and lends itself in general to a certain number of confusions, can nevertheless serve as the basis for the determination of two polarized human impulses: EXCRETION and APPROPRIATION. In other words, during a period in which the religious organization of a given country *is developing*, this division represents the freest opening for excremental collective impulses (orgiastic impulses) established in opposition to political, juridical, and economic institutions.

2. Sexual activity, whether perverted or not; the behavior of one sex before the other; defecation; urination; death and the cult of cadavers (above all, insofar as it involves the stinking decomposition of bodies); various taboos; ritual cannibalism; the sacrifice of animal-gods; omophagia; the laughter of exclusion; sobbing (which in general has death as its object); religious ecstasy; the identical attitude toward shit, gods, and cadavers; the terror that so often accompanies involuntary defecation; the custom of exchanging brilliant, lubricious, painted, and jeweled women; gambling; heedless expenditure and certain fanciful uses of money, etc. . . . together present a common character in that the object of the activity (excrement, shameful parts, cadavers, etc. . . .) is found each time treated as a foreign body (*das ganz Anderes*); in other words, it can just as well be expelled following a brutal

rupture as reabsorbed through the desire to put one's body and mind entirely in a more or less violent state of expulsion (or projection). The notion of the (heterogeneous) *foreign body* permits one to note the elementary *subjective* identity between types of excrement (sperm, menstrual blood, urine, fecal matter) and everything that can be seen as sacred, divine, or marvelous: a half-decomposed cadaver fleeing through the night in a luminous shroud can be seen as characteristic of this unity.[1]

3. The process of simple appropriation is normally presented within the process of composite excretion, insofar as it is necessary for the production of an alternating rhythm, for example, in the following passage from Sade:

Verneuil makes someone shit, he eats the turd, and then he demands that someone eat his. The one who eats his shit vomits; he devours her puke.

The elementary form of appropriation is oral consumption, considered as communion (participation, identification, incorporation, or assimilation). Consumption is either sacramental (sacrificial) or not, depending on whether the heterogeneous character of food is heightened or conventionally destroyed. In the latter case, the identification takes place first in the preparation of foods, which must be given an appearance of striking homogeneity, based on strict conventions. Eating as such then intervenes in the process as a complex phenomenon in that the very fact of swallowing presents itself as a partial rupture of physical equilibrium and is accompanied by, among other things, a sudden liberation of great quantities of saliva. Nevertheless, the element of appropriation, in moderate and rational form, in fact dominates, because cases in which eating's principal goal is physiological tumult (gluttony or drunkenness followed by vomiting) are no doubt unusual.

The process of appropriation is thus characterized by a homogeneity (static equilibrium) of the author of the appropriation, and of objects as final result, whereas excretion presents itself as the result of a heterogeneity, and can move in the direction of an ever greater heterogeneity, liberating impulses whose ambivalence is more and more pronounced. The latter case is represented by, for example, sacrificial consumption in the elementary form of the orgy, which has no other goal than the incorporation in the person of irreducibly heterogeneous elements, insofar as such elements risk provoking an increase of force (or more exactly an increase of *mana*).

4. Man does not only appropriate his food, but also the different products of his activity: clothes, furniture, dwellings, and instruments of production. Finally, he appropriates land divided into parcels. Such appropriations take place by means of a more or less conventional homogeneity (identity) established between the possessor and the object possessed. It sometimes involves a personal homogeneity that in primitive times could only be solemnly destroyed with the aid of an excretory rite, and sometimes a general homogeneity, such as that established by the architect between a city and its inhabitants.

In this respect, production can be seen as the excretory phase of a process of appropriation, and the same is true of selling.

5. The homogeneity of the kind realized in cities between men and that which surrounds them is only a subsidiary form of a much more consistent homogeneity, which man has established throughout the external world by everywhere replacing *a priori* inconceivable objects with classified series of conceptions or ideas. The identification of all the elements of which the world is composed has been pursued with a constant obstinacy, so that scientific conceptions, as well as the popular conceptions of the world, seem to have voluntarily led to a representation as different from what could have been imagined *a priori* as the public square of a capital is from a region of high mountains.

This last appropriation – the work of philosophy as well as of science or common sense – has included phases of revolt and scandal, but it has always had as its goal the establishment of the homogeneity of the world, and it will only be able to lead to a terminal phase in the sense of excretion when the irreducible waste products of the operation are determined.

6. The interest of philosophy resides in the fact that, in opposition to science or common sense, it must positively envisage the waste products of intellectual appropriation. Nevertheless, it most often envisages these waste products only in abstract forms of totality (nothingness, infinity, the absolute), to which it cannot itself give a positive content; it can thus freely proceed in speculations that more or less have as a goal, all things considered, the *sufficient* identification of an endless world with a finite world, an unknowable (noumenal) world with the known world.

Only an intellectual elaboration in a religious form can, in its periods of autonomous development, put forward the waste products of appropriative thought as the definitively heterogeneous (sacred) object of speculation. But in general one must take into account the fact that religions bring about a profound separation within the sacred domain, dividing it into a superior world (celestial and divine) and an inferior world (demoniac, a world of decomposition); now such a division necessarily leads to a progressive homogeneity of the entire superior domain (only the inferior domain resists all efforts at appropriation). God rapidly and almost entirely loses his terrifying features, his appearance as a decomposing cadaver, in order to become, at the final stage of degradation, the simple (paternal) sign of universal homogeneity.

7. In practice, one must understand by religion not really that which answers the need for the unlimited projection (expulsion or excretion) of human nature, but the totality of prohibitions, obligations, and partial freedom that socially channel and regularize this projection. Religion thus differs from a practical and theoretical *heterology*[2] (even though both are equally concerned with sacred or excremental facts), not

only in that the former excludes the scientific rigor proper to the latter (which generally appears as different from religion as chemistry is from alchemy), but also in that, under normal conditions, it betrays the needs that it was supposed not only to regulate, but to satisfy.

8. Poetry at first glance seems to remain valuable as a method of mental projection (in that it permits one to accede to an entirely heterogeneous world). But it is only too easy to see that it is hardly less debased than religion. It has almost always been at the mercy of the great historical systems of appropriation. And insofar as it can be developed autonomously, this autonomy leads it onto the path of a total poetic conception of the world, which ends at any one of a number of aesthetic homogeneities. The practical unreality of the heterogeneous elements it sets in motion is, in fact, an indispensable condition for the continuation of heterogeneity: starting from the moment when this unreality immediately constitutes itself as a superior reality, whose mission is to eliminate (or degrade) inferior vulgar reality, poetry is reduced to playing the role of the standard of things, and, in opposition, the worst vulgarity takes on an ever stronger excremental value.

THE HETEROLOGICAL THEORY OF KNOWLEDGE

9. When one says that heterology scientifically considers questions of heterogeneity, one does not mean that heterology is, in the usual sense of such a formula, the science of the heterogeneous. The heterogeneous is even resolutely placed outside the reach of scientific knowledge, which by definition is only applicable to homogeneous elements. Above all, heterology is opposed to any homogeneous representation of the world; in other words, to any philosophical system. The goal of such representations is always the deprivation of our universe's sources of excitation and the development of a servile human species, fit only for the fabrication, rational consumption, and conservation of products. But the intellectual process automatically limits itself by producing of its own accord its

own waste products, thus liberating in a disordered way the heterogeneous excremental element. Heterology is restricted to taking up again, consciously and resolutely, this terminal process which up until now has been seen as the abortion and the shame of human thought.

In that way it [heterology] *leads to the complete reversal of the philosophical process, which ceases to be the instrument of appropriation, and now serves excretion; it introduces the demand for the violent gratifications implied by social life.*

10. Only, on the one hand, the process of limitation and, on the other, the study of the violently alternating reactions of antagonism (expulsion) and love (reabsorption) obtained by positing the heterogeneous element, lie within the province of heterology as science. This element itself remains indefinable and can only be determined through negation. The specific character of fecal matter or of the specter, as well as of unlimited time or space, can only be the object of a series of negations, such as the absence of any possible common denominator, irrationality, etc. It must even be added that there is no way of placing such elements in the immediate objective human domain, in the sense that the pure and simple objectification of their specific character would lead to their incorporation in a homogeneous intellectual system, in other words, to a hypocritical cancellation of their excremental character.

The objectivity of heterogeneous elements is thus of purely theoretical interest, since one can only attain it on the condition that one envisage *waste products* in the total form of the infinite obtained by negation (in other words, the shortcoming of objective heterogeneity is that it can be envisaged only in an abstract form, whereas the subjective heterogeneity of particular elements is, in practice, alone concrete).

11. Scientific data – in other words, the result of appropriation – alone retain an immediate and appreciable character, since immediate objectivity is defined by the possibilities of intellectual appropriation. If one defines real exterior objects it is necessary at the same time to introduce the possibility of a relation of scientific elaboration. And if such a relation is

impossible, the element envisaged remains in practice unreal, and can only abstractly be made objective. All questions posed beyond this represent the persistence of a dominant need for appropriation, the sickly obstinacy of a will seeking to represent, in spite of everything, and through simple cowardice, a homogeneous and servile world.

12. It is useless to try to deny that one finds there – much more than in the difficulty met with in the analysis of the process of excretion and appropriation – the weak point (in practice) of these conceptions, for one must generally take into account the unconscious obstinacy furnished by defections and complacency. It would be too easy to find in objective nature a large number of phenomena that in a crude way correspond to the human model of excretion and appropriation, in order to attain *once again* the notion of the unity of being, for example, in a dialectical form. One can attain it more generally through animals, plants, matter, nature, and being, without meeting really consistent obstacles. Nevertheless, it can already be indicated that as one moves away from man, the opposition loses its importance to the point where it is only a superimposed form that one obviously could not have discovered in the facts considered if it had not been borrowed from a different order of facts. The only way to resist this dilution lies in the practical part of heterology, which leads to an action that resolutely goes against this regression to homogeneous nature.

As soon as the effort at rational comprehension ends in contradiction, the practice of intellectual scatology requires the excretion of unassimilable elements, which is another way of stating vulgarly that a burst of laughter is the only imaginable and definitively terminal result – and not the means – of philosophical speculation. And then one must indicate that a reaction as *insignificant* as a burst of laughter derives from the extremely vague and distant character of the intellectual domain, and that it suffices to go from a speculation resting on abstract facts to a practice whose mechanism is not different, but which immediately reaches concrete heterogeneity, in order to arrive at ecstatic trances and orgasm.

PRINCIPLES OF PRACTICAL HETEROLOGY

13. Excretion is not simply a middle term between two appropriations, just as decay is not simply a middle term between the grain and the ear of wheat. The inability, in this latter case, to consider decay as an end in itself is the result not precisely of the human viewpoint but of the specifically intellectual viewpoint (to the extent that this viewpoint is in practice subordinate to a process of appropriation). On the contrary, the human viewpoint, independent of official declarations – in other words as it results from, among other things, the analysis of dreams – represents appropriation as a means of excretion. In the final analysis it is clear that a worker works in order to obtain the violent pleasures of coitus (in other words, he accumulates in order to spend). On the other hand, the conception according to which the worker must have coitus in order to provide for the future necessities of work is linked to the unconscious identification of the worker with the slave. In fact, to the extent that the various functions are distributed among the various social categories, appropriation in its most over-whelming form historically devolves on slaves: thus in the past serfs had to accumulate products for knights and clerks, who barely took part in the labor of appropriation, and then only through the establishment of a morality that regularized for their own profit the circulation of goods. But as soon as one attacks the accursed exploitation of man by man, it becomes time to leave to the exploiters this abominable appropriative morality, which for such a long time has permitted their own orgies of wealth. To the extent that man no longer thinks of crushing his comrades under the yoke of morality, he acquires the capacity to link overtly not only his intellect and his virtue but his *raison d'être* to the violence and incongruity of his excretory organs, as well as to his ability to become excited

and entranced by heterogeneous elements, commonly starting with debauchery.

14. The need – before being able to go on to radical demands and to the violent practice of a significant moral liberty – to abolish all exploitation of man by man is not the only motive that links the practical development of heterology to the overturning of the established order.

In that they are manifested in a social milieu, the urges that heterology identifies *in practice* with the *raison d'être* of man can be seen in a certain sense as anti-social (to the same degree that sexual corruption or even pleasure is seen by certain individuals as a waste of strength, like, for example, the great potlatch rituals of the Pacific Northwest tribes or, among civilized peoples, the pleasure of crowds watching great fires at night). Nevertheless, the impulses that go against the interests of a society in a state of stagnation (during a phase of appropriation) have, on the contrary, social revolution as their end: thus they can find, through the historical movements by means of which humanity spends its own strength freely and limitlessly, both total gratification and use in the very sense of general conscious benefit. Besides, whatever the reality of this ulterior benefit might be, it is no less true that if one considers the submerged masses, doomed to an obscure and impotent life, the revolution by which these masses liberate force with a long-restrained violence is as much the practical *raison d'être* of societies as it is their means of development.

15. Of course, the term *excretion* applied to Revolution must first be understood in the strictly mechanical – and moreover etymological – sense of the word. The first phase of a revolution is *separation*, in other words, a process leading to the position of two groups of forces, each one characterized by the necessity of excluding the other. The second phase is the violent *expulsion* of the group that has possessed power by the revolutionary group.

But one also notes that each of the groups, by its very constitution, gives the opposing group an almost exclusively negative excremental character, and it is only because of this negativity that the sacrificial character of a revolution remains profoundly unconscious. The revolutionary impulse of the proletarian masses is, moreover, sometimes implicitly and sometimes openly treated as sacred, and that is why it is possible to use the word *Revolution* entirely stripped of its utilitarian meaning without, however, giving it an idealist meaning.

16. *Participation* – in the purely psychological sense as well as in the active sense of the word – does not only commit revolutionaries to a particular politics, for example, to the establishment of socialism throughout the world. It is also – and necessarily – presented as moral participation: immediate participation in the destructive action of the revolution (expulsion realized through the total shattering of the equilibrium of the social edifice), indirect participation in all equivalent destructive action. It is the very character of the revolutionary will to link such actions not, as in the Christian apocalypse, to punishment, but to the enjoyment or the utility of human beings, and it is obvious that all destruction that is neither useful nor inevitable can only be the achievement of an exploiter and, consequently, of morality as the principle of all exploitation.[3] But then it is easy to ascertain that the reality of such *participation* is at the very basis of the separation of socialist parties, divided into reformists and revolutionaries.

Without a profound complicity with natural forces such as violent death, gushing blood, sudden catastrophes and the horrible cries of pain that accompany them, terrifying ruptures of what had seemed to be immutable, the fall into stinking filth of what had been elevated – without a sadistic understanding of an incontestably thundering and torrential nature, there could be no revolutionaries, there could only be a revolting utopian sentimentality.

17. The *participation* in everything that, among men, is horrible and allegedly sacred can take place in a limited and unconscious form, but this limitation and this unconsciousness obviously have only a provisional value, and nothing can stop the movement that leads human beings toward an ever more

shameless awareness of the erotic bond that links them to
death, to cadavers, and to horrible physical pain. It is high
time that human nature cease being subjected to the autocrat's
vile repression and to the morality that authorizes exploitation.
Since it is true that one of a man's attributes is the derivation of
pleasure from the suffering of others, and that erotic pleasure
is not only the negation of an agony that takes place at the
same instant but also a lubricious participation in that agony,
it is time to choose between the conduct of cowards afraid of
their own joyful excesses, and the conduct of those who judge
that any given man need not cower like a hunted animal, but
instead can see all the moralistic buffoons as so many dogs.

18. As a result of these elementary considerations, it is
necessary from now on to envisage two distinct phases in
human emancipation, as undertaken successively by the different revolutionary surges, from Jacobinism to Bolshevism.

During the revolutionary phase, the current phase that will
only end with the world triumph of socialism, only the social
Revolution can serve as an outlet for collective impulses, and
no other activity can be envisaged in practice.

But the postrevolutionary phase implies the necessity of a
division between the economic and political organization of
society on one hand, and on the other, an anti-religious and
asocial organization having as its goal orgiastic participation
in different forms of destruction, in other words, the collective
satisfaction of needs that correspond to the necessity of provoking the violent excitation that results from the expulsion
of heterogeneous elements.

Such an organization can have no other conception of
morality than the one scandalously affirmed for the first time
by the Marquis de Sade.

19. When it is a question of the means of realizing this
orgiastic participation, [such] an organization will find itself
as close to religions anterior *to the formations of autocratic States* as
it is distant from religions such as Christianity or Buddhism.

One must broadly take into account, in such a forecast, the
probable intervention of blacks in the general culture. To the

extent that blacks participate in revolutionary emancipation, the attainment of socialism will bring them the possibility of all kinds of exchanges with white people, but in conditions radically different from those currently experienced by the civilized blacks of America. Now black communities, once liberated from all superstition as from all oppression, represent in relation to heterology not only the possibility but the necessity of an adequate organization. All organizations that have ecstasy and frenzy as their goal (the spectacular death of animals, torture by degrees, orgiastic dances, etc.) will have no reason to disappear when a heterological conception of human life is substituted for the primitive conception; they can only transform themselves while they spread, under the violent impetus of a moral doctrine of white origin, taught to blacks by all those whites who have become aware of the abominable inhibitions paralyzing their race's communities. It is only starting from this collusion of European scientific theory with black practice that institutions can develop which will serve as outlets (with no other limitations than those of human strength) for the urges required today by worldwide society's fiery and bloody Revolution.4

NOTES

1 The identical nature, from the psychological point of view, of God and excrement should not shock the intellect of anyone familiar with the problems posed by the history of religions. The cadaver is not much more repugnant than shit, and the specter that projects its horror is *sacred* even in the eyes of modern theologians. The following passage from Frazer very nearly sums up the basic historical aspect of the question: ". . . These different categories of people differ, in our eyes, by virtue of their character and their condition: we should say that one group is sacred, the other filthy or impure. This is not the case for the savage, for his mind is much too crude to understand clearly what a sacred being is, and what an impure being is."

2 The science of what is completely other. The term *hagiology* would perhaps be more precise, but one would have to catch the double meaning of *hagio* (analogous to the double meaning of *sacer*), *soiled* as well as *holy*. But it is above all the term *scatology* (the science

of excrement) that retains in the present circumstances (the specialization of the sacred) an incontestable expressive value as the doublet of an abstract term such as *heterology*.

3 For example, imperialist war.

4 As is always the case with theories based on generalizations about race, Bataille has here wandered into some dangerous territory. It would certainly appear from the content of this paragraph that his view of racial difference was, at least in part, affected by the completely invalid, erroneous, and decidedly racist "scientific" theories popularized (both in Europe and the US) during the mid- to late nineteenth century by such dubious investigators as Paul Broca, Gustave Le Bon, Cesare Lombroso, and Samuel George Morton (See Stephen Jay Gould, *The Mismeasure of Man*, W. W. Norton, 1981).

The emphasis on racial characteristics here may also be explained by the immense cultural interest in primitivism in France at the time Bataille wrote this essay: a primitivism that had already exercised considerable influence on numerous artists, including Picasso, Modigliani, and Matisse. In this regard, it should also be noted that Bataille's surrealizing ethnographic pretentions were exemplified by the Dakar-Djibouti expedition of 1931–33, in which Michel Leiris – one of Bataille's fellow dissident Surrealists – participated. The aestheticizing aspects of these ethnographic efforts resulted in the devotion of the entire second issue of the Surrealist art and culture review *Minotaure* to the expedition, as well as in the publication of Leiris's *L'Afrique fantôme* (See James Clifford, "On Ethnographic Surrealism," in *The Predicament of Culture*, Harvard University Press, 1988). [Eds.]

CHAPTER 2

Sade, or the philosopher–villain

Pierre Klossowski
(Translated by Alphonso Lingis)

It shall be our task here to envision Sade's experience as it was conveyed in writing.[1] First, we shall try to define the philosophical position he took, or made a pretense of taking, in his novels. The question shall be: What does thinking and writing – as opposed to feeling or acting – mean for Sade?

Sade himself, so as to definitively disavow authorship of his *Justine*, declares that all the "philosophers" in his "own" works are "decent people," whereas "through an inexcusable clumsiness that was bound to set the author [of *Justine*] at loggerheads with wise men and fools alike," "all the philosophical characters of this novel are villains to the core."[2]

The confrontation of the philosopher–decent-man with the philosopher–villain dates from Plato. The philosopher-gentleman sets forth *the act of thinking* as the sole *valid* activity of his being. The villain who philosophizes merely accords thought the value of favouring the *activity of the strongest passion* – which in the eyes of the gentleman is but a *lack of being*. If the summit of villainy consists in disguising one's passion as thought, the villain for his part finds in the thought of the gentleman nothing but the disguise of *an impotent passion*.

To do Sade justice, we should take this "villainous philosophy" seriously. Since it is set forth in such a voluminous work, it puts a sinister question-mark over the decision to think and to write – particularly to think through and to describe an act *instead* of committing it.

This decision does not, however, resolve the dilemma: how can one give an account of an irreducible depth of sensibility,

33

except by acts that betray it? It would seem that such an irreducible depth can never be reflected upon or grasped except in these acts perpetrated outside of thought – unreflected and ungraspable acts.

THE ACT OF WRITING IN SADE

The peculiarly human act of writing presupposes a generality which a singular case claims to join, and by belonging to this generality claims to come to understand itself. As such a singular case, Sade conceives his act of writing to verify this belonging. The medium of generality in Sade's time is the logically structured language of the classical tradition; in the field of communicative gestures this language re-produces and reconstitutes the normative structure of the human race in individuals. This normative structure is expressed physiologically by a subordination of the life-functions, a subordination that ensures the preservation and propagation of the race. To this need to reproduce and perpetuate oneself at work in each individual there corresponds the need to reproduce and perpetuate oneself by language. Thus the reciprocity of persuasion, which allows the exchange of individual singularities in the circuit of generality. This reciprocity is brought about only in conformity with the principle of identity or of non-contradiction, which makes logically structured language one with the general principle of understanding, i.e. universal reason.

With this principle of the normative generality of the human race in mind, Sade sets out to establish a counter-generality which would obtain for the specificity of perversions, making exchange between singular cases of perversion possible. For the existing normative generality, these perversions are defined by the absence of logical structure. Thus Sade comes to conceive the notion of integral monstrosity. But Sade takes this counter-generality, valid for the specificity of perversion, to be already implicit in the existing generality. He thinks that the atheism proclaimed by normative reason, in the name of man's freedom and sovereignty, is destined to reverse the existing generality into this counter-generality. Atheism, the supreme act of normative reason, is thus destined to establish the reign of the total absence of norms.

By choosing perversity of feeling and acting, devoid of logic, as testimony to rationalistic atheism, Sade immediately puts universal reason into question insofar as he renders it contradictory by applying it. On the other hand, he puts human behavior into question inasmuch as it proceeds from the subordination of the life-functions.

SADE'S CRITIQUE OF ATHEISM

How does reason arrive at atheism? By deciding that the notion of God would once again alter reason's autonomy in an illogical, hence monstrous, way. It declares that from the notion of God, which is itself arbitrary, all arbitrary, perverse, and monstrous behavior would derive. If atheism can prevail as a decision of autonomous reason, it is because this autonomy claims it alone maintains the norms of the species in the individual; also, it ensures human behavior is in conformity with these norms by subordinating the life-functions in each individual in the name of equality and freedom for all. How could autonomous reason include phenomena contrary to the preservation of the species, and foreign to its own structure, without altering the very concept of autonomous reason? But it is precisely in this respect that Sade changes the concept, by working out, if only implicitly, a critique of normative reason. For Sade this atheism is still nothing but an inverted monotheism, only apparently purified of idolatry and scarcely distinguishable from deism. Just as the deist certified the notion of God, this atheism stands as a guarantee of the responsible ego, its agency, and individual identity. For atheism to be purified from this inverted monotheism, it must become integral. What then will become of human behavior? One thinks that Sade will answer: "See my monsters." No doubt he himself shuffled the cards sufficiently for one to suppose him capable of giving so naive an answer.

In expressing himself in accordance with the concepts of universal reason, Sade can never account for the positive content of perversion, or even polymorphous sensibilities, other than with negative concepts that derive from this reason. Thus, while diametrically opposed to the "tonsured henchmen," he cannot avoid the reprobation of right-thinking atheists, who will never forgive him for having, through the detour of atheism, rejoined the monstrosity of divine arbitrariness. Reason would like to be wholly freed from God. Sade – but in a very underhanded way – wishes to free thought from all preestablished normative reason: *integral atheism would be the end of anthropomorphic reason.* Although this obscure will is at work in him, Sade does not, and does not seek to, distinguish the act of thinking from the act of referring to the universal reason, hypostatized in his concept of nature. This distinction is only expressed in the aberrant *acts* he describes, since in this context thought has only an experimental bearing. Whether through heedlessness or out of malicious pleasure taken in contradictory situations, the characters of his novels are given the aspect of "philosophers who are villains to the core."

If these characters happen to refer their anomalous acts to normative reason, they do so in a way that lays waste the autonomy of reason. They deride and demonstrate the vanity of a reason that in its supreme act, atheism, claims to guarantee human forms of behavior. Unless atheism is reconceived on the basis of phenomena which reason rejects, it will continue to consolidate the existing institutions based on anthropomorphic norms. One then has this dilemma: either reason itself is excluded from its autonomous decision (atheism) which is to forestall monstrosity in man, or else monstrosity is once again excluded from all possible argumentation.

SADE'S DESCRIPTION OF THE SADEAN EXPERIENCE

The description Sade gives of his own experience through the characters he created covers a twofold experiment: (1) trying to represent the sensuous in an aberrant act; (2) trying to describe representation.

There will then be a relationship between the *actualization* of what is sensuous in an act *through writing* and the *performing of the act* independent of its description.

With Sade, this writing is not purely descriptive (objective), but *interpretive*. In interpreting the aberrant act as a coinciding of sensuous nature with reason, Sade demeans reason with sensuous nature, and demeans the "rational" sensuous nature with a perverse reason. Perverse reason is nonetheless the rejoinder of reason which censors sensuous nature. As such, perverse reason retains censorship and introduces punitive sanction as *outrage* into "rational" sensuous nature understood by Sade as the transgression of norms.

For Sade the fact of sensing, the irreducible element in perversion, does not have to be justified. It is the aberrant act that issues from sensuous nature that Sade wishes to moralize. This act is aberrant in the eyes of Sade himself, inasmuch as reason – even atheist reason – cannot recognize itself in it.

The sensuous in Sade is described only as a propensity to act. From this description Sade passes progressively to the moral explanation of the act. He establishes a twofold relationship between a perverse way of sensing and of acting; namely, that between one's own inwardness and (1) *the exteriority of an Aberrant Act*, and (2) *the exteriority of Normative Reason*. Then the distinction between *deliberate sadism* and an *unreflecting sadistic act* can be made only through the intervention of normative reason. The result is an indissoluble whole, in which the sensuous (that is, the experience peculiar to Sade) is obscured to the extent that discourse must justify the act.

It is because Sade conceives of the act as stemming from the perverse way of sensing that he declares himself an atheist. Conceiving the perverse act as obedience to a moral imperative, an idea, he constructs a new conception of perverse sensibility from this idea. He explicitly reorganizes the insubordination of the life-functions on the basis of atheist reason, and implicitly disorganizes normative reason on the basis of this functional insubordination.

WHY SADE DID NOT SEEK A POSITIVE CONCEPTUAL
FORMULATION OF PERVERSION (THAT IS, OF SENSUOUS
POLYMORPHY). THE NECESSITY OF OUTRAGE.

If Sade had sought (supposing that he could have ever been concerned with such a thing) a positive conceptual formulation of perversion, he would have eluded the enigma he sets up; he would not have intellectualized the phenomenon of sadism, properly speaking. The motive for this is more obscure, and it forms the node of the Sadean experience: this motive is *outrage*. In outrage, what is violated [*outragé*] is maintained to serve as a support for transgression.

Sade shuts himself up in the sphere of normative reason not only because he remains dependent on logically structured language, but because the constraint exercised by the existing institutions comes to be individuated in the fatality of his own existence.

If one removes from consideration the intimate connivance between the expressive forces and those that are subversive – a connivance that is established in Sade's mind because he forces reason to serve as a reference for anomaly, and forces anomaly to refer to reason via the detour of atheism – then outrage will no longer be necessary in order that there be transgression. It becomes a purely intellectual transgression which is one with the general insurrection of minds on the eve of the Revolution. Sadism itself would then be but one utopian ideology among others.

But if, in Sade, outrage is necessary, then transgression must prevail over the postulates that derive logically from his atheist declarations.

THE THEME OF TRANSGRESSION MAKES SADE'S
POSTULATES OF INTEGRAL ATHEISM CONTRADICTORY

Integral atheism means that the principle of identity itself disappears along with the absolute guarantor of this principle; the property of having a responsible self is thus morally and physically abolished. The first consequence will be the universal prostitution of beings. And this is but the counterpart of integral monstrosity, which rests on the insubordination of the life-functions in the absence of any normative authority of the species.

The need for transgression, however, paradoxically opposes this twofold consequence of atheism. For the expropriation of the corporeal and moral self, the condition for universal prostitution, is still something that could be instituted, in the utopian sense of Fourier's phalanstery (community house) which was based on the "interplay of the passions." As soon as this pooling-together of the passions was established, there would no longer be the tension necessary for outrage, and sadism would dissipate – unless one knowingly created rules to be broken, this being the "game" (as is indeed done in the secret societies imagined by Sade).

Transgression presupposes the existing order, the apparent maintenance of norms, under which energy accumulates, thereby making the transgression necessary. Thus, universal prostitution has meaning only in function of the moral property of an individual body. Without this notion of ownership, prostitution would lose its attraction, and the outrage would beat the empty air. Unless, that is, in the state of institutionalized prostitution the outrage would consist in inflicting the intrinsic ownership of a body on an individual who had been excluded from the universal pooling-together.

The same holds true for integral monstrosity as a counter-generality implicit in the existing generality. Perversion (the insubordination of the life-functions), in the acts it inspires (particularly the sodomist act), derives its transgressive value only from the *permanence of norms* (such as the *normative differentiation of the sexes*). To the extent that perversion is more or less latent in individuals, it serves only as a model proposed to "normal" individuals as a way of transgression, just as the fact that one pervert may find a kindred spirit in another makes possible a mutual transcendence of each as a particular case.

If the human race as a whole "degenerated," if there were no one left but avowed perverts – if integral monstrosity were thus to prevail – one might think that Sade's "goal" would have been reached, that there would no longer be any "monsters" and "sadism" would disappear. This perspective is precisely the snare of an "optimistic" interpretation of Sade, which, in its desire to credit the "psychopathological" – and therefore therapeutic – "value" in Sade's work, conjures away the enigma. But the ruse in the phenomenon which forms Sade's physiognomy lies in pretending to have a "goal," even a "scientific" one. This ruse resides in the underlying intuition that integral monstrosity can be realized only within the conditions that made sadism possible, within a space composed of obstacles, that is, in the logically structured language of norms and institutions. The absence of logical structure can be verified only through the given logic, even when it is false logic, which, by refusing monstrosity, provokes it. Monstrosity or anomaly in turn brings out the given norms, and affirms itself if only in a negative way. It is then not surprising that in Sade's descriptions the norms, the existing institutions, structure the very form of perversions. Nor is it surprising that Sade made no effort to formulate the positive content of perversion with new concepts. It is not the concept of nature in Sade – a concept originating in Spinoza and which Sade takes as "nature destructive of her own works" – that will explain the phenomenon of transgression. For, he says, nature destroys because "she seeks to recover her own most active power." This concept serves only as an argument for murder – for the insignificance of murder – as well as for refuting the law of the propagation of the species. It does not elucidate the transgressive pleasure, which aspires after *nothing* save to renew itself.

Transgression (outrage) seems absurd and puerile if it does not succeed in resolving itself into a state of affairs where it would no longer be necessary. But it is the nature of transgression never to find such a state. Transgression is then something other than the pure explosion of an energy accumulated by means of an obstacle. It is an incessant recuperation of the possible itself – inasmuch as the existing state of things has eliminated the possibility of another form of existence. The possible in what does not exist can never be anything but possible, for if the act were to recuperate it as a new form of existence, it would have to transgress it in turn. The possible as such would thus have been eliminated and would have to be recuperated yet again. What the act of transgression recuperates from the possible in what does not exist is *its own possibility of transgressing what exists*.

Transgression remains a necessity inherent in Sade's experience, independent of his interpretation. It is not only because it is given out as a testimony of atheism that transgression must not, and never can, find a state in which it could be resolved; the energy must constantly be surpassed in order that its level may be verified. It falls below the level reached as soon as it no longer meets an obstacle. One transgression must engender another transgression. But if it is thus reiterated, in Sade it reiterates itself principally only through *the same act. The act itself can never be transgressed; its image is each time represented as though it had never been carried out.*

SADE'S CRITIQUE OF THE PERVERT; THE PRELIMINARY STAGE FOR THE CREATION OF A SADEAN CHARACTER

To arrive at his notion of integral monstrosity, and to create an original character-type to represent it, Sade first had to undertake a critique of the pervert as such.

The pathological sense of the term "perversion" is not to be found in Sade. His terminology in this domain remains that of moral psychology, of the *examination of conscience* developed by the casuists.

In *The 120 Days of Sodom* the different cases of perversion are designated as passions, advancing from the "simple passions" to the "complex." The whole set forms that genealogical tree of vices and crimes that had already been evoked in *Aline and Valcour*. The subject affected with perversity is termed vicious, depraved, a "lecherous criminal," indulging in "murders in debauchery." The recurring term that is closest to notions of modern pathology is the term "maniac."

Indeed, the pervert Sade observes and describes in *The 120 Days* – that is, in the narration of anecdotes and episodes in brothels, which serve as themes that the four principal characters will be able to vary and improvise on – does behave essentially as a monomaniac. He subordinates his pleasure to performing a single gesture.

The pervert is thus distinguished, in the midst of ordinarily licentious company, by a *determinate fixed idea*. This is not yet the "idea" in the sense that Sade will work out. In the context of what is now called "libertinage," nothing is less free than the pervert's gesture. For if one means by libertinage the pure and simple propensity for orgy, free of scruples, the pervert's desire would be sated only in the scrupulous taste for, and search for, a detail – sated only in a gesture that advances scrupulously to this detail. This kind of concern would escape those who deliver themselves over to outbursts of crude appetites.

The pervert pursues *the performance of a single gesture*; it is done in a moment. The pervert's existence becomes the constant waiting for the moment in which this gesture can be performed.

The pervert as such can *signify* himself only by this gesture; executing this gesture counts for the *totality of his existence*. As a result, the pervert has *nothing to say* about his gesture that would be intelligible on the level of reciprocity between individuals. The pervert is both below and beyond the level of "individuals," which level constitutes a set of functions subordinated to the norms of the species. He presents an arbitrary subordination of the habitual life-functions to one sole insubordinate function, a craving for an improper object. In this respect he is not yet at the level of the crudest individuals. But inasmuch as this insubordination of one sole function could only be concretized, and thus become individuated, in his case, he suggests to Sade's reflections a manifold possibility of redistribution of the functions. Beyond individuals "normally" constituted, he opens a broader perspective, that of sensuous polymorphy. In the conditions of life of the human species, the pervert can affirm himself only by destroying these conditions in himself. *His existence consecrates the death of the species in him as an individual*; his being is verified as a suspension of life itself. Perversion would thus correspond to a *property of being* founded on the *expropriation of life-functions*. An expropriation of one's own body and of others would be the meaning of this property of being.

By his gesture, the pervert – whatever his perversion – seems to set forth a definition *of* existence and to pass a sort of judgment *on* existence. To verify the fact of existing in this way, his gesture must correspond to a representation. What the gesture designates is not comprehensible in itself. Though it is produced in a sphere of licentiousness, the pervert's gesture can be understood only as *diverted* from its incomprehensible content. But in this gesture one only discerns a detour to the sating of an appetite, which then apparently finds the same solution as "normal" appetites.

In Sade's eyes, the perverse gesture must have a signification that gets obscured in the closed circuit of any one determinate case of perversion. The perverse gesturing is a deaf-mute language. Deaf-mutes possess a memory of their code, but the pervert's gesture does not yet belong to any code. His perversity is its own memory. It is not so much that the pervert recalls his gesture so as to unleash it again, as that the gesture itself recalls the pervert.

If this gesture signifies something intelligible, if it answers to a representation, if finally it is a judgment, this means that this gesture *interprets* something. To make it explicit, Sade will interpret the supposed interpretation of the pervert. He will do so on the basis of what he deciphers in the pervert's gesture.

Sodomy is the absolutely central case of perversity, which Sade will take as the basis to interpret all the others, i.e., as the principle of affinity in what will form integral monstrosity.

This Biblical term, consecrated by moral theology, covers an action which is not limited to homosexual practice. Homosexuality, which is not an intrinsic perversion, must be distinguished from sodomy, which is. Like heterosexual forms of behavior, homosexual practices admit of giving rise to institutions, as has been seen many times in the history of human societies. But sodomy is formulated by a specific

gesture of counter-generality (and this is most significant
in Sade's eyes): it is what strikes precisely at the law of
the propagation of the species, and thereby *bears witness to
the death of the species in the individual*. It evinces an attitude
not only of refusal but of aggression; in being the *simulacrum*
of the act of generation, it is a *mockery* of it. In this sense it is
also a simulacrum of the destruction that a subject dreams of
ravaging upon another of the same sex by a sort of reciprocal
transgression of their limits. When perpetrated on a subject
of the other sex, it is a *simulacrum of metamorphosis*, always
accompanied by a sort of magic fascination. The sodomist
gesture, transgressing the organic specificity of individuals,
introduces into existence the principle of the metamorphosis
of beings into one another, which integral monstrosity tends
to reproduce and which universal prostitution, the ultimate
application of atheism, postulates.

To decipher the pervert's gesture Sade will set up a code
of perversion. Its key sign is revealed by the constitution of
the sodomist gesture. For Sade, all things gravitate about
this gesture. It is the most absolute because of the mortal
threat that it poses for the norms of the species, and also
because of a kind of immortality the repetition gives it. It
is the most ambiguous in that it is conceivable only because
of the existence of these norms – as well as being the most
qualified for transgression, which can be brought about only
through the obstacle constituted by these norms.

One can see that Sade in no way seeks to know the origin
of perversion with respect to norms, nor to explain how these
norms could become depraved in the individual. He takes
perversion as a given (constitutional or congenital) phenomenon which, like everything that nature manifests, is to be
explained rationally. This is why Sade introduces logically
structured language into perversion, which is with respect to
this language a structure apparently devoid of logic.

This code, now translated into words, will be specifically
affected by the perverse gesture, upon which it will be structured, while logical language will restructure the perverse
gesture and shape Sade's written expression of it. What

logical language, as the language of reason, will adapt to the coded gesture of the pervert is atheism – as an "act of good sense," of "common sense." On the other hand, what the perverse gesture thus coded introduces into the language of "common sense" is the non-language of monstrosity, which subsists under this code. Between the rational language of norms and anomaly there is a sort of osmosis that only Sade could carry off: atheism will become integral only insofar as perversion seeks to be rational, and only insofar as it seeks this will it become integral monstrosity.

Sade will inaugurate his original creation by a decisive masterstroke at this point: to create imaginative characters corresponding to the type of the pervert he conceives, Sade takes the pervert out of conventional licentious society, and in particular out of the brothel. Here Sade breaks with the libertine literary tradition and introduces the theme of perversion into the depiction of common manners. Sade camps his characters in the everyday world; he finds them at the very heart of public institutions, in the fortuitous circumstances of social life. Thus the world itself appears as the locus in which the secret law of the universal prostitution of beings is verified. By the same token, Sade conceives the counter-generality to be already implicit in the existent generality, not to criticize institutions, but to demonstrate that of themselves the institutions ensure the triumph of perversions.

Sade invents a type of pervert who speaks from his singular gesture *in the name of generality.* If this gesture counts as a judgment, the judgment is pronounced only at the moment when the notion of generality intervenes. If the gesture is singular, undecipherable, it is so only in relation to the generality of gestures. The generality of gestures is confounded with that of speech. And if his gesture has a meaning for the pervert, there is no need of speech to express what it signifies. But the singular gesture of the pervert is precisely not formed in the medium of generality which may accompany speech; it is sometimes substituted for words, and sometimes even contradicts them. The singular gesture of the pervert immediately *empties speech of all content since it is for him the very fact of existence.*

But once set up as Sade's character-type, the pervert explicates his singular gesture in accordance with the generality of gestures. The very fact that he speaks requires the reciprocity involved in persuasion, and invokes the fact of his belonging to the human species.

It follows that at the moment he speaks, he disavows the singularity of his gesture (which was the motive of his discourse) because such singularity is unique to each individual. The content of his gesture, then, is no longer singular: in silence it had no meaning – and now it acquires meaning in speech. If, as the pervert says, the singularity of his gesture is proper to each, he still has to show that each one can act in the singular way that he acts. Yet each time the pervert speaks about this it is only because he is convinced of the contrary, that he alone acts in this way. From the very fact that he speaks, he is mistaken about the object of his demonstration and he encounters the obstacle already established in himself. For the pervert who speaks, the obstacle is not to be singular but to belong to generality in his own singularity. How can he overcome this obstacle? If he does speak, can he show, *in the name of generality*, that there *is no* generality and that the norms of the species have no real existence? If that were true, one could no longer say that this singularity was proper to each individual. How could one show that the norms do not exist? The singularity of the gesture is reestablished without its opaqueness being in any way cleared up. The pervert (who is the only one to have to show the validity of his gesture) hastens to perform that gesture.

Due to the very fact that it invokes one's adherence to common sense, the pervert's discourse remains sophistic: one does not get away from the concept of normative reason. Persuasion can be effected only if the interlocutor is in turn led to reject norms in himself. It is not by arguments that Sade's characters can obtain the assent of their interlocutors, but by complicity.

Complicity is the contrary of persuasion in accordance with

universal understanding. Those who know themselves to be accomplices in aberration need no arguments to understand one another. Yet the characters Sade depicts, despite the affinities that they discover in one another through the unique gesture (of sodomy), owe it to themselves to always proclaim the absence of a God, the guarantor of norms. Thus they profess integral atheism, which they claim to bear witness to by their acts. But among themselves, the coded gesture is disengaged from logically structured language which, as an oratorical precaution, conceals it, and the key sign that represents this gesture reappears in its *true locus: the secret society*. Here the gesture becomes a simulacrum, a rite, which the members of the secret society do not explain to one another other than by the non-existence of the absolute guarantor of norms, non-existence they commemorate as an event that can be represented only by this gesture.

For the normal interlocutor to feel complicity with the pervert, he must first suffer a certain disintegration as a "rational" individual. This is possible only by the impulse – or the repulsion – which the pervert's speech provokes in him.

How could the pervert recognize complicity in this "normal" interlocutor? By a gesture the subject makes, in the generality of gestures, in contradiction to what he says. The interlocutor who rejects the pervert's sophism makes a contradictory gesture: for, notwithstanding the disavowal it expresses, it physically, hence corporeally, bears witness to his own singularity – latent in him as in everyone. For if the rejection of the sophism is made in the name of the generality of common sense, what does the interlocutor (who at this moment becomes a passive subject) disclaim, if not this latent singularity in himself? He can make this gesture of disavowal and defense only by thereby avowing his own singularity. The pervert lies in wait for this contradictory gesture, this reflex gesture, this corporeal (and thus mute) gesture, which he deciphers in these terms: "Consider all the fatalities which unite us and see if Nature does not offer you a victim in my individual nature."

HOW INTEGRAL MONSTROSITY CONSTITUTES A MENTAL SPACE: THE ASCESIS OF APATHY

For Sade the act of sodomy is the supreme form of transgressing norms (which supposes their paradoxical maintenance). Since it is at the same time a mode of transgression common to different cases of perversion, it thus constitutes the principle of affinity among the perversions. For, like a callipygian test, this act suppresses the specific frontiers between the sexes and, according to Sade, constitutes the key sign for all perversions.

Having interpreted this act morally as a testimony to atheism and thus, as a declaration of war on the norms inherited from monotheism, Sade then projects perversion into the domain of thought. There, integral monstrosity forms a sort of mental space for communication with one another by the mutual understanding of this key sign.

Hence the doctrinal character of Sade's work and of the didactic situations he lays out; hence, above all, the preparatory discernment and discrimination carried out in this singular academy, according to which the doctors of monstrosity recognize one another, distinguish themselves from the casual pervert, and choose their disciples.

No candidate for integral monstrosity is recognized to be qualified who has not conceived this way of acting as a profession of atheism. No atheist is recognized who is not capable of passing immediately into action. Once such disciples have been chosen, they are subjected to a progressive initiation which culminates in a specific ascetic practice: the ascesis of apathy.

The practice of apathy as Sade suggests it supposes that what is termed "soul," "conscience," "sensibility," "the heart," are only diverse structures taken on by the concentration of the same impulsive forces. These forces can be structured as an instrument of intimidation under the pressure of the institutional world, or as one of subversion under the internal pressure of these forces – and always instantaneously. But it is always the same impulses that intimidate us *at the same time* as they raise us up in revolt.

How does this intimidating insurrection or this insurrectional intimidation act in us? On the one hand, by the images that precede the acts, inciting us to act or undergo. On the other hand, by the images of those acts, already committed or omitted, which come back to us at a later date and give us a guilty conscience: i.e., whenever the impulses themselves become inactive, the guilty conscience can reemerge. Thus the consciousness of oneself and of others is a most fragile and most transparent structure. Since our impulses intimidate us in the form of "fear," "compassion," "horror," or "remorse," by images of acts that have been or can be realized, we must substitute the acts for their repellent images whenever these images tend to substitute themselves for the acts and thus forestall them.

Sade does not use the term "image" here; we substitute it for the terms "fear" and "remorse" since his terms presuppose a representation of the act that has been or is to be committed. In any case, an image intervenes not only in the form of remorse, but also in the form of a project.

Reiteration is at first the condition required for the monster to remain on the level of monstrosity. If the reiteration is purely passionate it remains ill-ensured. For the monster to progress beyond the level he has already reached, he has first to avoid falling back short of it, and he can do so only if he reiterates his act in absolute apathy. This alone can maintain him in a state of permanent transgression. By imposing this new condition on the candidate for integral monstrosity, Sade introduces a critique of the sensuous, and especially a critique of the primary benefit of transgression – the pleasure inseparable from the act.

How can the same act committed in intoxication, in delirium, be reiterated sober-mindedly? For there to be any possibility of reeffecting this act, must not the image which re-presents itself to the mind, however repellent it be, function as a lure, a promise of pleasure?

What Sade takes as understood beneath his maxim of the apathetic reiteration of an act we can reconstitute as follows: he recognizes the alternation of the diverse structures which the impulsive forces take on in both their insurrectional and intimidating movements. But in one of the structures that these forces, individuated in the subject, have developed under the pressure of the institutional environment – that is, of norms – he seems also to have recognized *self-consciousness*. This structure undergoes variations and suffers instability, though this becomes clear only after the fact. Sometimes these forces put the subject *outside of himself* and make him act *against himself*, and thus they transgress the structure of consciousness and decompose it. Sometimes, especially when they have made him act against himself, they recompose the consciousness of the subject during his inaction (i.e. by remembering); in this case these same forces are inverted. The inversion of the same forces constitutes the consciousness that *censors* the subject. What exercises censorship is the feeling the subject has that *being put outside of oneself* is a threat to the subject insofar as he depends on the norms of the species. This censorship is already felt in the very act of transgression, and is the necessary motive for it. For Sade moral conscience simply corresponds to an exhaustion of the impulsive forces (the "calm of the senses"); this state of exhaustion opens an interval in which the repellent image of the act committed represents itself in the form of "remorse."

In fact, the first time the act was committed, it presented a promise of pleasure *because* its image was repellent. If, now, the reiteration of the same act is to "annihilate" conscience, the same forces that act will also undergo inversion and reestablish conscience. Inverted into a censorship, they will then provoke the act *anew*.

Sade's formulation of apathetic reiteration is the expression of a deeper apprehension: he feels quite clearly that transgression is bound up with censorship, but the purely logical analysis which his formulation presupposes does not grasp the *contradictory simultaneity* of the two. Sade describes and decomposes this simultaneity into successive states: insurrection–transgression–intimidation; but intimidation and transgression remain in close interdependency, each provoking the other. This is why he wishes to eliminate intimidation by the apathetic reiteration of the act. He then apparently empties transgression of the benefit it would yield: pleasure.

The elimination of the sensuous element should then block the return of moral conscience. But in preventing its return, this ascesis seems to uproot the motive for transgression. The sodomist act (which forms the key sign of all perversion) has no significative value save as a conscious transgression of the norms represented by conscience. The desire to be cast *outside of oneself* is, in practice, equivalent to a disintegration of the subject's conscience by means of thought. Thought must reestablish *the primitive version of impulsive forces*, which the conscience of the subject had inverted. For the disciple who will practice the doctrine (and this is not for the casual pervert) monstrosity is the zone of this being *outside of oneself, outside of conscience*; the monster can maintain himself in this zone only by the reiteration of the same act. The "voluptuous harshness" which, according to Sade, is its fruit, is no longer something sensuous. "Harshness" presupposes a distinction between thought and moral conscience; and "voluptuousness" alludes to the ecstasy of thought in the representation of the act reiterated "coldly" – an ecstasy here opposed to its functional analog, orgasm.

In effect, the orgasmic moment amounts to a fall of thought outside of its own ecstasy. It is this fall outside of ecstasy which ends in the orgasm of the body's functions that the Sadean characters wish to prevent through apathy. He knows that orgasm is but a tribute paid to the norms of the species, and is thus a counterfeit of the ecstasy of thought. It is not enough that orgasm in the sodomist act is but a loss of forces, a *useless* pleasure; when the act, this time separated from orgasm, is reiterated, this useless pleasure is identified with the ecstasy of thought.

The apathetic reiteration of the act brings to light a new factor: number. It brings to light the relationship between quantity and quality in sadism. The act passionately re-iterated on the same object is *depreciated* (or diversified) for the benefit of the *quality of the object*. As the object is multiplied and the very number of objects depreciates them, the *quality of the act itself*, reiterated in apathy, is the better affirmed.

THE LESSON OF APATHY: IS TRANSGRESSION OF THE ACT POSSIBLE?

It could be that for thought, apathetic reiteration is but a parable, and that transgression ends by transgressing the act: "Virtue itself will safeguard you from remorse, for you shall have acquired the habit of doing evil at the first virtuous prompting; and to cease doing evil you shall have to stifle virtue."[3]

Let us see if this second maxim contradicts or corroborates the maxim of apathetic reiteration. We take note that it says "You shall have acquired the habit of doing evil . . . and to cease doing evil." There are here two ways of acting such that the first substitutes itself for the second and makes non-repentance into virtue, which will now consist in "ceasing to do evil."

The co-ordinate clause introduced by "for" (*qua re*) incriminates "the habit of doing evil at the first virtuous prompting" as the motive for repentance. Hence there is a connection between two kinds of reaction: repentance, which is but a reaction undergone by the subject; and the habit of doing evil upon sight of virtue, which is a habitual *reflex*, that of reacting *immediately through outrage*. A first conclusion to be drawn is that repentance and the habit of doing evil are equally *negative reflexes*. If that is the case, the second maxim (to stifle virtue) aims to substitute for the reflex of outrage a reaction to this reflex (a reaction against the necessity of outrage), which would then be a positive action.

"You shall have acquired the habit of doing evil . . .": is not this the purpose of the deliberate apathetic reiteration? Then when will this reiteration no longer be a habit of doing evil? If it is a transposition, a *deliberate* reflex, how can it be distinguished from the habit of doing evil, the habit of perpetrating an outrage? If the deliberate reflex cannot be distinguished from the habit, then the second injunction would appear to be in fact the refutation of the apathetic reiteration. On the contrary, for the second injunction to explain that reiteration, one has to see how it disengages from the simple reactive character of outrage a positive act without outrage, all the while stifling virtue. How does virtue show itself – in what intolerable aspect? It shows itself as consistency (that of the conscious subject); consistency represents the Good. According to the principle of identity which follows from individuation, inconsistency is Evil. But for the impulsive forces that are opposed to individuation, inconsistency is Good. Since the impulsive forces sustain inconsistency but only manifest themselves in function of consistency, which is intolerable to them, they must then acquire *constancy* in inconsistency. In a word, Sade wished to transgress the act of outrage by a permanent state of perpetual movement – the movement Nietzsche much later termed "the innocence of becoming." But Sade caught sight of this transgression-by-transgression-itself for only a moment; the hyperbole of his thought brought him back to the core of his irreducible sensibility, bound to its representation of an outrageous act – which excludes the very notion of innocence. That is why the impulsive forces can prevent virtue (that is, consistency) from showing itself only through the *constancy of an act*. This consistency (i.e. the reiteration of the act), however apathetic, is but a reiterated reconstitution of virtue's intolerable aspect and of the outrage it provokes.

ANDROGYNY IN THE SADEAN REPRESENTATION

In Sade, the principal types of perversion are generally represented only by men; the number of unnatural women found among them do not really represent anomaly as such. Man, because he alone traditionally exercises reflection, represents the rational sex. Therefore he alone is also called upon to give an account of reason. However monstrous, perverse, or delirious a woman may be, she is never considered "abnormal," for it is written in the norms that by nature she lacks reflection, possesses no equilibrium or measure, and never represents anything but uncontrolled sensuous nature, more or less attenuated by a reflection prescribed by men. Indeed, the more monstrous or mad she is, the more fully a woman she is, according to the traditional representation, always colored by misogyny. Nonetheless, she has resources that a man will never possess, resources she shares with the pervert.

Now, the integral monstrosity conceived by Sade has as its immediate effect an exchange of the specific qualities of the sexes. The result is not only a simple symmetrical reversal of the schema of differentiation within each of the two sexes, giving active and passive pederasty on the one side, lesbianism and tribadism on the other. In integral monstrosity – as a didactic project for sensuous polymorphousness – the two representatives of the species, male and female, will in their relationship with each other face a twofold model. Each of the two sexes interiorizes this twofold model not only because of the ambivalence proper to each, but also because of Sade's embellishment of this ambivalence.

Although man as the Sadean pervert-type apparently retains rational primacy, he is henceforth presented as the affirmation of sensuous nature, which is given to him in a mental perspective: the perspective of the imaginary. Perversion, we said at the beginning, insofar as it confirms the fact of its being by a suspension of the life-functions, would correspond to a property of being whose meaning would be the expropriation of one's own body and the body of the other.

Integral atheism, the suppression of an absolute guarantor of the norms, would corroborate this *expropriation* ideologically. For in abolishing the limits of the responsible and self-identical ego, it logically abolishes the identity of one's own body. In itself the body is the concrete product of the individuating impulsive forces, according to the norms of the species. Since we are now in fact dealing with denomination in language, we can say these impulsive forces speak to the pervert in these terms: the language of institutions has taken over this body – or more particularly, taken over what is functional in "*my*" body – for the better preservation of the species. This language has assimilated the body which "I am" to the point that "we" have been expropriated by the institutions from the beginning. This body has been restored to "me," corrected in certain ways; that is, certain forces have been pruned away, and others subjugated, only through language. "I" then do not possess "my" body save in the name of the institutions; the language in "me" is just their overseer put in "me." The institutional language has taught "me" that this body in which "I am" was "mine." The greatest crime "I" can commit is not so much to take "his" body from the "other"; it is to break "my" body away from this "myself" instituted by language. What "I" gain by "myself" having a body "I" immediately lose in reciprocal relations with the "other," whose body does not belong to "me."

The representation of having a body whose state is other than one's own body is clearly specific to perversion. Although the pervert feels the *alterity* of the alien body, he has a stronger feeling that the *other's body is his own*, and that the body which is normatively and institutionally his, he experiences as being really *foreign to himself*, that is, foreign to the insubordinate function that defines him. To conceive the effect of his violence on the other, *he must first inhabit the other*. It will be in the reflexes of the other's body that he verifies its foreignness; he will experience the irruption of an alien force within "himself." He is at once within and without.

How can this be brought about? Not at first, indeed not at all, by recourse to violence that could go as far as murder, but rather by the workings of the imagination that precede every violent act. The imaginary will have primacy over the rational. We can see this primacy of the imaginary in the representation of pleasure, where the impulse redoubles in projecting its own image, that is, by extending pleasure to organs excluded from the propagative function and by reducing the organs' proper function, thereby producing pleasure without utility.

The imagination prerequisite for the perverse gesture is constituted in correspondences between intensities that the functional reason had to exclude in order to set itself up by subordinating the life-functions of the species. While reason (logical language) both expresses and guarantees the *equilibrium* that the species found in its empirical habits, imagination apprehends the *schemas* of an illusory function in which the *existing organ takes the place of* the absent – hence ideal – "functional" structure. In these schemas, the absence of the imagined structure is evidently the factor that excites; the existing structure offers a terrain in which *outrage* is inflicted *in the name of something absent*: the ideal structure of androgyny.

If the presence of this imaginary structure in the pervert and his disconnection from his body are strong enough for him to behave as a woman with his masculine counterpart, he will feel feminine passivity in himself more profoundly. He then can conduct himself *actively* only if he deals with his masculine counterpart as with a woman, or deals with a woman as with a boy.

Out of this latter case, Sade elaborates the synthetic simulacrum of the androgynous being: not a woman–man, but a man–woman. He conceived Juliette as such a being. In fact, the Sadean heroine is the contrary of a man, more particularly the contrary of the Sadean pervert who, in his integral monstrosity, functions as the definition of sensuous nature: she expresses reason. She uses reason only to better recover her own being, traditionally defined as sensuous nature, and does so only insofar as she progresses into insensibility. She presents the perfect example of the morality of apathy. This morality is one of the secret expedients of women, set up as a doctrine; the morality of apathy is feminine frigidity methodically put to use. Finally, and most importantly, it is the Sadean heroine who carries atheism to its integral affirmation, dissociating it from normative and anthropomorphic reason, freeing thought itself in the experimental sphere of monstrosity.

The abolition of norms, which this thought implies, is more important to the woman than to the pervert, in whom the norms exist only in a state of decay. For as woman she remains subject to the norms (at least organically), principally by reason of her fecundity. Then apathy will all the more be the source of her conduct; its first effect is the extirpation of all maternal instinct. Here again we see verified the fact that the norms themselves (here corporeal norms), just as much as institutions, structure the forces that are to destroy them. "Normally" prostitutable, "normally" vicious, "normally" lesbian and tribade – it is once again reason, here "good sense," that dictates to her that she be all this coldly. In learning to undergo coolly the perverse acts committed on her own body, she develops the virile energy of a consummate callipygian.

Juliette thus presents herself to the Sadean pervert as the simulacrum of what the sodomist act designates. In this figure formed by the reversal of sensuous passivity into active intellection, the preeminent act of transgression finds its complementary image.

HOW THE SADEAN EXPERIENCE RENDERS ITS CONVENTIONAL FORM OF COMMUNICATION UNREADABLE

In what has preceded I sought to examine the *interpretive* character of the description Sade gives of his own experience. This experience appeared to include a twofold experimentation: the representation of sensuous nature in an aberrant act, and its representation as described. We have to remember the fact that Sade writes books. What is the literary character of his work? How does its singularity set it apart not only from its contemporary literary context, but from everything one defines as literature? Is it essentially modern, or does it elude this definition also? Let us look more closely into the question formulated earlier: how does writing actualize sensuous nature in an aberrant act, and what is the *relationship* between this actualization *and the perpetration of the act* independent of its description?

Dealing with a personal experience which was condemned by its very nature to remain incommunicable, Sade chooses to translate this experience into the conventional form characteristic of all communication. By the same token, conventional communication becomes "unreadable" each time the incommunicable experience is *asserted*, but becomes all the more readable when the same experience disappears again. How then does Sade's experience render his conventional form of communication "unreadable"? In that it is entirely built on reiteration. The object of reiteration is to arouse ecstasy. This ecstasy cannot be conveyed by language; what language describes are the ways to it, the dispositions that prepare for it. But what is not brought out clearly in Sade's conventional form of writing is that the ecstasy and the reiteration are the same thing; in the description the fact of reiterating and that of undergoing the ecstasy are two different aspects. For the reader there remains only the reiteration described and the wholly exterior aspect of the ecstasy, the orgasm described, which is counterfeit ecstasy.

Sade seems to think of his reader as someone he must continually hold breathless with the promise of yet another shock. Yet what the reader is ultimately seeking at the expense of his reading is a sort of lapse of attention at a moment when the whole text wants sustained attention, a lapse of the thought pursued so laboriously. Here what is required is that we compare the practice of writing with the principle of the apathetic reiteration of acts. This principle immediately affects Sade's literary expression; it is at work in what the literary expression contains that is apparently non-literary, unreadable in the broad sense of the term. The apathetic reiteration conveys Sade's own struggle to regain possession of what is irreducible in his experience. It defines the bottom layer of this experience: writing's actualization of the aberrant act corresponds to the apathetic reiteration of this act perpetrated apart from its description. In actualizing the act, writing stimulates the ecstasy of thought. *Reiterated* on the level of language, the ecstasy coincides with the transgression reiterated by fictitious characters. Thus the logically structured language with which Sade expresses himself becomes the *terrain* of outrage, as it is the terrain of norms.

If Sade expressed himself in logically structured language, it is because this language also has structured the depth of Sade's own experience in advance. In order to make that experience clear to himself through his writing, he could apprehend it only in accordance with the laws of this language – albeit by transgressing them. He never transgresses these laws except in the gesture whereby he reproduces them *in* their transgression. Is it then the logical structure of language – or is it the very core of the experience – that wills the reiteration of outrage? No doubt it is this core of experience, already structured by language but restructuring its logic on the basis of the aberrant act.

The traditional language, which Sade himself uses with amazing effect, can endure anything that conforms to its logical structure. It corrects, censors, excludes, or silences everything that would destroy this structure, all non-sense. To *describe* aberration is positively to articulate the absence of those elements which would make a thing, a state, or a being not viable. Sade accepts this logical structure and maintains it without discussion; what is more, he develops it, systematizes it, even to the point of outrage. For outrage conserves it only as a dimension of aberration – not because aberration is *described* in this logically structured language, but because the aberrant act is *reproduced* in it.

To reproduce the aberrant act in this way amounts to giving language as a possibility of action; hence the irruption of non-language in language.

When Suetonius describes Caligula's or Nero's aberrant acts, it is not to maintain apart from these figures the *possibility of these acts through his text*. Nor is it to identify his text with the maintenance of this possibility.

Sade's text maintains and supports the possibility of the aberrant act, inasmuch as the writing actualizes this act. All the same, this *actualization by writing* functions as a censor which Sade inflicts on himself, namely, to censor an act that could be perpetrated independently of its description. The image of the aberrant act has first become a logically structured aberration. Thus structured in discourse, the aberration exhausts reflection; the words again become what the discourse had for a moment prevented them from being: a propensity for the very act that reestablishes the image of its perpetration in muteness. Why in muteness? Because the *motive* of the act to be done, the outrage, is not recognized in the sort of monumentalization of the possibility for action that speech, words, the phrasing of discourse produce. The discourse buried the act that was to be committed, even as it exalted its image. The propensity for the aberrant act then destroys this funerary image and once again requires obedience to its motive. Thus it precipitates anew the description of the act that here *stands for* its perpetration, but can do so only as *recommenced*.

The parallelism between the apathetic reiteration of acts and Sade's descriptive reiteration again establishes that the image of the act to be done is re-presented each time not only as though it had never been performed, but also as though it had never been described. This reversibility of one and the same process inscribes the presence of *non-language* in language; it inscribes a *foreclosure* of language by language.

"Foreclosure" means that something remains outside. That which remains outside is, once again, *the act to be done*. The less it is perpetrated the more it knocks on the door – the door of literary vacuity. The blows struck on the door are Sade's words, which, if they now reverberate within literature, remain nonetheless blows struck from without. The outside is precisely what of itself dispenses with any commentary. What gives Sade's text its disturbing originality is that through him this outside comes to be commented on as something produced within thought.

Do we in fact read Sade as we read Laclos, Stendhal, Balzac? Clearly not! We would not look to the bottom of the pages of *Splendeurs et misères des courtesanes* for notes which would give prescriptive formulas and recipes for the procedures to follow or ways to act in the bedchamber. We do find here and there this sort of quite pragmatic note at the bottom of the pages of *Juliette*. Perhaps some of these notes have been added with a commercial aim in view; perhaps they are not even from Sade's hand. Yet they do figure in the editions published during his lifetime. It would be false discretion to wish to drop them from the text; they do belong with the subject-matter of the book. To say that they are devoid of literary interest would be to show one understands nothing of Sade's originality. These pragmatic notes reveal the exercise of his purest irony. The irony would be pointless if these notes were without real pragmatic use. In any case, they function to indicate the outside. This outside is not at all the interior of the "bedroom" where one would philosophize; it is the inwardness of thought which *nothing* separates from the "bedroom".

In fact the term "bedroom" is merely banter; in Sade, it designates the bloody cave of the Cyclops, whose single eye is that of voracious thought.

Thus the foreclosure of language by itself gives Sade's work its singular configuration: first a set of tales, discourses, then a series of tableaux which slyly invite the reader to see outside what *does not seem to lie in the text* – whereas *nothing appears anywhere except in the text*. His work, then, is like the vast layout of an urban showroom within a city, one with the city, where without noticing it one passes from the objects exhibited to objects accidentally included but not really exhibitable. In the end, one recognizes that it is to *these* objects that the exhibition corridors lead.

NOTES

1 Elaborations, and digressions, on a paper entitled "Sign and Perversion in Sade" read to "Tel Quel" on May 12, 1966.

2 Cf. "Note relative à ma détention" in The Marquis de Sade, *Cahiers personnels* (1803–1804). Unpublished texts edited, with preface and notes, by Gilbert Lély (Paris: Corréa, 1953). Trans. Richard Seaver and Austryn Wainhouse, "Note concerning my detention", in The Marquis de Sade, *The Complete Justine, Philosophy in the Bedroom, and other Writings* (New York: Grove Press, 1965).

3 The Marquis de Sade, *Juliette*, trans. Austryn Wainhouse (New York: Grove Press, 1976), p. 450.

CHAPTER 3

Libidinal economy in Sade and Klossowski

Jean-François Lyotard
(Translation by Iain Hamilton Grant, slightly modified)

In Sade, the group of relations surrounding the *value* of the monetary sign and its *intensity* is quite different from that found in prostitution. To begin with, the client's body is the same as the procurer's – and from this perhaps stems Sade's republicanism.[1] The Society of the Friends of Crime is not the society of procurers. The criminal milieu embodies the duplicity of signs: adultery of money with *jouissance*, fraud of *jouissance* when it is converted into currency. The sign of these exchanges becomes the accomplice of untransmittable phantasms; the consumption of the libidinal singularity is bought at the price of universally estimable sums in the form of money. Like Hegel's *Mitte*,[2] the criminal milieu assures the institution's permeability to desire. In this respect there is little difference between it and the Police. "Perverse" drives are channeled by it towards the social body, the body of exchanges, towards the circuit of the communication of exchanges and goods. It is a milieu of duplicity and dissimulation *par excellence*, even though it has no need to hide itself, just like the Police, since it too is concerned with the detection and regulation of allegedly socially perverse partial drives. We would dearly love to write about the *policeman's discourse*, the dissimulated–dissimulating speech *par excellence*, not because its real aim is other than its declared aim, which is not its distinguishing characteristic, but by virtue of its *interest* in the *passions* of the interrogated: the comprehensive desire of the commissioner, always more comprehensive, more embracing, molding itself into, connecting onto the most intense regions of the interrogated's desire, his most unknown desires (for example, passivity, submitting to beatings), thus inscribing itself in an arousing, erotic, perverse, infantile relation – but always with a view to *concentrating* all these partial drives in the circle of trade and in the total body, one of the producers of which is the policeman. "Making someone talk" in this case is nothing other than the reestablishment of *jouissance* in the place assigned it by order.

The pimp is an element of the same figure, working more on the side of the passions than of interest, thus complementing the preceding case.3 His function still remains to distil the libido from the fragments of the negotiable body of prostitutes, to heighten its quality by a continual exercise of release rendering them available at every moment to the flows of strongest energy. *This availability at every moment* is what produces vertigo in great prostitution: it is, like the creations of the pimp on the woman's body, at once the mark of her *signification* as a communicable and negotiable sign, the remarkable madness of her disappearance as a person and of her abolition in the anonymity of libidinal drives. Within the *power* relation, such availability is called slavery or at least servitude [*Knechtschaft*], but at the same time and interior to the order of *powers*, it is a force and anonymity that surpasses every domination. There is no dialectic between the two positions, since there is no interval: for example, the same *arrogance* of *Jacques le Fataliste* counts both as an outburst against the position of the master and, therefore, an attempt to reverse it on the one hand, and on the other as the anonymous production of a libidinal "knowledge" passing beyond every hierarchy; this arrogance being that of the inflexible partial drive, and in this sense, never aggressive, never receptive to social reasons for struggle. In the story of *F.B.*, or *O.*, everything marks the dizzying heights of the pimp in a similar manner, the master of bodies reduced to registered initials, a region of routes for nameless intensities. The woman's initial and the prisoner's registration number result from a supplementary labor on the proper name, by which it is almost effaced, as every corporeality closed up on itself, and as every subjective reserve, must be; but also maintained in its effacement, since it is by the anonymity lodged in the name that the aberration makes itself noticeable.

But there is none of this in the Society of the Friends of Crime. This is a society cut off from the social body, neither catching the perverse passions nor concentrating them in it. Compared to the pimp and the cop, the criminal is a very rich man, 25,000 *livres* of annual income, 10,000 francs in expenses per victim bought for the purposes of *jouissance*. And his function is not at all the concentration of the partial drives: these, expended in profusion on the bodies of subjects, will never be inscribed on the social body, as money, due to the criminal's intervention. Conversely, the latter withdraws his revenues from the circulation of goods and devotes them to pure voluptuous consumption. If there is venality of *jouissance*, it is certainly not through poverty, but thanks to the greatest luxury and for the increase of lust. "The fantasy's equivalent (the sum paid)," writes Klossowski, "represents not only the emotion in itself, but also the *exclusion* of thousands of human lives. Value is even augmented by this scandal, from the gregarious point of view."[4] And he establishes criminal equations, which cannot be those of the procurer, in the following way: "*Exclusive voluptuousness = famine = annihilation = the supreme value of the fantasy . . . One fantasy = an entire population.*"[5]

It might be said that subordinating the libidinal force of the arrangements of the Château de la Forêt-Noire to the fact that they cost the price of the lives of thousands of mouths to feed is still to conceive of Sade in a nihilist fashion. Is it not enough for the purchased victims to be destroyed inside the château in order that we may begin to understand the mortifying stupidity of the libido, without any need to calculate, into the bargain, what it costs those outside? But the function of this infamy is not "supplementary." Instead, it must be linked to the peculiar status of the criminal; he is both pimp and client, or rather, neither one nor the other. The pimp diverts the client's partial drive back into the lap of society, under the form of the monetary equivalent; the client, in consuming his libidinal energy in the production of his fantasies with the help of the prostitute, produces a *libidinal equivalent of currency*. But it is essential that the criminal leave the system of equivalence between drives and money; if money remains present in its libidinal "accountancy," it is no longer as the substitute or the simulacrum, it comes under the heading of a *bodily region* (which can no longer be, then, the alleged social body, but the great libidinal surface), which, like any other, can and must be grasped by the libido and submit to its consummatory irradiation. Currency, language itself, becomes the object of the libertines' operations in the same way as the body. We know that from *Day* to *Day* Duclos "tells the story" of her monstrous life, which is simply the diachronic development of the combinatory set of infamies; this villainess's "narrative" is to language what the money spent for crime by the four master libertines is to political economy. Her narrative is not the substitute in words for "real" arrangements – we know that they practice this in abundance. Rather, it is a *reality* well beyond the supposedly "practical" (unduly endowed by a nihilist tradition with the exclusive privilege to determine reality), which extends into those regions occupied, according to this same tradition, by substitutes for things and persons, i.e. the regions of money and language. The criminal perpetrates, on the *skin of currency* as on that of beings and words, the same plan of extreme intensification, the execution of which can only be followed by the ossification of the excited surfaces. That is why signs of exchange here, as opposed to what happens in prostitution, are not taken out of the circuit of communication, but are devoted to destruction, to such an extent that one wonders if the Society of the Friends of Crime is economically viable. In any case, it is not capitalistic, and what it accumulates is a wealth of ruins.

Nevertheless, Klossowski understands this ruinous use of monetary signs in a very different, more "progressive" way: it constitutes, he says, a protest against the prostitutive function of cash value in society. Whereas the pimp establishes a relation between perversion and the social body, between the tensor sign and the intelligent sign, and when he thus proves to be the only really institutive connection to the commercial body itself, the criminal *disrupts* this relation. The withdrawal of his fortune and its squandering on untransmittable pleasure are provocations destined to give rise to the alternative, before which *dissimulation* or duplicity of signs necessarily places a politics of the libido: either recognize that "the institutional repudiation of complete monstrosity is *converted into de facto prostitution, material and moral*,"[6] thus admitting that the generalized system of commodities is the system of prostitution under the cover of trade in objects and services, – or "affirm that there is only one authentically universal communication: *the exchange of bodies by the secret language of bodily signs*."[7] Sade's woman criminal provides the principle for this and illustrates one of its effects, that of insurrection or perpetual disturbance of the circle of exchanges by the passions, as Blanchot would say.[8]

It is from posing the libidinal political problem under this alternative – either the beings communicate through the exchange of their bodies, i.e., "perversion," or prostitution is sanctioned under the sign of dead currency (which is capital, or in any case, mercantilism) – that Klossowski forges his impossible fiction of a living currency. "One should imagine for an instant," he writes,

an apparently impossible regression: that is, an industrial phase where the producers have the means to demand payment from consumers, in the form of objects of sensation. These objects are living beings. According to this example of barter, producers and consumers thereby constitute collections of "persons" allegedly destined for pleasure, emotion, sensation. How can the human "person" fulfill the function of currency? How could the producers, instead of paying for women, ever come to be paid "in women"? How would the entrepreneurs, the industrialists, pay their engineers, their workers? "In women". Who will keep this living currency alive? Other women. And this presupposes the reverse: women pursuing a career will be paid "in boys." Who will "keep", that is to say, who will sustain this virile currency? Those who have feminine currency at their disposal. What we are saying here in fact exists. For, without literally returning to barter, all of modern industry rests on an exchange mediated by the sign of inert currency, neutralizing the nature of the objects exchanged; it rests, that is, on a simulacrum of exchange – a simulacrum which lies in the form of manpower resources, thus a living currency, not affirmed as such, but already existent.[9]

Before we marvel at this fantasy, let's measure the exact range
its author attributes to it:

As living currency, the industrial slave stands as both a sign
guaranteeing wealth and this wealth itself. As a sign, it stands for all
kinds of other material riches; as wealth, however, it excludes every
other demand that is not the demand of which it is the satisfaction.
But satisfaction, strictly speaking, is equally excluded by its quality
as a sign. This is how living currency essentially differs from the
condition of the industrial slave (personalities, stars, advertising
models, hostesses, etc.). The industrial slave could not lay claim
to the category of the sign, since she differentiates between what
she is prepared to receive as inert currency, and what she is worth
in her own eyes.[10]

The creature who has become living currency occupies a quite
different position from that held by the woman Klossowski
calls the "industrial slave." This latter offers, on the whole,
nothing really new if one compares her with the status of the
labor-force-commodity as it is employed in the production
industries in the broad sense. The model whose bodily image
accompanies the offer of commodities, hosiery, refrigerators,
ice cream bars, is simply one component element of the commodity constituting the advertising medium (poster, "blurb,"
commercial). The same goes for the air hostess etc., all things
being equal. Of course, the interest which this economic power
shows in this body and this face appears to be indissociable
from a consideration of their libidinal force. But *de facto*, this
last fact is basically ignored; the images offered to the potential
consumer do not have as their function the stimulation of his
phantasmatic forces, but the stimulation of his propensity to
buy the ice cream bar or the refrigerator; they do not claim to
make him spend his libido, but his money. It is not a question
of intensive force here, it is only a matter of psycho-economic
power: but the libido is not a psycho-economic "motivation."
The industrial slave, therefore, by her position as a meta-
commodity, is subject to the libidinal neutralization which
is standard practice in the constitution of all objects in play
in industrial production and exchange. The consummation
it suggests is not consumption. This remains ignored by the

financial system which employs the woman for the purposes of advertising; the *price* that may be accorded to the intense *jouissance* of her body in its unexchangeable singularity is not realized in the financial system, it remains "priceless"; or rather, it would be better to say, it is beyond monetary value altogether. The industrial slave is therefore committed to the most classical split between the merchant's possessions and the lover's concerns.

In a living woman-currency, it would be, on the contrary, the emotional force of her body that would directly determine her libidinal *price*. Klossowski says this is determined "immediately" (but we will see that this immediacy is impossible). In this way she would be "wealth" inasmuch as (a) she "excludes all other demands," and (b) she cannot count as the substitute for something else. If you eliminate any transfer this implies the destruction of any remainder. Here Klossowski suggests an analogy with gold, in which he sees a political-economic metaphor of libidinal *price*: for like the latter, gold is useless, and it is precisely because of this that it is precious, being opposed to all instrumentality; its uselessness may recall the futility of the passions in the practical sphere. This pretentious referent nevertheless serves as a standard for the value of currencies, according to Klossowski, and it does this in the most arbitrary way. It is by the same unpredictable situation that the libidinal *price* of the money – body ("concrete currency") determines both the negotiable value of goods and the impossibility of deciding either how price follows from value, or of making any sort of comparison between them.

We here discover the two traits – indissociability and non-deductibility – which reunite and confuse the tensor sign and the intelligent sign in one and the same "thing." Woman-currency would be dissimulation itself; she is not only the point of intersection of more or less divergent signifying chains, a polysemic and overdetermined anchoring point; *beyond this* she appears as the infinity of a deadly tension which the libertine tracks like a beast over the plains and valleys of her body. Between its function as value and its potency as tensor, bodily money reiterates a duplicitous relation of incompossibility and indissociability. Because the order of intensities is not translatable or *convertible* into the order of value, this money (even if it serves as the subject matter for "perverse" fantasies) cannot help but remain abstract or dead. Klossowski, in these few words, *contradicts* his whole project. Besides recognizing her libidinal singularity (i.e., "she rules out any other claim, if not the claim whose satisfaction she represents"), Klossowski also allows for her neutralization into an intelligible sign: "as for satisfaction properly speaking, her nature as a sign rules that out as well." In this regard, the question of pleasure is exposed as a dilemma by this aporia of money brought to life. As a body of intensities, this money seems to lend itself to pleasure, but as cash intended for payment, it can only defer pleasure – precisely because the prostitute's skin can't stir with emotion under the client's caresses.

How does the Klossowskian system thus differ from prostitution? It differs in that the use of the woman is not bought with money, since this use is on the contrary authorized by a debt of which the "client" is the beneficiary vis-à-vis the woman's "master." The prostitute's body is entirely maintained within the network of venal values, even if it happens that the *jouissance* that it obtains for the client fraudulently "escapes" this network to be consumed as intensity. But the living body does not refer to dead money, and in this sense, it is not merchandise but just money; since, at least its acquisition, if not its enjoyment, is equivalent to the discharge of debts and the cancellation of credits.

Is there now a split between the organization imagined by Klossowski and the houses Sade dedicates to the debauchery of men and women in the pamphlet "One more effort, Frenchmen . . ."?[11] The split concerns an important point, republicanism. In Sade's houses, which are public property, every citizen, whatever their sex, has the power to convene there, to enjoy, however they please, every citizen, male or female. The "motive" of the convocation is not, for Sade, in any way economic, and the *jouissance* gained from the object, which Klossowski called phantasmatic, never results from settling a debt. The sole debt Sade recognizes and counts in his houses is a debt of *jouissance*, which is political, and by which every citizen is potentially and continually burdened with regard to all other citizens. This independence, forcefully maintained by the Marquis, of the libidinal with regard to the economic, split with Klossowski's fantasy: the Sadean theme is a political theme; the production and exchange of commodities plays no part in this. The houses of debauchery are civic institutions, and as such have an indirect but essential function, concentrating the libido on the circle of the body *politic*. There are two versions of this:

If . . . no passion needs the full extension of liberty more than this one, none probably is as despotic . . . every time you do not give man the secret means for giving vent to his heart, he will fall back on the objects that surround him to exercise it, and he will disturb the government. If you want to avoid this danger, give free reign to his tyrannical desires, which, despite himself, torment him ceaselessly.[12]

Thus, one vents perversion in peripheral establishments, faithful, on the whole, to the Greek model.

But Sade also says exactly the opposite: that a republican government always menaced by the despots surrounding it must have as its sole moral objective to maintain itself by any means. It is ruled out that the means are all moral; that, on the contrary, it must be *immoral* men, who by their movement of perpetual *insurrection*, keep the republican government on the alert. Thus the houses of which he spoke, far from having the function of appeasing the excitations provoked by the drives in the citizens, rather replenish what sustains them. These houses of lust have a fundamental duplicity with regard to the political sphere itself – they both charge it with and discharge it from libidinal energy. Villainy, the perpetual restlessness of those whom Plato called "hornets" in *The Republic*, and whom he wanted to eliminate, helps the government in two ways; by pressuring the latter with its peculiar excesses, and by obliging it to set up zones of debauchery that are points of discharge, for both itself and the government. Here Sade revives the great Machiavellian tradition of the connivance of the politician and the beast, the tradition of Chiron the Centaur, instructor to Princes, the duplicitous policy *par excellence*.

For Klossowski, there is nothing of a city or government; he is a modern man, the republic no longer exists, and the only body with totalizing pretentions is the body of capital. It is an open secret that today's politicians are only the executors of the impulsive imperatives of capital, and that they have no need to receive the great excess of stupidity or bestiality from a Chiron as the endowment of political genius; they are secure enough if they are endorsed by the National School of Administration. It is in economics that the post-Marxist Klossowski seeks the conspiracy of the drives on the "social body." But he is not content to protest as Marx does against the indirect extension of prostitution into all activities through the intervention of commodities. He further draws out the implications of this fact: he sees within capitalism the return (though denied, unrecognized) of the libidinal intensity which it rejects, at the very heart of even the most apparently neutral exchanges. (An analysis which, at first sight, does not appear to be unrelated to that of Baudrillard, for whom commodity fetishism, denounced and largely ignored by Marx himself, is the transcription, in the order of political economy, of the *foreclosure* underlying this order, at the same time as it institutes it.) Consequently, Klossowski claims there is *little left to do* ("What we are talking about here exists in fact") to ensure that what presently happens in ignorance (which ignorance stems from the fact that the production and exchange of goods, under the screen of dead money, cloaks the exchange and consummation of phantasies) is publicly exposed, and that production and exchange immediately become the circulation of pleasures. To conceive of *living money* has no other function than to try to reestablish libidinal intensity upon the circuit of trade itself, and thus to cease treating desire as an outlaw. Rather, it is to use the body of capital as a convenient angle for attaining, in this case, his unacknowledged ends (i.e., "paying for women"). But since the Klossowskian idea of intensity is not affirmative (at least not in *La Monnaie vivante*; *Le Cercle vicieux* is another matter), the full establishment of pleasure within the circuit of trade can take no other form in his eyes than that of a kind of *money*, indeed a kind of living money, and thus be pregnant with the ancient heritage of prostitution and substitution, that is, with the dualism that we, libidinal economists, wish to end. This is further borne out by his insistence (as we clearly see from what he judges to be an important corrective, in this regard, in "The philosopher–villain") in keeping within the nihilist tradition of transgression (of propagation), of perversion (of the henchman), of deviation (of energies), and concurrently, if not in the tradition of the fantasy as substitute, at least of the simulacrum as duplicating the fantasy.

As soon as one admits the inexchangeability of phantasms, one must accept decisively the necessity of the conservation of political economy and capital. The result of this inexchangeability is that a substitution of copies or simulacra for these fantasies is inevitable. Thus, libidinal "wealth" is betrayed by the economic signs which represent this wealth, and which also continually defer its consumption. On the other hand, the fact that the money is living does not change the fact that it is money. By being extended to erotic bodies, the newly conceived political economy transforms them into simulacra, appearances, and composes a kind of *terrestrial city* out of the body parts – in those illustrated "tableaux vivants" that Klossowski favors – which is but the *duplicatum* of another city, forever out of reach. In this sense, *La Monnaie vivante* continues the Augustinian religion of *The City of God*, and the "life" which excites this currency and these tableaux is a kind of death, in conformity with the tradition of the Church Fathers.

We must nevertheless pay homage to this fiction at the very moment that we distance ourselves from it. For what is sought in the fantasy of these *golden bodies* is also totally opposed to the teaching of Augustine. The exchange of libidinal zones in excessive arrangements ("priceless" fantasies) can and must be understood, in the work of Klossowski himself – and this is explicitly the case in *Le Cercle vicieux* – not as an exchange in the sense of two contracting parties each intending to swap two objects of equivalent (marginal) utility, but as a metamorphosis in which the invested regions (and we have seen that, according to Sade, whom Klossowski follows here, this might be language *or even money*) exist only to the extent that they are crossed by energy, by the greatest or the most delicate or the most gentle tension and pain, unpredictably and ceaselessly. This "exchange" is the passage of intensities running from one proper name to another, from one initial to another, from one reference number to another, without a return to the same and therefore without capitalization, without which there can be no instance, structure, base Zero of input/output matrices, no Memory, to register the energies expended and amassed. Understood in this way, "life" is in fact currency in the sense that there is nothing but simulacra, signs of course, but without reference to *another order*, to a signified. This is assuredly a political economy, but one which, far from being a betrayal and misrepresentation of the libidinal economy, *is* this libidinal economy – i.e., a political economy without a betrayed or alienated "origin", without a theory of value. This is a currency, therefore, in the sense of Roman paganism and theatrical theology, which admits only tensor signs, only masks hiding no faces, only surfaces without a backstage, only *prices* without *values*.

It is undoubtedly because he has not broken with the problematic of *alienation*, which is Augustinian just as much as it is Marxian, that Klossowski hesitates in his evaluation of capitalism and therefore over the exact range to give to a libidinal use of signs. He may indeed insist on the strict analogy which reigns between the useful ("instrumental") product and the fantasy, between the consumption of the product and the voluptuous emotion, between the "industrial world" and the perverse society – but this move is just as much a way of declaring that it must be suspected: "Strictly speaking there exists no economy of voluptuousness which would benefit from industrial means." And it even serves to superimpose an overtly "perverse" relation into this analogy: "a purely analogical relation leads to nothing, if one does not start from the point of view of *objects* and *needs* in order to detect the struggle of affects against their *inadequate formulation*, *materially* reconverted *to the state of a demand for goods* which only corresponds to them in a contrary way."[13] Now, is it not obvious that this contrary relation stems from a return to the thought of alienation in the heart of the erotic? Elsewhere, Klossowski says that the drives are always in conflict with themselves. Therefore, capitalism does not enter into their "inadequate" formulation. It remains that this inadequacy, wherever it comes from, exists only with regard to a manner of thinking concerned *with*, and determined *by*, *truth*. Between the intelligent sign and the tensor sign, between the currency and the drives, we say that the relation is not of formulation, expression, translation, or betrayal, but of coexistence and dissimulation. And the problem of capital, that of money, cannot be one of *freeing* desire from its grotesque masks, those of capital being neither better nor worse, neither more nor less "authentic", than any others. It is of decisive importance to recognize that for some time now, new "signs" have been emerging, new statements – in the first rank of which are those by Klossowski himself – new "practices," new "works," that libidinally as well as economically call for the destruction of the distinction between feelings and dealings, between affect and labor. *Just like the signs of capital*, these signs are duplicitous, and there is no question of declaring *urbi et orbi* that with their appearance semiotics and political economies are ruined, and desire would be freed from the shackles of the system of values. Their intensity is new, in the manner in which they are inscribed into established regions, by the distances which they emboss and sketch. Their relation to sign-values, to intelligent signs, is wrapped in a new duplicity. Rather than greeting a dawn, we should honor the new dissimulation in them. Where there are only surfaces, conspiracy and secrecy reign.

NOTES

1 As is the case for Klossowski in *Roberte ce soir*, in which Antoine and Octave are as one.
2 *Realphilosophie I* (Iena, 1803–04).
3 On Lyotard's use of "figure" (*figure*), see his *Discours, Figure* (Paris: Klincksieck, 1971), esp. pp. 9–23, and *passim*.

4 Pierre Klossowski, *La Monnaie vivante* (Paris: Eric Losfeld, 1970), p. 84.
5 Ibid.
6 Ibid., p. 79.
7 Ibid.
8 *L'Inconvenance majeure* (Paris: Pauvert, 1965). But Blanchot, like Sade, sees rather a principle here.
9 *La Monnaie vivante*, p. 89.
10 Ibid.
11 *Philosophy in the Bedroom*, pp. 296–339.
12 Ibid., p. 317.
13 *La Monnaie vivante*, pp. 26–29.

CHAPTER 4

A political minimalist

Philippe Roger

There is perhaps no question concerning Sade more difficult to address than that of his political thought. He has been the subject of the most contradictory interpretations in many domains (such as the ethical and the philosophical). But it is in the face of the exasperating enigma of his politics that the number of conflicting interpretations reaches a peak. An anachronistic, or indeed untimely, contemporary of the Enlightenment, a protagonist of the French Revolution often despite himself, Sade has provided his critics with a set of paradoxical political declarations which seem to conspire to undermine all the premises generally admitted by those, from Aristotle to Rousseau, who tried to think "politically". But were they not all, in Juliette's terms, just "ordinary philosophers"?

The portfolio of ideological labels attached to Sade by his commentators, hagiographers or detractors is large, and so contradictory that it may be asked whether this ubiquitous Marquis, sometimes terrorist and sometimes counter-revolutionary, here a bolshevik and there a conservative, is one and the same character. In spite of their unanimous moral prejudices against him, nineteenth-century authors were immediately divided when dealing with Sade's relationship to revolutionary events. Jules Janin, the conservative literary critic, and Jules Michelet, the progressive historian, offer an almost comical contrast. Janin deems it natural to link Sade with Robespierre: "Oh, what a worthy couple, Sade and Robespierre . . .".[1] Being contradicted by the facts is no major hindrance to him: if Sade was jailed during the Terror, if he was indeed condemned to death on 8 Thermidor of year II (and saved by Robespierre's fall on the 9th), it all happened, explains Janin, because Sade was a terror to the terrorists themselves, because "he had frightened even the executioners of 1793."[2] Michelet, on the other hand, sees Sade as the perfect embodiment not of the Terror, but of the Thermidorean reaction and debauchery! And he uses the rather inelegant formulation, speaking of a man who almost died under the guillotine: "Nobody showed any restraint any longer. De Sade got out of jail on 10 Thermidor."[3] A comment not only unfair but inaccurate: Sade, imprisoned at Charenton, had to wait until June 1790 to recover his freedom.

Twentieth-century critics are no more in agreement than their nineteenth-century predecessors. Quite the contrary. In 1920, the red Marquis haunted the Congress of Tours, along with his radical commentator Maurice Heine, before being praised by Eluard in a French Communist Party magazine.[4] In 1945 Raymond Queneau wrote: "It is beyond dispute that the world imagined by Sade and desired by his characters (and why not by himself?) is an hallucinating prefiguration of the world where the Gestapo reigns, with its tortures and its camps."[5]

There are several reasons for such a critical imbroglio. The first lies in the confusion created by many analysts between Sade's political ideas and his acts during the French Revolution. Given his perilous status – as an aristocrat, the father and relative of émigrés, and a known pornographic writer – Sade's political gestures or claims must be interpreted very cautiously.[6] Although he often manages to imbue his "patriotic" contributions with his libertine sensibility (praising the ill-famed Franks and surreptitiously introducing libertarian intonations into his *Idée sur le mode de la sanction des lois*, and dwelling on the "androgynous" character of Charlotte Corday in his political pamphlet "Eulogy of Marat"), the "general trend" as well as the topics was dictated by a situation imposed on the writer, now given the civic title of "Secretary": the heavy responsibility of writing in the name of the people. As early as his *Adresse au Roi*, at a time (June 1791) when he was not yet a scrivener for the "Section des Piques," Sade already knew that an extraordinary political context predetermined his speech. In order to be received by its legitimate recipient (not the King, but "the French people"), it must in the first place be delivered in their name ("all speak by my mouth"). The same can be said of his letters. After years of authoritarian censorship by the governors of Vincennes and the Bastille, even those letters written after his release in 1790 show signs of self-censorship: "one must be careful in one's letters, as the regime of freedom opened many more of them than despotism ever did."7

On the one hand, we have contradictory professions of faith, spun out in a correspondence whose "private" nature is too unsure to allow for any possible conviction to be neatly expressed; on the other hand, there are sparse public interventions, often supportive and always "framed" by the exigencies of the revolutionary stance. Sade, with lucidity and some weariness, commented on the pressure exerted by a situation of almost permanent crisis and described how his political ideas had become more and more "mobile," due to "the necessity of working, day after day, sometimes for one party and sometimes in favor of the other."8 Indeed, screening Sade's acts or gestures during the French Revolution could prove as elusive as scrutinizing his political writings. Ambiguity prevailed from the very first, as he rebelliously shouted from his cell in the Bastille on 4 July 1789, an event he himself first derided in a letter of May 1790 ("a little fuss I made there . . ."), which he then rewrote for the sake of the Revolutionary Tribunal, presenting himself as the real "taker" of the Bastille.

A second reason for the interpretative confusion, which is of a textual nature, is no less important. The whole of Sade's œuvre possesses a fictional quality. And, as Pierre Klossowski once noted, it is in his fiction that Sade expresses "the foundations of his thought, inasmuch as it had any" – a situation acknowledged *de facto* by critics who, generally ignoring the handful of his "revolutionary" writings, build their theories on evidence drawn from the novels. *Philosophy in the Bedroom* itself, so often cited in support of various and divergent theses, grows out of one of those literary montages of which late eighteenth-century political pamphlets offer many an example. Critics almost always wrench a confession of Sade's "opinions" or of his supposed "systems" from the mouth of one of his characters, at the risk of forgetting the warning formulated in the "philosophical novel" *Aline and Valcour*: "Composed by different people, this collection offers, in each of its letters, the views of its [fictional] writer, or of the persons whom this writer sees and whose ideas he delivers."9 In this note, Sade is not satisfied with merely evoking the traditional terms of the contract with the reader, characteristic of the epistolary novel, for he adds the following invitation: "the reader must . . . laugh at or ponder the different systems proposed both pro and contra, and adopt those which best flatter either his reason or his fancy." The protocol of reading hereby suggested for fictional ideological discourses – a nefarious eclecticism – is one and the same as the guidelines offered to the reader in the Foreword to *The 120 Days of Sodom*: to choose whatever "passions" he likes, and leave the rest for other readers. Sade, as a writer, wants to deal individually with each and every one of his readers. While the notion of a *contrat de lecture* suggests a general agreement, Sade insists on one-to-one deals between author and reader, according to a type of individualized agreement mirrored in the social field, by a mechanism he calls "arrangement": a privately conducted arbitration of inter-individual litigations that would deter all conflicts in society without recurring to laws and punishments. Interestingly enough, his footnote in *Aline and Valcour* on how best to read his books appears on the same page on which Sade introduces a new character of crucial ideological significance, the gipsy chief Brigandos, who will soon explain the doctrine of "arrangement" to both heroines and readers.

Neither Sade's novels nor his philosophical tales have the univocal quality or the limpidity of principles that these forms assume in almost all of his contemporaries. The reader is not, as with Voltaire, Marmontel, or Rétif, firmly directed towards a "reading" which an omnipresent author strives to make convincing. As Sade insists, "views are offered," not imposed. While saturating the text with "dissertations," the decentered author takes the trouble to underline the polylogical nature of his narrative. This flexible protocol has been analyzed by some as a symptom of ideological indecision, while others have obeyed it only too well, choosing one or the other fictional "discourse" according to their fantasy – and claiming that discourse to be the sole and true vehicle of Sade's thought. And while the former fail to recognize Sade's intentional staging of political doubt, the latter fall into the trap of an ill-founded certainty about his political creeds. For, in making the "passions" of his reader the judges of the best proposed "system," Sade doubtless not only transgresses the ways and customs of "literature with a message." He also sabotages the basic assumption of Western political reflection, which regards the city, not the individual, as its object and as the cornerstone of its theoretical relevance. The inability to decide is more subversive than nihilism. Proposing politics as a choice which his reader can make according to reason *or* libido (as in the previously quoted footnote) is more devastating for political discourse than pronouncing them downright irrational.

Hence another major difference: while his contemporaries use fiction as a transparent veil and a coded convention to convey and promote ideas, Sade "fictionalizes" ideology to stir, displace, shock. Ambiguity prevails in all of his political declarations. In the first place, it is an ambiguity regarding the status of such declarations as: which one would he himself adopt? condone? laugh at?; secondly, it is an ambiguity as to their enunciative mode: are they serious or sarcastic? Are they really "great ideas" or just enormous jokes? Ruthless "leading on" or mystifying reformulations? Malignity or malice? In such a floating context, the most referential elements can no longer serve as references, for quoting an author can also be derisory. If some of the best commentators (Huxley, Klossowski) agree on the parodic, satirical and critical status of the revolutionary pamphlet in *Philosophy in the Bedroom*, why not cast a similar doubt on some outrageously anti-democratic tirades (Noirceuil's, for instance) which have often been used as evidence of Sade's political ignominy? Such doubt should be the companion of any venture into this minefield where so many ideas seem to explode as soon as they are exposed.

There are no political "treatises"; there are, however, "dissertations" which (not excluding the famous *Français, encore un effort si vous voulez être Républicains!*) draw their ambiguity from the fictional origin of their articulation; there is a correspondence which, if not muzzled, is at least wary; and there are political interventions written on the razor's edge of a highly uncomfortable personal situation.

However, if the dramatized, polylogical staging of political discourse is one major difficulty for the exegete, a no less important cause for confusion lies in the very violence of the Sadean text. The arabesques of modern interpretation would not be so profuse if it were not for Sade's effect on many a reader: a revulsion so strong that it suffices to legitimize, for many, a deciphering by way of an analogy the secret provenance of which is none other than the horror inspired by both terms of the comparison. The historical ban on his texts, together with their reputation of aberration, have only encouraged comparisons (some of them rather baroque) with social and political phenomena that have hardly anything in common with the Sadean œuvre, aside from exceeding or paralyzing the methods of investigation and the analytical gaze of critical rationalism.

Queneau, when he draws his parallel between Nazi concentration camps and "the world of Sade," does not feel any intellectual obligation to justify it by examining in detail the political structures or behaviors he compares. The analogy between the two "systems" lies in the "excess of evil" that both have come to signify. Yet this metaphorization of "sadism" in the historical-political world is not Queneau's invention. In every given period, Sade's name or "sadism" have been used to mark those political events which seemed beyond the reach of rational examination: for example, the French Terror in the eyes of Janin, or the savage massacre of King Alexander and Queen Draga in the 1903 Belgrade insurrection, described by Albert Moll (Krafft-Ebing's disciple) as "mob sadism." In our own times, with Nazism remaining the unthinkable political event *par excellence*, Sade has been regularly summoned to account for what could not be explained. Queneau in 1945 had tried to "read" the camps as a Sadean fantasy; Pasolini in his 1976 *Salò* was to "translate" the Italian *nazifascista* episode of the Repubblica di Salò into the Sadean idiom of *The 120 Days of Sodom*. As a result of these analogical games, Sade's œuvre has been de-historicized, at the same time as major historical events were being depoliticized.

These dangerous amalgamations, these ideological collages, signify specifically that fascination exerted by the textual violence of the Sadean fiction, which blurs most critics' understanding of both the enunciative intricacies and the contextual complexity of Sade's œuvre. Failing to recognize the text itself as the site of that violence, these critics make "violence" into a Sadean theme or theory and promote it as the kernel of Sade's thought. But cruelty is not violence, and even less is it politically motivated or state-sponsored violence. Such interpretations doubly miss the point: thematically speaking, Sadean libertinage is about cruelty as a natural offset of lust; it cannot be said to be thematized *in* the text, since this violence exists only *as* the text.

Identifying Sade with the most repulsive of historical formations has been a major trend since the nineteenth century. But fascination being ambivalent, Sade's misreadings have also taken another course, which might be called "retro-projective." One word indefinitely repeated by political commentators of Sade sums up the mechanism of ideological retro-projection: the term *precursor*. These apparently more positive or flattering interpretations are nevertheless a byproduct of fascination degraded into uncritical identification. They tend to present Sade as the forerunner of any possible political system ever conceived during the past two centuries. For lack of any careful integration of Sade's position in the political philosophy of his time, well-meaning critics have kept enlarging the list of the "theories" that he supposedly "anticipated," "preceded," or "foretold."

With "retro-projective criticism," Sadean thought takes

a bitter revenge: it becomes the manifold seed of every great ideological construct of the nineteenth century, if not the twentieth. The French scholar Jean Tortel finds in it the embryo of "the Marxist theory of work value."[10] For his part, Gabriel Habert, in the learned *Revue Internationale d'Histoire Politique et Institutionnelle*, makes Sade a precursor of "anarchy", "a forerunner of Malthus," while, without dismissing the unavoidable Nazi filiation, he finds Sadean redolences even in the work of Guizot, the French historian and statesman famous for his slogan and motto of "Enrichissez-vous!" ("Make money!").[11] This generosity in granting ideological paternities almost outstrips that of Paul Eluard, who thirty years earlier had explained to the young readers of the Communist Party student magazine *Clarté* that Sade was "the precursor . . . of Proudhon, Fourier, Darwin, Malthus, Spencer, and also of all modern psychiatry."[12]

Such excesses of honor are perhaps no less detrimental to Sade's political reputation than the indignities by analogy referred to above. A "thinker" can hardly be assigned such an eclectic lineage without serious doubts being raised as to his coherence – a coherence clearly denied him by Simone de Beauvoir, who dismissed Sade's œuvre, from a philosophical standpoint, as inane, "unreadable," and "escaping philosophical banality only to founder in incoherence."[13] Beauvoir's brutal denial (contradicted in the same years by the dissenting opinions of Blanchot, Klossowski, Bataille, and Paulhan) has one merit: it exposes the critical mechanism by which Sade, to become the password for anything, has first to be declared nothing. It also signals the most common flaw in political analyses of Sade's thought: they all presuppose a modern definition of politics entirely foreign to Sade, who clearly retains a pre-Enlightenment understanding of the word, the better to test the emerging notion that our commentators take for granted.

Hence, the last temptation of Sadean criticism, once rid of Sade as a thinker and unaware of the textual dimension of his political statements, is probably the temptation of reductive sociologism and hasty psycho-biographism. How tempting, indeed, to account for a political Sade either by his social condition or by the uniqueness of his unusual personality and destiny, or by a learned mixture of these ingredients. A sociology of the exception is, however, a dangerous temptation, even in its Sartrian version. Jean-Paul Sartre himself, in one of his rare comments on Sade, is hardly convincing when he offers Sade's "situation" as a necessary and sufficient key to the Marquis's thought, and tries to fix the reading of Sade's works around the simplistic cliché of the "aristocrat witnessing the decline of his own class."[14] His mechanistic opposition between "aristocrats" and "bourgeoisie" at the end of the Ancien Régime (itself a very disputable dichotomy) leads him to a caricature, verging on downright error, of Sade's positions on nature. While Sartre errs by an excess of dogmatic sociologism, many others do so through a biographical reduction focusing on the many years Sade spent in confinement. Sade thus becomes the Prisoner, *l'enfermé* (to borrow the nickname of the socialist activist Blanqui), and his stance is reduced to a short circuit between incarceration and the anarchism or libertarianism it bred.

The risks of such simplifications could be illustrated by an example bearing on a consistent feature of Sadean political discourse: his articulate hatred of the *parlements* which were, in pre-revolutionary France, both courts of law and political chambers inasmuch as they registered royal decrees. A socio-biological reading would tell us that Sade hated *parlements* because of his own ancient nobility. Born to a family which dated back to the Crusades, he would share the scorn of his caste for the well-scrubbed villains who preside over these ignoble institutions. Indeed, in his letters from prison, he can hardly find designations disparaging enough for his in-laws, who belong to the *noblesse de robe*. But the criticisms within his works (developed in *Aline and Valcour*, for instance) are not his own; such hostility spans many other social strata and circles of thought. This discourse is so pervasive that it is shared even by mortal enemies: historians like Boulainvilliers as well as Enlightenment spokesmen like Condorcet, and the entire Physiocratic school as well as the Physiocrats' *bête noire*,

Linguet. Sade's pages on the *parlements* should be read in that light, as his personal contribution to one of the major debates of the 1770s and 1780s. A bio-anecdotic reading, on the other hand, would certainly remind us that Sade had been condemned, after the Marseilles affair (a wild whorehouse party), by the *parlement* of Aix. Hence his hatred towards his judges (whom he likes to call "Aix's tuna-mongers") and, by extension, towards the institution itself. But in fact, it was not the regular *parlement*, exiled and dismissed at the time, that sentenced Sade to death *in absentia* on 11 September 1772. It was a "Maupeou *parlement*," filled by that authoritative Minister with hand-picked docile magistrates. And it was the regular *parlement*, put back in power in 1774, which transformed this condemnation into a simple "admonition." It was thus "ministerial despotism" (another buzz-word of Ancien Régime politics) and the order under the king's private seal (*lettre-de-cachet*), and not parliamentary tyranny, which kept Sade imprisoned.

Even though it combines aristocratic prejudice, family problems, and personal grievances, Sade's anti-parliamentarianism cannot be reduced to any of the above. It is an articulate historical and political discourse, borrowing both from the rich anti-parliamentary historiography of the eighteenth century and from the more recent Rousseauian critique of political representation.

Sade's political thought is undeniably elusive, as is proven by the wide spectrum of interpretations. In this context of so many flawed anachronistic projections, it might be wise to pose a preliminary question: how exactly did Sade understand "politics"?

The last decades of the eighteenth century were a time of semantic turmoil. The word *politique* (the feminine noun meaning "politics"; the masculine, "a man dealing in politics") was one of these numerous signifiers around which battles raged. Louis-Sébastien Mercier, a contemporary of the Marquis, provides us with an excellent summary of the debate around two notions of *politique*: the traditional one, referring to cunning and ruse; and the Enlightened one, aiming at the general good. "In the vulgar sense of the word," writes Mercier, "a political man is a man who is crafty, who takes covert paths, who deftly has recourse to subterfuge and sham; his ideas are complicated, his hatreds petty." Mercier writes in order to promote what he calls "the more general and reasoned acceptation" of the term, i.e., "a man who sees things in a wide perspective, who finds remedies where others have failed, who can understand the real disease of empires and its cure, who knows how to compute the degrees of resistance and feasibility . . ."[15] While praising this new *politique*, Mercier is perfectly aware that he is going against the generally received meaning, which, he owes, is the prevailing "point of view, giving a bad name to the political man."

In this semantic quarrel, Sade does not side with Mercier, champion of the progressive, but nonetheless Rousseauist, Enlightenment. He remains wedded to the old-fashioned, seventeenth-century, post-Machiavellian definition. It is quite remarkable that "politics," as he uses the word, never refers to a quest for "principles" (however much he admired Montesquieu in other respects), nor to a speculation on the ideal organization of the city. *La politique*, in his writings, is above all the management of affairs of state, considered as a power confronting other powers: a restrictive and pragmatic definition, stated in somewhat pejorative terms. Even the French Revolution and the new semantic habits it induced could not shake Sade's certainty that politics is nothing but a "human science . . . which strives only to cheat, whose only goal is to benefit one nation at the expense of another."[16] Such a "science," far from Mercier's computing wisdom, is but a strategy, indeed a simple battery of stratagems, conceived and executed by a power, or by the powerful, against external or internal enemies. The real-life Sade tells the Section des Piques that such or such a move would be "quite impolitic" in exactly the same tone used by the fictional Juliette toward King Ferdinand of Sicily, when stigmatizing the tactical awkwardness that might backfire against his own throne.

In Sade, politics are systematically denigrated, discredited, nullified. His attitude is not unique at the end of the eighteenth century. But here the rationale is different. Scores of reformer-utopians of the 1770s and 1780s willingly practice the elision of politics as such, fascinated as they are by "government projects," "police plans," and other such technocratic dreams that would substitute the administration of things for the government of men. A name was even coined for them, recorded by Mercier: *faiseurs de projets*. But Sade's hostility towards politics is not made of such a progressive, enlightened fabric. Radically deprived of any social optimism, Sade does not share these reformers' conviction that intellectual and technical progress will soon make speculative reflection on the governement of men or the forging of good institutions either obsolete or auxiliary. His invalidation of politics does not stem from an historical euphoria; it is rooted in a post-Hobbesian anthropology, in his materialistic metaphysics and in his historical negativism.

Maurice Blanchot might well have been summarizing the paradox of Sadean social relationships when he phrased the philosophical question: what can possibly be the relation of the exception to the exception? In a time fascinated by the dual figure of the monster and the genius, the question is indeed a pressing one, and Diderot's *Rameau's Nephew* is its finest literary exposition. In Sade, though, there are no monsters – because there are only monsters. "But that man of whom you speak is a monster," exclaims Justine, less and less surprised, yet a little weary to have encountered yet another one, even though only as a figure of discourse. Clément, the lewd monk, quickly corrects her mistake: "The man of whom I speak is the man of Nature."[17] The problem, from this moment on, can no longer be to know if society must accommodate itself to the exception, or "throw it overboard," as Rameau's nephew suggested for new-born geniuses. Sade enthusiastically inverts the conclusion: it is society, and not the individual (by definition exceptional) that he "throws overboard." Or would, if society were not still-born, non-existent, chimerical.

Sadean "impolitics" are thus rooted in a denial of the social link itself. What Klossowski terms the sovereign man is the metaphysical corollary of a socio-ontological thesis: *isolisme*. The notion is central to Sade's thought. And its elaboration, or reorientation from the *Infortunes de la vertu* (1787) to *Juliette* (1797), is of great import. The term appears as early as the first draft of the tribulations of Justine, but as a simple statement of fact, the description of a situation, the contingent result of a change in fortune. Orphaned and penniless on the very threshold of the narrative, Justine suffers two rebuttals, from a seamstress and a priest from whom she has solicited help. She is, in Sade's words, "twice rebuked as soon as condemned to isolism."[18] Isolism here is but a state into which one is thrown by a stroke of bad luck, and from which escape is possible (as for Juliette), given a better analysis of the social bond (which is nothing other than "the desire to fuck") and a willingness to abide by the laws of that market. In any case, the register is sociological, not ontological. The world of Justine is very similar to the world of Marivaux's young Marianne (in a 1731 novel by that name), who is also an orphan, and also the butt of male lust, with one difference: while Marivaux's heroine meets scores of guardian angels and white knights, there is a tragic scarcity of good Samaritans in Sade's fiction. Isolism, as professed in the story of Juliette, is utterly different. When Noirceuil declares that "all creatures are born isolated and with no need whatsoever for one another,"[19] it is clear that *isolisme* has become a philosophical thesis, which no longer designates a circumstantial lack, but rather the human condition *per se*, in its naked truth clumsily travestied by the tenets of the "alleged bond of fraternity." Isolism is no longer a synonym for either unhappiness or misfortune: it becomes the Stoic motto of the libertine, on whom it lavishes a thousand promises of pleasure.

Isolism is thus the core of Sadian "un-politics." In Sade's eyes, the best-ruled societies have never ceased to be asocial. Such a gathering of creatures – the "scum of the laws" of a stepmother nature – never becomes a city. Man was never the *zôon politikon* of Aristotelian fame, never will be, and has not the least interest in becoming so. (Noirceuil's tirade on isolism turns up in support of a remark on the cumbersome uselessness of laws – another example of the metonymic textual logic of Sade's montages.) The sovereignty of Sadean man is not inalienable; it is inexpiable, giving respite neither to the individual nor to the would-be societies. Such a sovereignty can neither relinquish itself, nor come to terms with itself. The Rousseauist *tour de force* of the institution of the Sovereign by the total alienation of private sovereignties assumes, at the very least, a kind of metaphysical equality of the sovereignties among themselves. The Sadean sovereignty permits no such computation. The state of war described by Noirceuil resembles the anarcho-despotic vision of the last period of humanity sketched by Rousseau at the end of the *Discourse on the Origins and Bases of Inequality*; yet it presents itself as the immutable condition of men, not as the final phase of a long degradation of their relationships.[20] Instead of a long genealogy of usurpation, the history of humanity offers Sade but the static image of a long and bad joke, a buffoonery without mystery.

Isolism is thus at the core of what could be called Sade's "negative anthropology," by reference to the phrase "negative theology." The denial of the *fil de fraternité* is essential to his thought, just as the affirmation of *pitié* is to Rousseau's. But Sade is not content with inversing the Rousseauist anthropological model; he also shakes off the cosmetic and fuzzy notion of "sociability" which has prevailed among anti-religious and anti-Rousseauist philosophers. While borrowing heavily from these latter, D'Holbach in particular, to reassert a dogmatic materialism, he takes a very different path in his radical critique of history.

A fervent admirer of D'Holbach, an impassioned reader (and rewriter) of his *Système de la nature*, Sade espouses the vision of a monist materialistic universe subject only to the laws, not of nature – albeit a "bad nature" – but of "movement". The impeachment of politics, so to speak, in Sadean thought is directly articulated on this materialistic metaphysics – an articulation Sartre fails to recognize, obsessed as he is by sociological categorizations. In his already-quoted comments, after presenting Sade as caught up in his disappearing privileges and the rise of the bourgeoisie, Sartre continues:

Sadism is a theory of inter-human relations; what Sade is seeking is communication. But he has to use the language provided to him by his time to express his thought. One century later, sadism could have defined itself as anti-physis. In the eighteenth century, this is impossible: Sade has to abide by the idea of nature. He will then build a theory of Nature identical to that of the bourgeois, with only one difference: instead of being good, nature is bad, she wants the death of man.

Let us pass over the monolithic vision that Sartre entertains of the many-faceted philosophies of nature in the eighteenth century. Contrary to Sartre's interpretation, Sade presents his reader with a systematic deconstruction of the idea of nature, ultimately diluted in the larger notion of "laws of kingdoms" and "laws of movement." Sade thus finds an original place in a complex philosophical tradition. On one hand, as previously said, he borrows from D'Holbach as well as from La Mettrie. On the other hand, he revives on his own terms the Hobbesian ambition (sketched as early as 1630 in the unpublished "Short Tract on First Principles" and elaborated in the *Elements of Law Natural and Politic*) of a general theory of nature, man, and society, based on mechanism and a true understanding of the nature of movement, combined with an anthropology focusing on the individual as the primary reality. In both cases, what Sade deliberately discards is these conciliatory or dynamic concepts which would allow for "natural" or imposed social cohesion: "sociability" or the so-called "natural moderation" of self-interest dear to the French atheists, and in Hobbes's case, the rational preference given to power, over struggle and war, to reinaugurate social peace. A selective combination of these traditions, along with a serious innoculation of neo-Stoicism, provide the philosophical background and backbone for Sade's immutable invalidation of politics in the Rousseauist (modern) sense of the term.

But such a description without another related aspect of his "impolitical philosophy" would be incomplete: namely, his historical pessimism. Interested by historical writing as a man of letters (he envisioned writing historical essays in the Bastille, then devoted years in Charenton to historical novels), Sade maintains positions which are neither those of the Enlightenment philosophers nor those of the reactionary historians à la Boulainvilliers. The former (with the exception of Voltaire) tend to favor purely "philosophical" analyses of society and to avoid history, a tainted genre filled with barbaric cruelties and the lies of power, an idiotic tale told by enslaved pen-holders on a script handed down by despots; they avoid history and despise most historians, the better to preserve their belief in a better tomorrow. Sade shares their gloomy vision, but he makes History, not historians, responsible for the atrocities they only record. But, on the other hand, while sharing a passion for the past with "aristocratic" historiographers, he distances himself from their ideological motivations and conclusions. Boulainvilliers and his successors had entered the historical field as crusaders fighting for the recognition of the "nobility" against the infringements of the monarchy and its allies (bourgeois and men of law); even though Sade sometimes copies their tirades, he is unwilling to draw lessons from history, whether or not they are profitable to his own caste. He is deaf to both the eschatology of progress and the ratiocinations of nostalgia. To him, history is meaningless, a farce played by puppets. "Of course rogues must get rich and idiots must be subjugated! Here, in a word, lies the whole secret of the civilization of men."[21] This pronouncement, in *Juliette*, is not conveyed by one of the characters; it appears in an author's note; and, interestingly enough, at the very moment when "isolism" is going to be philosophically redefined by Noirceuil.

History, in Sade's eyes, is but a flat repetition of the same, deprived of any significance or dramatic interest. (Hence also his theory of the absolute right, indeed the duty, for the novelist to rewrite history, thus instilling dramatic or moral sense into it.) Sade's certainty of the absolute meaninglessness of human history is such that, following his denial of any "meaning of history," even the French Revolution will not shake his creed. One of his "literary notes," written around 1800, clearly illustrates that point. Sade draws a parallel (quite paradoxical if taken as referring to the self-presentation of the Revolution) between the killing of the Swiss guards in 1792 by patriotic fighters and the massacre of the Parisian Huguenots on Saint Bartholomew's Eve, as reported by the French historian De Thou: "De Thou records that, the day after Saint Bartholomew, the women belonging to Catherine de Medici's court went out of the Louvre to see the naked bodies of the murdered and despoiled Huguenots which had been disposed of down the walls. On 10 August [1792], the Frenchmen of Paris came and saw, in the same way, the bodies of the Swiss guards strewn in the Tuileries."[22] Only Sade could have brought together, through the centuries, the Protestants fallen victims to French Catholicism and Monarchy and the last defenders of Louis XVI, the Most Christian King. The comparison, far-fetched and provocative as it is, is a perfect example of Sade's mistreatment of History – and of the French Revolution.

The commentators who have recognized the ironic nature of Sade's "political thought" are numerous. Several have uncovered the ambiguity of his out-and-out republicanism. The pamphlet *Français, encore un effort* . . . strongly contrasts with the copious polemical production of the post-Thermidorian years, not in formal qualities alone, but also in its scope. Pierre Klossowski suggested that it be read as an extensive allusion to the founding regicide. Before him, in a 1938 book, Aldous Huxley described the "nihilism" at work in Sade's pages as a "reductio ad absurdum of revolutionary theory."[23] No doubt Sade took pleasure in driving the wedge of a logical humor, worthy of Jonathan Swift in his *Modest Proposal*, into the virtuous phraseology of his fellow countrymen. Sade holds up the bloody mirror to the French Revolution.

However, Sade's political critique is not circumstantial. Neither can it serve as evidence of Sade's rallying to counter-revolutionary ideologies: as foreign to providentialism as he is hostile to the various myths of "sociability" used by the Philosophers as a "pineal gland" of the difficult union of the individual and the society, Sade keeps equally distant from Burke and Robespierre, from Saint-Just and Joseph de Maistre. Sade is all the more dangerous to the revolutionary creed or credo in that he "does not contradict the values of the new society born of the Revolution."[24] His satirical encouragement to an extra revolutionary "effort" – at a time when everybody else is demanding a winding-down of revolutionary excesses – is but the most spectacular avatar of his radical refusal to conceive the city – that is, as a philosopher, to give Laws to it or obey them. Barthes once called him a "logothetes," a founder of language; but he energetically refuses to dictate the law, to become a "thesmothetes."[25]

Yet it should be underscored that the cold glance he casts on the Revolution is no different from that which he threw on the Ancien Régime. At the core of his pamphlet is a very un-revolutionary view of what revolution is about: laws are useless, indeed nefarious; there should be as few laws as possible (while the French Revolution proclaimed no less than 3,400 laws in five years!); or, even better, no law at all. To achieve this demonstrative goal, Sade procedes by accumulation, delivers heaps of arguments, unscrupulously practicing a "logic of the kettle." Sometimes he accuses the law of creating the crime, for there is none in nature: "crimes are impossible to man"[26] before legislators' interference. And sometimes he reproaches the law for inhibiting crime, the free exercise of which is nonetheless indispensable to the "energy" of a republican government, which is warlike by necessity and constrained to seek ways to survive in a "necessary horror."[27] But as early as *Aline and Valcour* (a novel published in 1795, but written for the most part in jail, before 1789), Sade was already preaching a strange alliance or combination between law and crime. Exploiting the vogue for utopian constructions in the last decades before the Revolution, Sade offers his reader a description of the paradise island of Tamoé, run by good king Zamé. But, in a typical reversal of the utopian stereotype, which thrives on imaginary legislation of the tiniest aspects of life, Zamé explains at length to his French visitor that equality diminishing the number of vices and crimes, "law becomes useless." "Good Zamé" then makes the strangest and probably the most perverse suggestion ever phrased in a Sadean text in reference to the law: "the great art would be to combine crime and law, so that any crime whatsoever would offend the law but lightly, and that the law, less rigid, would weigh only on very few crimes."[28]

In a different time and a different setting, there still exists the same mechanism and the same goal, which is to deprive "society" of the right to punish offenses of which it is the cause (in the case of Ancien Régime France) or from which it draws benefits (in the case of Republican France). "Be fair, tolerate crime since the vice of your government leads to it,"[29] says Zamé to his guest newly arrived from monarchic Europe. And the author of the pamphlet bought by Dolmancé in the Palais-Royal will ask, in 1795, "how could one possibly demonstrate that in a state which is immoral in its obligations [the Republic at war], it would be essential that the individuals be moral?"[30]

Above and beyond the political convulsions and the patterns of a prose always ready to ironically espouse the trends of the times, one must nonetheless underline the constancy of a strategy which, by dint of its stability, points to the quintessential Sadean conviction: the illegitimacy of any form of collective coercion upon the individual in the name of his, or the general, good. This is precisely the denial of what we call politics.

Sade's argument develops according to two separate logics, one applying to human beings considered as a mass, where the key word is "equilibrium," and the other applying to individuals, through "arrangement".

"Arrangement," as previously stated, is a private, non-judicial technique of conciliation exposed by Brigandos, the gipsy "Solomon". It regulates inter-individual relations and conflicts. Simone de Beauvoir once noted that "nobody is more fond of the practical" than Sade. Such is the case with "arrangement." The gipsy's free association is really a counter-utopia; his nomadism is opposed to the closure of the imaginary islands; it is a parallel society, in the winding paths which it borrows, its network of hovels, clearings and hideouts; it permits a flight from society, but from the interior. The "arrangement" participates in this spirit of reality, it is concrete and applicable independent of the prevailing state of political institutions; it does not require a lost island in the South Seas; it assumes no overturning of human relations, no thorough reexamination of pacts, no redefinition of a hypothetical contract. In each case, taking into account every particularity and trying to establish a "compensation" for every damage acceptable by both sides, "arrangement" realizes the paradoxical demand of a law flexible enough to adjust to every single individual, phrased in *Français, encore un effort* . . .

Such a minimalist proposal evacuates politics by default: it takes more than two plus a referee to evoke the city and its good government. It is not by accident that the "case" solved by the new Solomon is that of an attempted rape, which will be "satisfactorily" settled by means of a sex-for-money contract – which in the "great societies" is called prostitution. What Sade is really concerned about with this minimalist proposition is decriminalizing a permanent and generalized access to sex – a less than political fancy which he will translate in very "political" terms in *Philosophy in the Bedroom*, suggesting compulsory prostitution for both men and women!

Turning away from individuals, however, and dealing with human groups on a collective scale, does not bring Sade back to "politics," which disappear once again, this time diluted in too much abstraction, as they were previously dismissed in the name of concrete reality. *Vel duo, vel nemo*: when Sade deals with more than two, he plays with numbers, not human beings; he computes figures and does not let himself be concerned with empirical, historical humanity. When King Zamé is pressed by his eager young guest to comment on the possible reformation of European societies, he immediately turns to an abstract computation, *more algebraico*, within the framework of the ideology of "equilibrium." Given the (naturalistic) premise of universal inter-devoration, or to say the least "oppression," the only task of a philosopher-king should be to "restore balance." Zamé thus imagines a State "composed half of whites and half of blacks." (The context does not allow for a racial interpretation, but suggests a chess game.) The former find their happiness in "a kind of oppression" imposed on the latter, with the bad solution consisting of putting the oppressed in the place of the oppressors, so that the general sum of damage and evil will be constant. The good solution, says Zamé, is to force the "wrongdoers" to make "reparations" to the "victims" in order "to preserve the equilibrium, since the union is impossible,"[31] without resorting to a collective punishment of the "whites," which would lead to reversal of oppression in favor of the blacks.

Between these macro-physics and micro-politics reduced to (mostly) sexual "arrangements," Sade leaves an immense void, which is clearly also a "window of opportunity": the opportunity to declare oneself, long before Barrès, "an enemy of the law". From the existence of such a theoretical void in Sade's thought, must we jump to the conclusion of a philosophical credibility gap? Not necessarily. First of all, Sade's denial of the political process is consistent with his "philosophy of nature" (as a materialism identifying "matter" and "movement"), as well as with his "philosophy of history" (as endless non-finalized repetition). Second, it can be read as a deliberate "exasperation" of the moral relativism of the late Enlightenment, as expressed in Diderot, Raynal, Helvétius, and so many others. It is interesting to note that Brigandos's modest proposal and Zamé's algebraical calculation are derived from a common rationale, which Sade calls "compensation". The Enlightenment's general effort towards decriminalization (through the critique of original sin, a deterministic physiology or a psycho-social approach to human behavior) logically leads to "systems of compensation" (based on "utility" and value, and finally on the only general equivalent, money) that would replace codes of punishment (unfair if guilt is obsolete and also non-productive, as underlined by all philosophers). Such systems of "compensation" have indeed existed since the nineteenth century; they compete with coercive systems for social regulation, forming what the French philosopher

François Ewald has called *la société assurancielle*,[32] the basic creed of which is that everything can be repaid, not through equal suffering or morally improving reclusion, but simply through pecuniary indemnization.

In our "fin-de-siècle" shaken by the collapse of revolutionary values and systems of reference, Sade has finally been recognized as the most penetrating critic, among his contemporaries, of "revolutionary reason." But his subtle satire on the philosophical approximations put forth by a benevolent Enlightenment is of no less value or interest. When so many "men of letters," before and after 1789, could not resist drafting plans, projects, or institutions, and offering them to the King of Prussia, the Polish People, the Intendant de Police, Catherine of Russia, or the National Assembly, we can certainly find merit in a Sade who abstains from "dictating laws," and who takes ideas seriously enough to confine himself to the proper role of the writer: a thoughtful critical exercise by means of that excess named Literature.

NOTES

1 J. Janin, *Le Marquis de Sade* (Paris: Chez les marchands de nouveautés, 1834), p. 12.
2 Ibid., p. 38.
3 J. Michelet, *Histoire de la Révolution française* (Paris: Calmann Lévy, 1899), vol. VII, p. 464.
4 Maurice Heine, a scholar and book collector, was one of the first serious commentators on Sade's works. A left-wing militant, he attended the famous Congrès de Tours (1920), where the French socialist movement split between communism and social democracy.
5 R. Queneau, *Front National*, November 3, 1945. (Reprinted in *Bâtons, chiffres et lettres*, Paris: Gallimard, 1950, p. 152.) In several other chronicles published the same year, 1945, in the same newspaper, Queneau insists on an analogy of purpose and structure between Nazism and "the world of Sade" – which, in two instances, he also associates with American gangster novels.
6 Being an émigré was made a capital crime in 1793–94, and again in 1797. Sade, who never emigrated, was not only endangered

by his sons' emigration, but also the victim of a Kafkaesque bureaucratic imbroglio. He had been put by mistake on the émigré list for the Bouches-du-Rhône, and had had great difficulty in rectifying the mistake. Meanwhile, the Département des Bouches-du-Rhône was split. An uncorrected version of the list, with his name on it, was forwarded to the newly created Département du Vaucluse (where his château was located). Sade was never able to overcome this very uncomfortable situation.

7 Letter to Reinaud, May 19, 1790, in G. Lély, *Vie du Marquis de Sade. Oeuvres complètes du Marquis de Sade* (Paris: Cercle du Livre précieux, 1966), vol. II, p. 290. (Sade's complete works will henceforth be abbreviated *OC*)

8 Letter to Gaufridy, December 28, 1791; *OC*, vol. II, p. 316.

9 Sade, *Aline et Valcour*, *OC*, vol. V, pp. 109–110, note.

10 J. Tortel, "La philosophie en prison ou l'agent provocateur," *Cahiers du Sud* 285 (1947), p. 374.

11 G. Habert, "Le Marquis de Sade, auteur politique," *Revue Internationale d'Histoire Politique et Institutionnelle* 25–26 (Jan–June 1957), pp. 1, 196, 200 and 190.

12 P. Eluard, "L'intelligence révolutionnaire du Marquis de Sade," *Clarté* 6 (Feb. 1927).

13 S. de Beauvoir, *Privilèges* (Paris: Gallimard-Idées, 1972), p. 12. First published in *Les Temps Modernes* 74 (Dec. 1951), pp. 1002–33, and 75 (Jan. 1952), pp. 1197–230.

14 Sartre's comments on Sade's thought, taken as an example of "synthèse subjective," are to be found in a 1966 interview with Bernard Pingaud, *L'Arc*, 30, pp. 87–96.

15 L.-S. Mercier, *Mon Bonnet de nuit* (Neufchâtel, 1784), vol. II, p. 376.

16 Sade, *La Philosophie dans le boudoir*, *OC*, vol. III, p. 516.

17 Sade, *Les Malheurs de la vertu*, *OC*, vol. III, p. 208.

18 Sade, *Les Infortunes de la vertu*, *OC*, vol. XIV, p. 337.

19 Sade, *Histoire de Juliette*, *OC*, vol. VIII, p. 173.

20 I deal with Sade's attitude towards Rousseau in "Rousseau selon Sade ou Jean-Jacques travesti," *Dix-Huitième Siècle*, 23 (1991), pp. 383–405.

21 Sade, *Histoire de Juliette*, *OC*, vol. VIII, p. 172, note.

22 Sade, *Notes littéraires*, *OC*, vol. XV, p. 16.

23 A. Huxley, *Ends and Means* (London: Readers' Union and Chatto and Windus, 1938), p. 271.

24 M. Horkheimer and T. Adorno, *The Dialectic of Enlightenment*, trans. J. Cumming (New York: Continuum, 1989), p. 85.

25 See J. Roger, "Le marquis de Sade et l'esprit républicain," in

L'Esprit Créateur, Actes du Colloque d'Orléans (4–5 sept. 1970) (Paris: Klinksieck, 1972).

26 Sade, *La Philosophie dans le boudoir*, *OC*, vol. III, p. 543.
27 Ibid., p. 522.
28 Sade, *Aline et Valcour*, *OC*, vol. IV, p. 268.
29 Ibid., p. 297.
30 Sade, *La Philosophie dans le boudoir*, *OC*, vol. III, p. 498.
31 Sade, *Aline et Valcour*, *OC*, vol. IV, p. 317.
32 See F. Ewald, *L'Etat providence* (Paris: Grasset, 1986).

CHAPTER 5

The Society of the Friends of Crime

Alphonso Lingis

SUBSTITUTIONS

An organ is *une machine*, an engine, that can be put to multiple uses. The mouth of an infant, with its strong jowls, couples onto the maternal breast and draws in the milk, but also takes in air, drools, slobbers, excites a nipple, kisses, hisses, pouts, spits, vomits, murmurs, whistles, sings, chatters, will formulate arguments and libertine sophisms. The anus ejects excrement but also holds it in, can absorb suppositories and medicines, releases gases, acquiesces, pouts, threatens, mocks, defies, and defiles. Body parts substitute for one another. An insect whose leg gets broken substitutes another and does not limp. When a patient born blind has vision given to his eyes with a corneal transplant, he does not at first, like the rest of us, see a visual field where the light leads but is not seen for itself; he has a visual field organized tactually, he uses his eyes like hands. During toilet training the column of fæces hardening and advancing is the new anal pleasure felt by the infant; when he learns to harden his penis it will substitute for that pleasure. Sometimes one wakes up in the morning with an erection and wonders what orgasmic fantasies dreamt had provoked it, until one goes to the toilet and feels the voluptuous sliding of a large stool. For Freud, substitution in the anal zone, substitution of blockage for movement, of the pleasure of retention for the pleasure of release, of delayed for immediate gratification, of public praise for private comfort, results in the constitution, paid for by praise and rewards and love from the outside, of the anus into a private part and the first private property. It is the substitution, for this *machine*, of the spiritual apparatus of obstinacy, prickliness, and possessiveness – which is character. It results in the constitution of orderliness, cleanliness, and parsimony – that is, the basic constituents of civilization.

Body parts also substitute for the body parts of another. A passerby stops and sees the fallen contact lens I have been peering in the leaves for. Standing behind him, she unbuttons his shirt and undoes his belt buckle for him. A team-mate spontaneously finds the right diagram with which to support my weight with his leg when I sprained an ankle. His fingers, hands, tongue, penis spontaneously find the pleasure-zones the other loves to masturbate.

TRANSUBSTANTIATIONS

The mouth lets go of the chain of its sentences, rambles, giggles, the tongue spreads its wet out over the lips. The hands that caress move in random detours with no idea of what they are looking for, grasping and probing without wanting an end. The body tenses up, hardens, heaves and grapples, pistons and rods of a machine that has no idea of what it is trying to produce. Then it collapses, leaks, melts. There is left the coursing of the trapped blood, the flush of heat, the spirit vaporizing in exhalations.

Lust is the posture become dissolute, the bones turning into gum. It is the sinews and muscles becoming gland – lips blotting out their muscular enervations and becoming loose and wet as labia, chest becoming breast, thighs lying there like more penises, stroked like penises, knees fingered like *montes veneris*. It is glands stiffening and hardening, becoming bones and rods and then turning into ooze and vapors and heat. Eyes clouding and becoming wet and spongy, hair turning into webs and gleam, fingers becoming tongues, wet glands in orifices.

The supreme pleasure we can know, Freud said, and the model for all pleasure, orgasmic pleasure, comes when an excess tension confined, swollen, compacted is abruptly released; the pleasure consists in a passage into the contentment and quiescence of death. Is not orgasm instead the passage into the uncontainment and unrest of mire, fluid, and fog – pleasure in exudations, secretions, exhalations? Voluptuous pleasure engulfs and obliterates purposes and directions and any sense of where it itself is going; it surges and rushes and vaporizes and returns. Lust is the dissolute ecstasy by which the body's glands, entrails, and sluices ossify and fossilize, by which its ligneous, ferric, coral state gelatinizes, curdles, dissolves, and vaporizes.

We fondle animal fur and feathers and both they and we get aroused, we root our penis in the dank humus flaking off dandelion fluff, we caress fabrics, come on silk and leather, we hump the seesaw and the horses and a Harley-Davidson. Lust does not transact with the other as a representative of the male or female gender, a representative of the human species; it seeks contact with the hardness of bones and rods collapsing into glands and secretions, with the belly giggling into jelly, with the smegmic and vaginal swamps, with the musks and the sighs. Lewd eyes fetishize the body lusted after, solidify the sweating lineman's body in those gleaming belts and boots, petrify in marble the gestures of the powdered face and arms of the stewardess, metalize the starched nurse's uniform. Wanton hands liquefy the dyadic oppositions, vaporize all the markers of *différance* into a sodden and electric atmosphere. Lust muddies and makes turgid the light of thought, vaporizing its constructions, petrifying its ideas into obsessions and idols.

TRANSACTIONS

Body Portions

The Sambia of Papua-New Guinea[1] live, without rulers, in autonomous compounds. Their combats, without battle-chiefs or strategies, are not wars – for territory, booty, or women – but feasts of ferocious individualism. The primary social act is that of the young man who goes to another compound to transact for a woman. For the sister he takes from them, he pledges to one of her brothers his niece for his son. And he will now give her younger brothers, those from seven to 16 years old, of his male essence; he will give them his penis to suck in order that they, weaned from the female milk of their mother, will have the male milk they need to become men.

For among the Sambia the essence of life is fluid, it is in blood, female milk, and male milk. The bodies are not producers of fluid but conduits of fluids. The milk-sap of the pandanus trees, the milk of female nature, is sucked by men; in their bodies it transubstantiates into the male milk of their penises. Men give the milk of their penis to boys that they grow into men. When these boys are filled with the milk of men to the point that the milk flows in their penises, they will give it orally to young girls, until the milk fills them and their breasts swell. Then when the excess blood of the women begins to flow from their vaginas, the husbands will pump into it their male milk. They will fill them continually day after day as the child coagulates in this mix of female blood and male milk. Mature male and female bodies among the Sambia are parallel, both conduits of fluids, giving their milk to infants that they grow into women and men. Men are men when they give male milk to women and to boys; when it ceases to flow they lose their maleness, and become neuter or sexually indeterminate. Male and female identity is in the flow, and is itself a fluid identity.

Among the Sambia body fluids do not flow freely, they are coded, metered out. The fundamental act of association which organizes society is a transaction with portions of the self, fluid portions of a fluid self.

Sambia society is a dual economy; the men hunt, the women garden. Married men eat male food, the male milk of the pandanus trees they themselves cultivate and tend, and game from the hunt. They cook and eat together, in the men's house. Relations among men are fiercely egalitarian. Women garden, and eat what they raise. A wife, taken from another compound, remains bound to her own family, and in time of conflict she may lend her force to theirs. The transaction does not deliver over the whole woman to the ownership of the husband. The infant is their co-production. The parents do not educate their sons into the ways of men; they will be initiated by the whole clan into the skills and tasks of each stage of their development.

We both have careers. We have an apartment on the Upper West Side. It was done by a decorator. We have insurance on everything, including our lives, our deaths. We have networks of friends; the city is a compound of theaters, galleries, cafés, discos. But we live together. She does not cook, neither of us does housework; we go out or call in to eat, have a maid. We have no children. We fuck with a condom. We are not into phallocratic macho bullshit. We have our own rules. She has a vibrator, and a dildo, and rights to my ass. He gives head, I give head. He nibbles on my tits, I bite his. We frenchkiss in the elevator, in the taxi, at lunch break when we meet in the Japanese restaurant halfway between her office and mine. Her nervous circuitry is connected to the neon map of my Big Apple, his dreams navigate about the contours of my private movies, her steps move with the rhythms of the songs I have in my heart, his wit and nonsense ricochets off mine. Our talk is an idiolect of clandestine allusions, private jokes, whimsical taxonomies, perverse explanations. We team up for picaresque escapades in the halls and desks of office buildings, for island-hopping adventures on Caribbean cruise ships. We own a private Key Club: our apartment. Between us all the sophisticated and perverse and debauched emotions get rolled back and forth. An ocean in an illuminated plastic box with a small motor tilting it back and forth.

Body parts

A young man of the Eastern Highlands of Iran Jaya[2] walks with the arms of the most noble and fierce lords of the jungle in the perforated lobes of his ears, his nostrils, his arms, his penis: tusks of wild boars, the beaks of cassowaries with which he has contended, the claws and plumes of eagles, and shells he has braved long treks down the slippery paths of the dangerous jungle to obtain from alien people who plunge into the shark-patrolled ocean for them. He is a warrior. The combats in which he participates are Aztec flower-wars, or rather bird-of-paradise wars, exultant ceremonial feasts, where each is his own chief, elaborates his own strategy, and celebrates his own triumph. In the clash with the people on the other side of the ravine, he pursued and killed the one with boar's tusks through his nostrils and an array of glittering black bird-of-paradise plumes on his head, the bravest of their warriors. He cut off the head of the one he vanquished, stripped it of its flesh and brain, and has hung it over his door. He has eaten of the cadaver, whose pride and ferocity now dwell in him. Now he is going to the other settlement – with which one season and against which another season the men of his settlement fight – for a wife. He is bringing her father and brothers the tusks, fangs, shells, and plumes he will amputate from the body. These he will graft to their nostrils, ears, arms, head, enhancing their male power as hunters, incorporating in them the weapons and power of the most lordly animals of the mountains and seas. They will take him as a son and as their brother and give him a daughter and their sister.

The high valley in the Eastern Highlands of Iran Jaya is wet from the rains that collect about the mountains above and the melting ice. The people have dug deep trenches and created raised flats for gardens. It is very laborious, but the only season here is springtime and the crops do not fail. The women do not gather foodstuffs from the forest; they are skilled in the arts of gardening. They have learned to maintain the fertility of the soil by throwing the weeds into the trenches, and scooping up the rotted masses to spread back on the flats for the new planting. They raise yams, rich in nutrients, as the staple, and many kinds of vegetables to garnish them. All the labor, save for the actual digging of trenches and turning over the flats after a harvest, is done by women. The men depart into the forests above and return with feasts of game. Men are hunters, and head-hunters.

Out of the enormous number of postural diagrams a child forms – rolling, sprawling, crawling, creeping, wallowing, tumbling, flailing, rocking, snuggling – I had to eliminate most of them, and out of the selection remaining I had to rectify them, adjust them to the representative paradigms. I had to learn the vocabulary, the grammar, the phraseology, the rhetoric, the intonations of voice. I fitted myself with jeans and motorcycle boots, and learned to stride and sprawl in them. With a skirt and heels. With stubble left by a special razor, and a tattoo. With depilated legs and a nose job. With musculature built in a gym and a scar from the football field. With fluttering eyelashes and liquid hand movements. I am straight, I do not want a careerperson, I want a woman. I do not want an interlocutor and housemate, sisters are not enough; I want a man. Those of taste know one another's taste; I know her taste in perfume and she mine in aftershaves. It becomes "a relationship" when he gives me a bottle of Joy or I give him a bottle of Brut. It gets serious when he gives me see-through panties and I give him a cock-ring. Immanuel Kant defined marriage as a contract for the reciprocal use of each other's genital organs.

Having paid him millions, we, sprawled before our television sets, copulate with Michael Jackson as he pirouettes, singing and thrusting into our bedrooms. In order to do that, our demiurgic imagination has to substitute, for the feel and smell and look of our actual scrawny groupie and couch-potato bodies, bodies that would not weigh him down, trip him on the disco floor, bodies of his partners on MTV.

The family jewels

Where this young man lives, in the high valleys of the western cordillera, pigs are raised and gardens are very large and their yields abundant. The women are rich. He has undergone the seventh-stage initiation, and has been accepted into the clan, knows the secret myths and rituals of the men. It is the daughter of an important man he sets out to acquire for a wife. He does not long to drink the semen of men; it is their blazons and connections that draw him to them. He is a man, now he will become a "big man". By entering into the household of a man of status and wealth and guardian of sacred rituals, he will be able to acquire more wives, and more wealth. The women are expensive. He will wait, will transact with men indebted to him, until he can put before the important man and his sons a pile of rare shells, ritual objects or insignia of status, and large quantities of foodstuffs, roast pigs and beverages. They will demonstrate his male power to acquire things. The shells, ritual objects, and insignia will not be grafted to the bodies of the father and brothers; they will be added to their hoard of prestige. The foodstuffs and beverages will be consumed in potlatch feasts in which the connections of and obligations to his father-in-law's family will be increased.

The herding of pigs and extensive cultivation of crops in the Western Highlands of Papua New Guinea make female labor not complementary to male hunting but in disequilibrium with it. The dominant discourse is here not women's generative role in social reproduction, but women as producers of external wealth.[3] The ritual and the ideological superstructure are spheres of male power. With their political organization, the men control the surplus agricultural production, and engage in financial transactions that issue in the concentration of wealth. With status in the ritual and political sphere, men can traffic with other men for the acquisition of many women.

In this century such Melanesian societies have entered into relationship with Western societies. Food production in the village is supplied by the women; with game scarce and headhunting suppressed, the young men are drawn off to the plantations and the mines of the white men. They work for wages while the white men control the productive resources and the equipment. They really cannot use their wages to acquire productive wealth, plantations, or mines; the profitable plants cannot be grown in their Highland homes. What they use their wages for is metal-buckled belts, wrist watches, gaudy and macho clothing, eventually motorcycles, which they will take back to their villages to offer as bride-price in exchange for women, the local wealth-producers. The fathers-in-law add these things to the hoard of shells, ritual objects, and insignia that represent status within male society. Filling his compound with the sumptuary objects of white male prestige, the big man extends his prestige to white male society also. For the greatest male power a father can have is to be the headman of the village which the white labor-recruiter will have to deal with.

The white men have a society in the region. They contract with other white men for productive property and for refined women. Offering not their body portions or body parts but their money, they enter into transactions with the native big men for black laborers for their plantations and their mines. The raw materials these extract, and the commodities they harvest, the white men market for a profit, which they invest in equipment for more profit.

The fundamental social transaction is not for reproductive bodies but for things that produce more things; the transactions among men produce not children but "big men." For these things that produce more things in place of bodies, produce persons in those places. As resources they supply one's needs; as property that produces more property they materialize one's independence, freedom of initiative, status. They are representatives of self.

TRANSACTIONS WITH REPRESENTATIVES

Lounge bar in São Paulo. Skyview restaurant in Berlin. Disco in New York. Where we professional, affluent, broad-minded, health-conscious, cultivated, sensitive white males meet educated, financially independent, street-wise, liberated, caring women. We are not just, like savages, or like fiancés, transacting with body parts. One has to present oneself, represent oneself, the in way. Like on a talk-show, images of Hilary Clinton and Larry King, H. Norman Schwartzkopf and Anita Hill, Michael Jackson and Oprah. Our bodies with their contact lenses and hair implants, designer gowns or leather jackets, and diamond chokers or razor blade, represent us. We amuse ourselves over the tvs, the starlets and the nerds, who also deck themselves out with these things, the instant-executive, instant-fashion-model or instant-punk from Kansas or Belgium, come from an afternoon's shopping in the Upper East Side or in Soho. It is by going to certain clubs, stepping out of limousines or off Harley-Davidsons, by the suave or swaggering choreography of our gestures, by an intricate rhetoric of allusion and multiple things never alluded to, that one materializes a representation of oneself. The invisible raiment one's choreographed movements weaves about oneself and the sophisticated lighting one's sparkling allusions project upon oneself are representations not of our bodies but of our training, education, business acumen, and connections. That, high on cocaine, we will prove our love by copulating our depilated and perfumed bodies, is not discussed now or reported on later. Those who are into basic instincts go slumming.

It helps to really have a degree from Princeton, an executive job at McIntosh, to be an editor of *Ms* or a dancer in Chippendale's. You get established in a career, you build up a business, you build a home that represents success. With these you have credit, can get loans and can transact for more productive wealth. The business, the home, represent you, not as a body but as a name that means something in the real world. What Aristotle Onassis produces with all his wealth-generating wealth is Aristotle Onassis. A name with which he gets a Kennedy, not the hottest woman there is but the woman that represents all that Camelot America is.

The self that advances from the body is not its representative, but a representative of a trend, a caste, the action, an empire. Vassar graduate on a date with Formula-1 racer. Hollywood surgeon on a date with British novelist. Not heads of state, feudal lords who meet for hand-to-hand combat before their assembled troops, but chancellors – representatives of Paris, Washington, Moscow, Tokyo; representatives of Prime Ministers who are elected representatives, not of the people (that Brownian movement of individual interests) but of the nation, *la Gloire* that is France, the baby-boomers, or Japan, Inc.

When we meet, we lay out hands strapped with Rolexes and fingers ringed in old jade and complement a silk necktie or a recherché chain of Navajo beads. We discuss the menu, what wines we like, what songs that we love the band is playing. We check out whether we liked the film that won all the Oscars, verify that we both love the new director of the Philharmonic or the new Madonna MTV. Lover's talk.

The person loved is overdetermined with roles in the conversation and activity of society, the theater of femininity and masculinity, one's future and past family, and the songs, chronicles, and epics of the social and civic order. Love, more than sex, would be this exorbitant attention directed to a nexus of a categoreal network. Love is a spiritual devotion to the carnal; when one loves someone it is an ideal one is captivated by or pursues. Transaction with body parts is only the way to keep score.

In our postindustrial, postindustrious society the mass media are not, as in the so-called developing countries, controlled by ministries of propaganda and filled with what they deem public education. They are satellites in orbit in outer space, circulating above laborious and lascivious continents, generating the precession of representations, contexts, trends, the order, Baudrillard says, of seduction. Or the enchanted empyrean of love.

CORRUPTION

The social order, whether a system of regulated transactions of body portions, body parts, or of representatives of self, is subject to corruption, and exposed to crime.

The tolerated publication of smut which displays the combinatorium of simple and compound passions every social order is set up to limit – child prostitution, police brutality, the wasting of the nation's wealth in the debaucheries of the court, the alliances of FBI and Mafia, of Japan Inc. and the Yakusa – are phenomena of social decay. The regulated and policed order of transactions undergoes a kind of rot, that of the dead octopus with which *La dolce vita* ends. Normative reason, the necessary, the workable, and the politic lose their evidence. The enormous resources of the mass media pour into the social body a slow intoxication with the unscrupulous, the fraudulent, the servile, the venal. Before the spectacle of athletes and politicians bought and traded for enormous sums that melt away in conspicuous consumption, that exorbitant devotion to the nexus of a categoreal network: love – personal love of idolized bodies, patriotic love of society – softens, turns sentimental, and begins to smell. Resignation turns into positive fascination with the irresponsible, the hedonist, the immediately gratified, the insubstantial, and the precession of simulacra. The social body acquiesces in the transubstantiation of a generalized lust.

THE CRIMINALIZATION OF SOCIETY

Donatien Alphonse François, the Marquis de Sade, does not wish to reverse the evolution of society that advanced from transactions with body portions to transactions with body parts and to transactions with representatives of self, and bring it back to a paradise of transubstantiation. A dissolute lord living in an epoch of the generalized corruption of society, Sade does not write in order to feed the corruption: he wishes to reverse the very nature of lust, to make it serve his reason; he aspires to be the mastermind of an unprecedented criminal enterprise. He argues for the overthrow of corrupt society and its replacement by the Society of the Friends of Crime.

Only the naive, or rather those who want to wilfully dupe themselves, see in "One more effort, Frenchmen, if you are to become Republicans" a protodocument of modern political liberalism. In fact, Sade's pamphlet is a piece of propaganda not for liberalism but for libertinage, and those who elect to take propaganda at face value are cowardly accomplices of the masterminds of Machiavellian strategies. The one more effort will not make Frenchmen, or us, free; it is Sade who wants to be freed by one more effort of the Frenchmen, and freed from them; Sade who, while taking office in the Commune, judges it as yet another Bastille. Sade wants to appropriate, and make into characters of his own plays and novels, all the representations of which the self is a representative in the theater of society. This hereditary aristocrat become magistrate in the Commune wants to misuse all the rules for the regulated transactions with body parts so as to acquire all the body parts of others as his own property and to treat his own body parts as the property of his criminal will. This consummate rationalist wants to subvert the rules for the regulated exchange of body portions so that blood, milk, urine, and shit flow wherever he wills. (The naive, the wilfully duped, take at face value one letter in which Sade complained that the guillotine set up under his window disturbed his sleep.)

Libertines are men of principle; libertinage is defined formally by its relationship with law. Libertinage is not a particular perversion; Sade's sodomy is not simply a perverse use of an organ, it is an imperative of universal perversion. The libertine as imagined by Sade is constituted in essential criminality by violation of every form of social contract, in essential sacrilege by the incessant aggression against God, in essential monstrosity by violation of nature. Libertinage is the singular, and singularizing, will to violate the law for the sake of violating the law.

The representations of society, industry, the civic order have been in the West laid out in a field of coordinates whose focal point is God. The God of Genesis is the formula for generating the generic norms governing transactions with body fluids and body parts. The Kingdom of God is the formula for regulating the transactions with representations of the body politic. The God of Abraham, Isaac, and Jacob, of Saul and Paul, is the formula for generating the transactions with representations of self, selves that are representatives. The formula for generating transactions with ideals, with nexuses of categorial networks, is the Word of the God that is the God of love.

In the libertine pedagogy the inclinations of the unsophisticated and the virginal to obey divine law are sapped by a rationalist argumentation which demonstrates the arbitrary nature of the law by assembling massive empirical evidence of promiscuity, incest, infanticide, matricide, and torture wherever nature holds sway. The family, economic, and indeed linguistic codes are stripped of their authority by an appeal to nature. The outcries and screams of nature are hypostatized into incontrovertible law in order to discredit positive, ethical, and civic codes. But the libertine reason affirms its sovereignty by then proceeding to a generalized discrediting of laws in nature. Its syllogisms are, to be sure, essentially sophistical. It proves itself by becoming practical; it issues in the performing with impunity of unnatural acts, in which its voice is reduced to outbursts of malediction, blasphemy, and derision shouted at God.

An act that gives rise to an after-image of the act can find itself substituted for by that after-image. Prudence and remorse are the substitutive effects of these after-images. They cannot be counteracted by the impulse on the part of the libertine to act passionately; the passions cannot be trusted. Neophyte libertines can come to voluptuously acquiesce in the regulated order of transactions and the representations of the social order, which they can use to idolize and break into fetishes, liquefy and vaporize. The libertine must make the pure thought of a crime immediately imperative for his will, and short-circuit both imagination and feelings. It is repetition that will at length enervate the inventiveness of the imagination and dissipate the thickness of passion. In the resulting apathy, a thought, as soon as it takes form, will be able to trigger acts of cold-blooded depravity.

The imagination, when left only to its natural operation of reproducing and combining what is sensibly impressed, is servile and limited. The pornographic imagination will be replaced by the much more extensive powers of calculating and compounding reason. These exercises of reason generate the tableaux of debauchery whose exhaustive computation Sade attempted in *The 120 Days of Sodom*.

The personages in the House of Sodom are not really phallic and significant individuals who, once identified by a libertine act in which they accede to sovereignty, then pursue a certain activity, discourse, or destiny. They are without character, without history, ciphers of a single act: they are the matricide, the infanticide, the coprophagist, the sodomite, personages whose whole reality is exhausted in the indulgence of their mania. Save for naming his vice, the libertine has nothing to say; his life has nothing to promulgate but his singular depravity. His existence consists in subsisting until the moment when he can again perpetrate his transgression. The libertine is not an invert living according to the codes of an underground or damned brotherhood; his existence consists in nothing but the compulsive repetition of a single act going each time to the limit of outrage against the normative: disemboweling the other in the course of an assault on the genus as such.

Sadism is wholly concentrated in sodomy. Sade will need an interpretation to turn the anal eroticism his argumentation finds universal in nature into the consummate outrage. The erected penis, an instrument to bond in giving pleasure and to serve the reproduction of the species, is the body part that had become representative of the whole body in the society that regulated transactions with body parts. In the society that transacted with representatives, it had become a representative of virility, power, armies, corporations, nations, Shiva, God the Father. Sade will use this representation with which advanced society has invested the erected male penis as the basis for giving it all rights. It will be turned by Sade into an absolute and a weapon aimed at the species as such.

Sade interrupts coitus with the maternal womb, and drives the erected penis into the private part, the private property of the one of character – the zone of conscientiousness and trust, the original locus of order, cleanliness, and parsimony. The phallic arm, the clenched fist of the libertine, plunges into the anus to despoil the gold fæces of character and the vaults that contain them. Sodomy for Sade is the use of the erected male organ to release the germ of the race only in its excreta, and to gore, to disembowel, the receiving partner.

One can want to be sodomized. The libertines are pedagogues; their sentimental education corrupts the soul of the neophyte to the point of wanting to be a prey. The master libertines sodomize one another. One must not confuse the libertine pleasure with gratification, that is, with plenitude, equilibrium, and contentment simmering over a final state. The libertine pleasure consists in the squandering of a surface flow; the pleasure of the libertine will consists in the discharge of an excess, in the dying away of a surplus, of that redundancy in a material system which is life itself.[4] Libertine pleasure is then nowise the opposite of pain and death. There is also the brazen pleasure of the outrage. As the privacy of their person is sacked, the economy of character and its treasures despoiled, the vast intercorporeality of the genus in their own body torn apart, the very extremism of the torments of the victims blazes like a black splendor and gives rise to the satanic pleasure of pride in the outrage they are enduring. The sodomized one, in the midst of his screams and imprecations, comes.

The libertine as conceived by Sade exists as the sign of the destruction of signs, the clamor in which every demand made to another and every demand put on another is made incomprehensible. Hard, erected, bigger than life, he is invested with feral compulsions freed from the limitations of imagination and feeling. He comes as plunderer, Cossack and Hun, to every order of persons associated in an economy of exchange. A sodomite, violating the imperative of the genus, of common humanity in himself and in every body, he leaves room in himself only for bestiality. Singularity, solitude, is essential; the dark hero of Sade's revolt is a mutant, a deviation from every law of the genus, of common understanding, of every interchange and every discourse. He is the extreme limit of the stranger, the exception and the outlaw. Exhibitionism, ostentation, is essential: he is not a sign that speaks within a semiotic system, an exchange system operating among individuals; he is the outbreak and the outrage, the derision and the blasphemy shouted out at God, the universal cosmic witness. The lord of the House of Sodom is constituted in integral monstrosity. The followers of the libertine pedagogy are driven by a lust for association with what is most dissociated, a singular concupiscence addressed to the sovereign monster, for the extreme pleasure of contact with him who is a stranger anywhere in humanity.

The Society of the Friends of Crime is neither a fraternity nor an estate; it is a conspiracy of singular ones whose existence is nothing but subversion of the community of the species as well as of every social economy. It is true that the magnitude of their lusts requires unlimited resources, in wealth, power, and victims. Inexhaustible resources that they have acquired gratuitously. The libertine republic could exist only as a conspiracy diverting, for its spectacular rituals, immense resources of a compulsively reproductive race and an overheated productive society. The inexpiable evil done to their victims can only mobilize ever more the instincts of the race and the powers of civilization against them. But they can also acquire unlimited resources through their very libertinage; it is through a career in debauchery that Juliette has become fabulously rich and has the most powerful lords of church and state in her subjection. The libertines are dissolute lords of a society in an advanced state of corruption.

Within the Society of the Friends of Crime, too, every law exists to be violated: each libertine is for the other the permanent excitant to violate his physical integrity, his character, his private personage, his generic body. There is no outrage he inflicts on another that he does not inflict on himself; the torments of the other function for him as excitants to be sodomized. It is true that just as the rational discourse of universality is inverted into a speech reduced to outcries of blasphemy, which maintains God at a distance just this side of inexistence in order to subsist as the unitary and ultimate term of the violation, so also the libertines must maintain their own bare existence without which a society of friends of crime cannot subsist. In Sade's Society of the Friends of Crime, the "Everything is permitted" of its secret Constitution decrees a limit: everything is permitted the libertine on the body of another libertine – save murder. But this interdiction, simply by being, as it must be, legislated, immediately produces the imperative motive for its transgression: the purely formal imperative to violate the law for the sake of violating the law is the pure and *a priori* motive of all libertine action. The asceticism of apathy removes every obstacle in the way of its immediate translation into effect.

It would be imperspicacious to conclude that such a society cannot exist, or cannot subsist, because it immediately engenders the agency of its decomposition. As though the Society of the Friends of Crime were a friendship for the sake of society, and not society for the sake of crime. The disorder it introduces may be irreparable. Sade identifies Jesus as the impostor who taught that every sin, even original sin, can be redeemed. Sade's Juliette lives only to perpetrate a crime which would disturb the civic and cosmic order so irrevocably that its consequences would continue indefinitely, after her death, a death itself she wishes to occur by crime.

Sade wants to subvert the social orders established in transactions with body portions and body parts and representatives of self, by a conspiracy of integral monsters. They use the representatives of self which are themselves representatives of representations to construct weapons to release the germ of the race in its excrement. They use the body parts with which individuals transact to appropriate the body parts of others, in order to spread about themselves a wasteland of mutilated and discarded genitals, crushed limbs, decapitated torsos. They appropriate the body fluids of others in order to rot the earth itself with spilt blood, slashed breasts, mutilated vaginas, urine, and shit. They have big brains; they are to be found in key positions in mass media, industry, and the Intelligence Division of governments.

Tribes in Melanesia, the European Enlightenment of the eighteenth century, the French Revolution, and the sodomite utopia written on toilet paper by the Marquis de Sade – all that has completely ceased to exist. All the white or black utopian images that goaded the four-million-year-long advance of the human species – which has avoided the irrevocable disorder plotted by criminal masterminds by a periodic aimless collapse into lust and by the regulated forms of transactions for the reproduction of individuals – were incinerated at Hiroshima. We, now with a thermonuclear arsenal of 1,500,000 times the explosive power of the Hiroshima bomb – enough to obliterate a Hiroshima-size city every day for the next 550 years – stand before the imminent possibility of the instant reduction of the human species to extinction, a possibility in the hands of any of the ten nations that have nuclear arsenals, those of their allies to which their hands are held hostage, and those of any terrorist group now able to invent or steal a thermonuclear device. The past is for us but a quaint museum of images.

A future had existed as an array of possibilities which we could laboriously discern in the obscure lines of the present. The release of quasi-unlimited nuclear energy for industrial production has made the future cease to exist. We live in an infantile world where any demand for equipment and gratifications can be satisfied and any possibility of sexual mutations brought about on ourselves or on others, or racial extinction, can be realized immediately. Our present has swallowed up the future as merely one of the infinite array of possibilities open now.

Our transactions with representations of self which were representatives of the action, the trend, a caste or an empire, have become simulacra. In each of us, the self is but a representative of the precession of fifteen-minute celebrities generated and satellite-broadcast by the mass media. Humans used to transact with body parts, *machines* susceptible of multiple uses that incorporated the arms of the lords of the jungle and the seas. Now the lords of the technopoles are only eyes fixed on computer screens and fingers touching the keyboards; robots that do all the productive labor have dismembered our muscled arms, legs, and our body fluids, uncoded, unmetered, are waste products.

High over the blood-splattered streets, in our high-rise protected with electronic surveillance systems in all the corridors, like Pablo Escobar in his prison, we sniff a line of coke and settle into our plastic leatherette sofas and fix our eyes on television screens. There we view customized snapshots and hear sound-bites of the neighborhood where urban guerrillas with crack-soaked brains prowl with switchblades and assault rifles. We view customized snapshots and hear sound-bites of Northern Ireland, the West Bank, Lebanon, El Salvador, Afghanistan, Cambodia, Bosnia. We view customized snap-shots and hear sound-bites of Amazonian Indians being hunted down in the rain forests, Papuans being napalmed in their jungle retreats, Brazilian slums being covered with mudslides and Tibetan monks being exterminated with assault rifles. We view customized snapshots and hear sound-bites of deserts advancing and famine ravaging across marginal lands, hear sound-bites of coral reefs being dynamited and poisoned with industrial wastes, view computerized animations of the ozone shield gaping open over the polar icecaps.

In [Catherine's] sophisticated eyes, I was already becoming a kind of emotional cassette, taking my place with all those scenes of pain and violence that illuminated the margins of our lives – television newsreels of wars and student riots, natural disasters and police brutality which we vaguely watched on the color TV set in our bedroom as we masturbated each other. This violence experienced at so many removes had become intimately associated with our sex acts. The beatings and burnings married in our minds with the delicious tremors of our erectile tissues, the spilt blood of students with the genital fluids that irrigated our fingers and mouths. Even my own pain as I lay in the hospital bed, while Catherine steered the glass urinal between my legs, painted fingernails pricking my penis, even the vagal flushes that seized at my chest seemed extensions of that real world of violence calmed and tamed within our television programs and the pages of news magazines. (J.G. Ballard, *Crash!*, p. 37)

In our bedrooms our bodies are thrown in the transactions with hi-tech equipment – Porsches embraced by languid women, handguns extending the penises vasectomized by AIDS of men with virile Marlboro jaws and Marlboro lungs, by the glamorous and feline femininity of the Stealth bomber advanc-ing, like *Penthouse* lesbians, in mists seen by vaseline-coated camera lenses. The technological artifacts seduce us only by images of lascivious thrills that will shiver across the moribund musculature and surveillance and decision circuitry of our prone and concupiscent bodies. But it is illusory to hypoth-esize that the last backwaters of life stagnating in us in the final form of simple libido are the universal polymorphously perverse power to probe into reality and continually discover new sexual possibilities. It is only the cold touch of death in the fingernails that prick our penises, in the handguns and motor-cars in our masturbating hands, simulacra of the thermonuclear arsenal in our collective landscapes, that gives us a sense of our own bodies. We lasciviously welcome into our private parts the electronic weapons devastating the locus of obstinacy, prickliness, and possessiveness that is our character, the carnal locus of the order, cleanliness, and parsimony that is civilization. We acquiesce to the release of the germ of the race into the electronic and radioactive excrement. We lasciviously acquiesce to being disemboweled.

NOTES

1 Gilbert H. Herdt, "Fetish and fantasy in Sambia initiation," in *Rituals of Manhood* (Berkeley: University of California Press, 1982), pp. 17–27, 52–53; and Gilbert H. Herdt, *Guardians of the Flutes: Idioms of Masculinity* (New York: McGraw-Hill, 1981), *passim*.

2 Shirley Lindenbaum, "Variations on a sociosexual theme in Melanesia," in Gilbert H. Herdt, ed., *Ritualized Homosexuality in Melanesia* (Berkeley: University of California Press, 1984), pp. 337–61.

3 Ibid, p. 349.

4 The *mystery* of sexuality is that we seek not only to get rid of this shattering tension but also to repeat, even to increase it. In sexuality, satisfaction is inherent in the painful need to find satisfaction. It is therefore not a question of deciding whether or not cruelty – or more specifically now, masochism as the "ground" of all the forms of the cruel – operates independently of the erotogenic zones, or even of seeking out the "mutual influences" to which cruelty and sexual development would somehow both be subject . . .

The investigation of human sexuality leads to a massive detachment of the sexual from both object-specificity and organ-specificity. We desire what nearly shatters us, and the shattering experience is, it would seem *without any specific content* . . .

According to what I have called the counter-argument of the *Three Essays* – the argument which runs against the teleological position – sexuality would not be originally an exchange of intensities between individuals, but rather a condition of broken negotiations with the world, a condition in which others merely set off the self-shattering mechanisms of masochistic *jouissance*. It is from this perspective that the exceptional importance of Freud's genealogy of sadism and masochism in the 1915 essay on "Instincts and Their Vicissitudes" can best be understood. In order to account for the mystery of sadistic sexuality – that is, how we can be sexually aroused by the suffering of others, as distinct from the easier questions of why we wish to exercise power over others – Freud is led to suggest that the spectacle of pain in others stimulates a mimetic representation which shatters the subject into sexual excitement. Sadism is defined in "Instincts and Their Vicissitudes" as a masochistic identification with the suffering object. Sexual pleasure enters the Freudian scheme, Laplanche has noted, "Within the suffering position" and he suggests that fantasmatic representation is in itself *ébranlement* and is therefore "intimately related, in its origin, to the emergence of the masochistic sexual drive." The suffering of others provides – to return to a passage already quoted from the *Three Essays* – a "relatively powerful emotion, even though it is of a distressing nature," an emotion which produces sexuality. Thus sadomasochistic sexuality would be a kind of melodramatic version of the constitution of sexuality itself, and the marginality of sadomasochism would consist of nothing less than its isolating, even its making visible, the ontological grounds of the sexual.

Genetically, sexuality is inseparable from the experience of failure; or, in other terms, the possibilities of instinctual pleasures in the past were already, from the very beginning, inseparable from and finally vanquished by, the actuality of pain. Sexuality comes "at the wrong time" in human life – but, as I have been suggesting, it is *created by* that wrong time . . . Human sexuality is constituted as a kind of psychic shattering, as a threat to the stability and integrity of the self – a threat which perhaps only the masochistic nature of sexual pleasure allows us to survive . . .

Leo Bersani, *The Freudian Body* (New York: Columbia University Press, 1986), pp. 38, 39–40, 41, 60.

CHAPTER 6

Sade, mothers, and other women

Jane Gallop

Nero played a superior Oedipus.

Sade, *The New Justine*

On the surface, the work of the Marquis de Sade appears to be a systematic transgression of every interdiction weighing upon civilized man. The anthropologist Claude Lévi-Strauss posits the incest taboo as the fundamental interdiction, the primal taboo which founds society.[1] Not surprisingly, incest is prevalent in Sade's novels. In *The New Justine*, Verneuil, whose entire household is allied through multiple incests, argues in defense of his pet crime: "Let a father, a brother, idolizing his daughter or his sister, descend to the bottom of his soul and interrogate himself scrupulously about what he feels: he will see if that pious tenderness is anything other than the desire to fuck."[2] As represented by Verneuil, incest is the passion underlying the relation between brother and sister or father and daughter. Likewise for Lévi-Strauss, it is intercourse with the sister or the daughter that must be abandoned so the brother or father can partake in the generalized exchange of women constitutive of society.

Whereas for Sadean libertine and structuralist anthropologist, incest means father–daughter or brother–sister sex, for Freud the central configuration of incest – figured by the oedipal myth – is between son and mother. In the vast tableau of forbidden passions making up Sade's opus, mother–son incest is sorely underrepresented. And in all but one case of its occurrence it is consummated through anal intercourse, thus avoiding contact with the locus constitutive of the mother as mother.

Still, the mother is not absent from Sadean libertine activity. She is a privileged victim: many libertines start their life of crime by killing their mother; others view the murder of their mother as their greatest accomplishment. In fact, Minski, the only character who successfully accomplishes incest with his mother, combines the incest with murder "on the same day" (vol. xxi, p. 299).

In point of fact, the reader cannot be positive that Minski actually penetrates the maternal vagina. In this exceptional instance Sade simply uses the verb *violer* (violate, rape), thus not specifying, as he usually does, the orifice. In the Sadean context the verb becomes ambiguous, thus leaving a final veil of uncertainty as to whether any character ever makes it into his mother's vagina. Since in most contexts *violer* implies vaginal penetration, the reader infers as much. But the fact that the sole case of successful mother–son incest should be accompanied by an ambiguity about the orifice gives some sense of the extent to which Sade's text avoids contact with a specifically maternal organ.

In the novel *The 120 Days of Sodom*, prostitutes recount sexual acts to libertines who are then moved to reenact them with their victims. The storytellers are to recount "all the passions,"3 a task they normally execute without showing personal taste or distaste – like the accomplished prostitutes they are. The first narrator nonetheless displays her lack of esteem for the seventh passion: "A young man whose mania, *although hardly libertine in my opinion*, was nonetheless singular enough . . . His cock seemed paltry to me and his entire person rather puny, and his discharge was as mild as his operation" (p. 143, emphasis added). In the universe of this novel to call a passion "hardly libertine" is the ultimate put-down. This young man's perversion consists in sucking the milk from a wet-nurse and discharging between her thighs. *120 Days* includes the narration of six hundred "passions" and is full of shit-eating and murder. Yet this enactment of mother–son incest, this attempt to repeat the primary satisfaction of suckling at the breast, is the sole occasion in the entire book when a storyteller expresses her disapproval.

This supposed tableau of "all the passions" has elicited from Sade's devoted biographer, Gilbert Lély, the remark that "we must nevertheless note that a dominant error comes to compromise in many a place the didactic value of such a work: we mean the monstrously exaggerated place that the author devotes to the coprophagic aberration carried to its final excesses."4 I would add to Lély's observation that not only is there an overemphasis on shit-eating in this supposedly encyclopedic work, but there is a shocking dearth of obsessions with breasts, menstruation, and female genitalia. To Lély's disappointment, far from being didactic and encyclopedic, *120 Days* bears the imprint of a living subject's desire rather than issuing from the omniscient position of an impartial observer.

Although they are seldom objects of desire for Sade, breasts and vaginas are favorite focuses of torture, just as mothers are favorite victims. Yet just as Minski raped *and* murdered his mother, throughout Sade's works a tight knot links lover and tormentor. Sade's text is haunted by the figure of Nero, in praise of whom Clairwil exclaims: "He had been very taken with Agrippina. Suetonius assures us that he had often jerked off for her . . . And he kills her" (vol. xxiii, pp. 273–74). The ellipsis here is Sade's. Oedipus did not just marry his mother, he also killed his father. Yet in Sade's classical myth, Nero expresses his desire for his mother by killing *her*.

Of all Sade's characters, Bressac most nearly repeats Nero's story. In the first two versions of Justine's adventures (*Les Infortunes de la vertu* and *Justine*), Bressac is a confirmed woman-hater and devotee of sodomy who murders his mother. The link between Bressac's misogynistic homosexuality and his desire to kill his mother is presented as merely contingent: Bressac's mother disapproves of his sodomistic activities and controls the fortune which Bressac wishes to squander on his passion. In the second version (*Justine*) she is actually an aunt but is otherwise identical to the first and third versions. Perhaps this revision is another strategy to avoid contact with the mother.

In the third and last version (*The New Justine*) – as if through repetition Sade gets closer to something he is trying to say – Bressac buggers his mother before he kills her. This is the only woman his member has ever penetrated. It is specified in this third version that in his sodomistic acts Bressac "was always the woman" (vol. xv, p. 148). Banished from his sexual life, woman returns in the guise of Bressac's mimicry. Bressac says to Justine: "There is not one of your [women's] pleasures that is not known to us, not one we cannot enjoy" (vol. xv, p. 164). By consummating the oedipal incest in the anus, Bressac is denying that his mother, that woman, has any pleasure "that is not known to us." However, this parodic attempt to deny her femininity is not sufficient; he must kill her, for her maternity, her otherness, remains inviolate, inappropriable.

According to Clairwil's story of Nero and his mother Agrippina: "he had often jerked off for her . . . And he kills her." Bressac repeats the Roman emperor's legendary bravado, filling in the ellipsis in Clairwil's account with a violation of the maternal anus. Bressac's representation of Suetonius' "he had often jerked off for her" is more elaborate than the original. Bressac faces his mother and masturbates at her while one of his "men" anally penetrates him. Before enacting this "scene," Bressac explains to his mother what will happen: "[While I am being fucked] you will be soaked with my cum, madame you will be inundated; that will remind you of the happy times when my esteemed father would smear your navel with it" (vol. xv, p.200). At once playing "the whore" – an epithet he applies equally to himself as buggered and to his detested mother – and representing his father, Bressac figures as the complete conjugal couple. In an attempt to transcend his subjective place as male child, Bressac figures as his own father and mother, thus denying his issue from the fact of sexual difference. It is not enough to combine the pleasure known to women and that known to men into a "delicious union" (vol. xv, p. 164), which sets him above either men or women. He must recreate the past and erase sexual difference as it preceded his individual existence, and free himself from his inscription into a series where father and mother are mutually exclusive alternatives. This attempt fails. A few days later he buggers his mother (not only his first sexual act with a woman, but his first active role) and then kills her.

Bressac's scenario is a compromise between the Oedipal myth and the Neronic myth. The ellipsis in Clairwil's version of the Neronic myth has been occupied by the dead father. First the masturbation is supplemented both by a man in the "background" and by an accompanying fantasy in which the dead father is invoked to mediate the son–mother relation ("that will remind you of the happy times when my esteemed father would smear your navel with it"). Then in the space of the ellipsis Bressac undergoes a transformation from mother-identified to father-identified, from buggered to bugger. Finally, returning to Clairwil's Neronic script, he kills her.

In the Neronic complex the mother–son relation remains dual, with no mention of a father-term, and this leap from masturbatory desire to murder is pure. The father is not simply dead; his name is missing. Only an ellipsis marks the locus of the absence of the name of the father.

A scenario which resembles the Neronic myth can be found in Freud's work. However, it is not the story of a boy and his mother. In 1925 Freud wrote "Some psychical consequences of the anatomical distinction between the sexes"[5] to remedy the lack of girls in his theory. Freud finds that the Oedipus complex in girls (desire for the father, hatred of the mother) is a secondary formation. The girl, like the boy, has a preoedipal object in her mother. However, there is a discontinuity between that early mother–daughter attachment and the Oedipus complex in which the daughter hates her mother as a rival. Between the two falls the so-called "discovery of castration," of something missing, an ellipsis.

In Freud's story of the little boy the pre-Oedipal attachment to the mother flows smoothly into the Oedipus complex where the father becomes the hated rival, and only then does the castration complex intercede, cutting off the little boy's potential for being his mother's lover, just as Oedipus himself succeeds in marrying his mother and *only later* discovers the facts of the situation. *Then* he loses his mother and is blinded (castrated). For the boy the ellipsis comes after the Oedipus complex as the anxious possibility that an ellipsis might intervene, that something will some day be missing. Nero's ellipsis is in the place of the girl's, not the boy's castration complex.

One mode of reception for the girl's discovery of the ellipsis, of "castration," is denial, which leads into what Freud calls a "masculinity complex." Bressac has anal intercourse with his mother, denying the vagina, denying the mother's "castration," in order to fill the ellipsis between masturbatory fantasy (pre-Oedipal, bisexual wholeness) and killing the mother. So too between the little girl's preoedipal desire for the mother and her oedipal hatred of her intervenes a denial in which the girl refuses to accept what Freud calls "the fact of being castrated" (*Standard Edition*, vol. XIX, p. 253).

In "Female sexuality" (1931) Freud once again takes up the question of the difference between the Oedipus/castration complex as it appears in the boy and in the girl. Freud tries to fill in the girl's ellipsis, to investigate what transpires between the girl's desire for the mother and her hatred of her. Considering the different reasons for the girl's hatred of the mother, he finds that it stems from experiences common to both sexes. He flirts with an assertion of "the ambivalence of emotional cathexes" as "a universally valid psychological law"[6] but then dismisses that as, albeit primitively true, not functioning in most adult emotional life. Freud then goes on to suggest that "boys are able to deal with their ambivalent feelings towards their mother by directing all their hostility on to the father." In trying to figure out *the girl's* hostility toward the mother, Freud comes up against *the boy's* hostility toward her, something Freud was ever loath to touch. He veers away, first gesturing toward the classic Oedipal structure, and then the whole investigation leaves off with an air of mystery: "we have as yet no clear understanding of these processes with which we have only just become acquainted."

At the beginning of the same article Freud writes: "we can extend the content of the Oedipus complex to include all the child's relations to both parents" (vol. XXI, p. 226).

"All the child's relations to both parents" includes not only the daughter's love of the mother and hostility toward the father but also the son's hostility toward the mother and love of the father. The simplicity of the "positive" Oedipus complex (boy loves Mom, hates Dad) will not hold. But Freud goes on to study only the details of the girl's penis envy, shying away from the intersection where the male and female positive and negative Oedipus complexes cross.

Universal ambivalence toward the mother is made up of a universal primary attachment to the mother as nurturer and universal disappointment in the mother. That universal disappointment has two sources: (1) "Childhood love is boundless; it demands exclusive possession, it is not content with less than all ... it has, in point of fact, no aim and is incapable of obtaining complete satisfaction" (vol. xxi, p. 231); and (2) discovery of the absence of the maternal phallus causes a devaluation of the mother who is thus considered incomplete, mutilated. In Freud's oedipal myth the ambivalent emotional cathexis is divided into a positive feeling fixed onto the mother and a negative feeling directed onto the father. In Sade's Neronic myth the ambivalence is kept intact and focused entirely on the mother. The ellipsis in Nero's story is the place of the absent father who reappears in Bressac's interpretation of the script.

This universal ambivalence toward the mother is reflected in the Sadean libertine's attitude toward Mother Nature, model and source of all crime. In Sadean philosophical discourses there are two natures. Nature vanquished includes ideological notions of what is natural: for example, normal sexuality and procreation. Nature triumphant is anything that actually occurs in nature, which includes all sorts of monstrosities. The libertines transgress the first nature, but the second nature they can only imitate – their petty, contingent crimes but paltry images of nature's universal, eternal destruction. Any violation of the weak nature leaves the criminal with an all-encompassing strong nature, whose agent he must be in any violation. Any possible transcendence of nature has already been coopted and inscribed within the domain of the impervious, complete Mother Nature: "Convince yourself completely . . . that were you to trouble and disturb the order of nature in every possible sense, you would never have done anything but use the faculties she gave you for that" (*Oeuvres Complètes*, vol. XXI, p. 126).

The first nature is the Mother after the discovery of her lack of phallus. This castrated, incomplete nature cannot encompass the universe of crime which the Sadean libertine aspires to. Nature triumphant is the preoedipal phallic mother, omniscient and omnipotent, whose ways are still dark mystery to the curious child. It is precisely the mystery, as yet impervious to the child's curiosity, which constitutes the maternal phallus.

Jacques Lacan defines the phallus as that which is interpreted as missing in the discovery of the fact of sexual difference which, according to Lacan, both sexes live as the discovery of the *mother*'s "castration." Lacan writes that "the phallus can only play its role veiled, that is, as itself the sign of the latency which strikes each signifiable, as soon as it is raised to the function of signifier."[7] When the subject has access to knowledge (discovery of sexual difference), the phallus is the sign of the still-latent "signifiable" (that which is mystery), the sign of what is lost once the veil is removed, once knowledge is revealed: once the mother is *known*, she is *known* as "castrated." The (veiled) phallus functions as the sign of what she potentially (latently) has, what she has as potential, when it is not known what she has – when she potentially has any/everything.

In *The New Justine* we meet Almani, who as a chemist is the curious child trying to learn what is under nature's skirts. Nature as phallic mother causes Almani to despair that "the whore [nature] mocked me . . . In offering me only her effects, she veiled from me all her causes" (vol. XVII, pp. 69–70). In the traditional theistic schema, only the knowable effects are attributed to nature; the veiled causes constitute God, whose being is mystery. However, in an atheist schema based upon the negation of God, "it is a misprision of nature to suppose she has an author; . . . God is nothing but nature" (vol. XXI, pp. 230–31). The existence of the Father is denied in favor of a Mother with a veiled phallus. Almani lives the Neronic rather than the oedipal myth.

Faced with phallic Mother Nature, the libertine is not subject to the disappointment which follows the discovery of the mother's "castration." He does not disparage her, but only hates her all the more for the older, preoedipal reason for hating mothers: "Childhood love is boundless; it demands exclusive possession, it is not content with less than all . . . it has, in point of fact, no aim and is incapable of obtaining complete satisfaction" (*Standard Edition*, vol. XXI, p. 231). The libertine hates nature and wants to be her tormentor, for he is not able to be her lover. Nature is a tease. She arouses desires, just like the mother who cares for her child and then doesn't "put out." In "Female sexuality," Freud writes: "The part played in starting [masturbation] by nursery hygiene is reflected in the very common phantasy which makes the mother or nurse into a seducer" (*Standard Edition*, vol. XXI, p. 232). The frustration caused by the teasing calls for revenge ("he had often jerked off for her . . . And he kills her").

In *Juliette*, the Pope, tired of always being Mother Nature's pawn, craves to violate her omnipotence, craves to unmask the maternal phallus which only exists as masked. Preserving a phallic mother necessitates an eternal desire to castrate her. The Sadean libertine despises the weak castrated nature, yet can be satisfied by nothing less than castrating the strong phallic nature: "When I will have exterminated on this earth all the creatures that cover it, I will be far indeed from my goal, since I will have served you . . . step-mother! . . . and I only aspire to avenge myself for your stupidity, or the wickedness you inflict on men" (vol. XXI, p. 310; Sade's ellipsis).

"Stepmother" is the epithet thrown at nature in anger and frustration. The "stepmother" usurps the loved mother's position, frustrating the child through "stupidity" or "wickedness." The negative component of the ambivalence felt for the mother is distilled into the evil stepmother. Just as in the oedipal myth the original ambivalence is divided into love for the mother and hatred for the father, so the Neronic myth (killing the beloved mother) degenerates into love for the good mother, hatred for the "stepmother."

The pure tension of passionate ambivalence cannot be maintained. Clairwil's Nero, Minski, and the third version of Bressac are rare moments in Sade's work. Usually the elements of the Neronic myth are separated, thus appearing either in a positive Oedipus complex (desire to be the mother's lover) or a negative Oedipus complex (desire to be the mother's killer). That split seems to run along the line dividing Sade's tame from his scandalous writings. Sade did not only write graphic, obscene texts. He wrote many works which remain within the bounds of proper, decent discourse. Mothers are often literally and graphically killed, but (except in the limit-instances where the penetration is accompanied by murder) incest with the mother is represented in veiled, that is decent, terms.

The principal representative of the good mother in Sade's work is Mme de Blamont in *Aline et Valcour*, one of his "decent" novels. Aline loves Mme de Blamont, her mother, more than she loves her lover Valcour. Valcour considers Mme de Blamont as his own mother. In the course of the novel, two total strangers, on separate occasions, wind up at Mme de Blamont's summer retreat, and both these young women turn out to be her daughters. To disregard these chance meetings as the extravagances of a baroque novel is to obscure the point that Mme de Blamont is everyone's mother. An observer describes her funeral: "one would have said that everything there was attached to her by some tie . . . it seemed they were all her children, everyone mourned her as a mother."[8] Like nature herself, Mme de Blamont is "the common mother of us all." But unlike Mother Nature, who inspires a Neronic ambivalence, Aline's mother receives only the positive component of that ambivalence.

Most of all, Aline loves Mme de Blamont. In a startling moment very early in the novel – long before the unweaving of M. de Blamont's treachery gives the book a fatal, somber air – Mme de Blamont speaks to Aline of a projected bequest upon the former's death. Aline, unable to bear the possibility of separation from her mother, throws herself into her mother's arms. Then they swear to love each other and to die together: a lover's vow (vol. i, p. 66).

At the end of the novel, when Mme de Blamont is in fact dying, the two reenact primordial mother–daughter union: "the doctor allowed Mme de Blamont to take a bit of creamed rice that she seemed to desire. Aline . . . shared this last food, pressed to the very breast (*sein*) of her mother" (vol. ii, pp. 444–45). After Aline partakes of the milky food at her mother's breast, the mother dies and Aline faints. The pair here comes close to merging (the vow to die together). An observer describes the scene: "[Aline] was bent over her. Alas: it is difficult to know which of the two still lived" (vol. ii, p. 447).

The hated father then arrives to tear Aline away from the preoedipal paradise, and offer her virginity up to his friend. In this oedipal variation, where the mother is unambivalently loved and the father hated as the one who frustrates the ultimate union between daughter and mother, Aline triumphs by killing herself and being laid to rest with her mother in her mother's tomb, preserving her preoedipal "innocence" through a denial of the father and patriarchal society constituted by the exchange of women between men.

Aline's wish to lie in her mother's tomb repeats a wish Sade expresses in a letter to his mother-in-law upon his imprisonment in Vincennes: "From the depths of her grave, my unhappy mother calls me: it seems I see her open once more her *sein* to me and invite me to return there as to the only asylum I have left. It is for me a satisfaction to follow her so closely and I ask you as a last request, Madame, to have me put next to her" (letter to the Présidente de Montreuil, February 1777).[9] In fact, like Aline, the marquis is swept away from the side of his dead mother and imprisoned. *Sein* has the double meaning of breast and womb, so that to return to the maternal *sein* is to return both to the womb and to the breast. Aline's meal "pressed to the very breast [*sein*] of her mother," the wet-nurse perversion in *120 Days*, and Sade's and Aline's wishes to be buried with their mother where she will "open once more her *sein* and invite me to return there" all bespeak the phantasmatically closed dyad of mother and child. That fantasy combines preoedipal "innocence," ignorance of sexual differentiation, with the "crime" of penetrating the mother's womb, of being the mother's lover. Any "return" to the womb is a penetration from outside, a repetition of the father's penetration which placed the child in the womb in the first place. Ignorance of sexual difference supports a belief in parthenogenesis, but the discovery of sexual difference is the revelation of how babies are made. The "original" mother–child intimacy is predicated upon a prior violation of that interior space by a third term.

In the same letter to Mme de Montreuil Sade writes "I asked you . . . if it was a second mother or a tyrant that I would find in you." Sade's mother has just died, and his mother-in-law would thus take her place, be a second mother. In fact his mother-in-law has had him imprisoned by *lettre-de-cachet*. The second mother usurps the good mother's place. That usurpation, the very fact of being the *second* mother, the "stepmother," is sufficient to constitute Mme de Montreuil as "tyrant." In this scenario the Neronic ambivalence toward the mother has been divided into love for the first mother and hatred for the second.

Mme de Montreuil is indeed primordially omnipotent for Sade. Paul Bourdin, editor of a volume of Sade's correspondence, writes that Sade "plunges like a child into the conviction that everything that happened corresponds to the plans of Mme de Montreuil."[10] Sade "plunges like a child into the conviction" that Mme de Montreuil is the phallic Mother, a belief which only exists in the mode of childish conviction. This conviction is based on a denial of Sade's more powerful enemies, of the third term outside the mother–son dyad. One of Sade's friends writes that "the dear présidente was not as guilty as we thought. [Sade] has earned enemies stronger still."[11] Sade believes every jailer and official he comes into contact with to be the agent of Mme de Montreuil. He is convinced that his entire universe is subjugated to her, his every thought suggested by her, just as the Sadean libertine's universe is ruled and encompassed by Mother

Nature, just as the infant's world seems to be ruled by the early mother.

Like his characters, Sade craves revenge. In a letter addressed "to the stupid scoundrels who torment me," Sade writes: "here is the hundred eleventh torture that I invent for [Mme de Montreuil]. This morning, while suffering, I saw her, the bitch, I saw her skinned alive, dragged over thistles, and then thrown into a vat of vinegar" (Vincennes, 1783).

The Neronic complex has been divided into love for the mother (wish to return to her womb/tomb) and hatred for the second mother (wish to be the torturer of the stepmother). This same split is expressed in a divergence in Sade's discourse. The wish to join the mother is cloaked in decent language; the wish to torment his mother-in-law is expressed in the graphic detail typical of *120 Days*. Yet the most powerful cloak of decency in Aline's and Sade's wish to lie with the mother is the prerequisite of the mother's death. If the mother is not to be despised, she must be "phallic." But the phallic mother is hated for her omnipotence. Nero kills his mother so he can continue to masturbate for her. Alive, she must elicit his hatred, for she disproves her (his) unlimited potential by being knowable. The phallus disappears when the mystery is unveiled. By entering the realm of death the mother enters the domain of mystery, of the unknowable. The living mother, as unfallen, uncastrated mother, cannot be possessed, understood, uncovered. Desire for the phallic mother is frustrated unless the mother is killed. The ambivalence of the Neronic myth is not some external marriage of love and hate, desire to possess (know) and desire to kill. The ambivalence is inescapable at that extreme of passion: the desire to know carried to its greatest intensity *must* kill. The existence of a real mother outside Nero's masturbatory fantasy is a threat to the integrity of that fantasy, and to Nero's feeling of mastery.

The dizzying precipices of this inextricable ambivalence are uninhabitable. Sade turns away after expressing his wish to lie with his dead mother, unable to bear the unassimilable knowledge of the truth of his desire: "One thing only stops me; it is a weakness, I admit, but I must confess it, I would want to see my children" (letter to the Présidente de Montreuil, February 1771). The fatal knowledge is obscured by hope (for the future). Sade is diverted from attempting to fulfill the desire for his mother by an interest in his children.

A similar turning-away occurs in Freud's story of the little girl. Trying to explain how the little girl's libido switches from mother to father (how the feeling for the mother turns from love to hate), Freud writes: "now the girl's libido slips into a new position along the line – there is no other way of putting it – of the equation 'penis–child.' She gives up her wish for a penis and puts in place of it a wish for a child: and *with that purpose in view* she takes her father as a love-object" (*Standard Edition*, vol. xix, p. 256). Although it appears that the child is a substitute for the penis, following Lacan's reading of Freud we find that both penis and child are equally inadequate substitutes for the always missing maternal phallus. Thus the Oedipus complex in girls which follows upon the knowledge of sexual difference is a denial of the phallus as always necessarily latent (never present) and an attempt to elect the child to the place of phallus, the locus signifying unlimited potential. Fulfillment through possession of the mother (maternal phallus), once it is accepted as impossible, is abandoned in favor of an attempt at satisfaction through the child. The child, like the phallus, "can only play its role veiled," as potential child. Sade wishes to *see* the children his imprisonment hides from his sight. The child wished for by Freud's little girl is a signifiable not yet signified, unlimited potential.

Freud renders the substitution of child for penis explicit only in the story of the little girl. Yet he himself mentions, in a relaxed moment (within a parenthesis), that "It is easy to see how the suppressed megalomania of fathers is transferred in their thoughts on to their children, and it seems quite probable that this is one of the ways in which the suppression of that feeling, which becomes necessary in actual life, is carried out."[12] The substitution is equally applicable to the boy's history, to Sade who turns away from the union with his mother so as to see his children. The replacement of precastration complex

mother-love by child-love as an (inadequate) substitute for the
desire to have (and be) the phallus (Freud's "megalomania")
is at play in both sexes.

The fact that incest with the mother, and perversions centered on the breasts and female organs, are underrepresented
in the Sadean tableau of "all passions" is symptomatic of the
turning-away from the Neronic myth, from the unbearable
ambivalent intimacy with the mother. The mother returns
– a mutilated, exposed, "castrated" mother – as object of
tenacious hatred, the obsessive hatred which stems from an
uncovered deception. The phallic mother returns in nature-
as-stepmother, hated for her mystery and potency, for her
ability to have and be the phallus that is lacking to any living
subject but also, and at the same time, admired and imitated
as everything the Sadean libertine aspires to be.

Sade's text is filled with a staggering multiplicity of passions: variations, repetitions, and substitutions, none sufficient to compensate for the missing phallus, the unfulfilled
mother–child union. The attempt to replace the eternal
concentration on one object with a multiplicity of crimes
and objects is represented in Clairwil's discourse: "Replace
the voluptuous idea that fills your head, this idea of a
prolonged torture of the same object, replace it with a
greater abundance of murders: don't kill the same individual for a longer time, which is impossible, but murder many others, which is very feasible" (vol. xx, p. 317).
In their number and their diversity, the passions present
themselves as all-inclusive, masking the underrepresented
center.

Clairwil in her pragmatism ignores the attraction of the
impossibility of impossible crime. Yet throughout Sade's text
some libertine will bemoan the petty contingency of any
possible crime. The only crimes worth doing are universal,
eternal, the domain of Mother Nature. Curval in *120 Days*
laments: "How many times, damn it, have I not desired that
one could attack the sun, deprive the universe of it, or use it to
set fire to the world, those would be crimes and not these little
faults we devote ourselves to that do no more than transform

in the course of a year a dozen creatures into lumps of earth" (p. 207).

Throughout Sade's work, the most wicked, most successful libertines utter this pathetic plea: why are my crimes individual, not universal? The most masterful and most powerful Sadean characters are despondent over the emptiness of their innumerable crimes. Yet apart from all these sad winners stands Juliette, whose story has a "happy ending." Juliette never bemoans her lack of omnipotence, never envies Mother Nature her phallus. Juliette expresses only positive feelings toward nature, and finds a happy union with a mysterious, maternal woman named Durand who knows nature's inner secrets. When Juliette and Durand travel together as lovers, Durand says to her, "I must pass for your mother" (vol. xxiv, p. 71). Durand is old enough to be Juliette's mother, but if she is a mother, she is a parody of a phallic mother. Her vagina is literally blocked, impenetrable. Thus her lack of phallus is permanently hidden, inaccessible. Durand must be penetrated anally – anal intercourse being the act preferred by Bressac and most other Sadean libertines for its denial of sexual difference. When Juliette first meets Durand, the latter is presented as a sorceress whose effects are seen, but whose causes, like Almani's nature, are veiled. Durand herself says to Juliette at this first meeting that "all nature is at my command" (vol. xxi, p. 226). She is omnipotent; she is Mother Nature's concealed cause; she is the (maternal) phallus.

Durand displays a remarkable ability to be resurrected. Twice in the novel she is believed dead – she is actually seen hanged – but she later shows up to everyone's astonishment. Durand's name sounds like the present participle *durant*, which means "enduring." Like Mother Nature she remains unaffected by creation and destruction, life and death. They are but phases for her: she is alternately dead and alive in this book. The phallus can be distinguished from the penis by being that which is inalienable, that which endures. The penis is a detachable object, not an intrinsic property. To be phallic is to be immune to the threat of castration (death). The phallus is not subject to the ups and downs of contingency, as the penis is. To discover the mother's "castration" is to discover she *never had* a phallus. To believe the mother phallic is to be ignorant of the possibility of castration.

Juliette (whose story is subtitled "the prosperities of vice") ends up happily with Durand, the mysterious phallic mother. Like Aline who commits suicide to join her mother, Juliette says to Durand what she says to no one else: "I like the idea of putting my life in your hands" (vol. XXIV, p. 70). At the end of *Juliette*, with the "mother" and "daughter" reunited, a veil is thrown over their lives. The narrator insists that nothing more can be known about Juliette except that she died ten years later. Her story ends like Aline's with the daughter triumphant in her union with her mother. Juliette's "mother" does not have to die, as is necessary with Aline's, Bressac's, Nero's, and Sade's mothers; she already possesses that mystery. So Juliette's story, which is composed of a plurality of passions and the principle of unmasking any prejudice that privileges one passion above another, can have an "ending," a closure, fulfillment. Yet the "happy ending" necessitates the ruse of a mysterious Durand, whose secrets are left concealed as the unique exception to the graphic detail that pervades a book in which the heroine's last line is "Philosophy should say everything" (vol. XXIV, p. 337).

If the chemist tries to look up nature's skirts to learn her hidden causes, the philosopher, who must say everything, is committed to the task of undressing nature for all to see. Juliette's final remark is made in defense of the project of publishing the story she has just recounted, "The Story of Juliette." Philosophy here means novel-writing. In "Ideas on novels" Sade writes:

don't lose sight of the fact that the novelist is nature's man; she created him to be her painter: if he does not become his mother's lover as soon as she gives birth to him, let him never write, we will not read him; but if he feels that ardent thirst to paint all, if trembling he opens up nature's *sein* . . . that is whom we will read.[13]

The novelist as would-be lover of Mother Nature, by his very project to "paint all" would also be nature's tormentor. The writer in his "ardent thirst" to paint all of nature, to know (possess) all of nature, "opens up nature's *sein*." In Sade's fantasy of a return to the mother's womb, it is the *dead* mother who "opens once more her *sein* and invites [him] to return there." Opening the mother's breast/womb and describing all that is found there is performing an autopsy. The penetration of the womb, the telling of all nature's secrets, is the uncovering of the Mother's "castration." If the philosopher/novelist could say all, he would castrate/kill Mother Nature.

Durand's womb is blocked, inaccessible. No novelist or philosopher can open it in order to depict all her secrets. Juliette can find happiness through this impasse, behind which is hidden the impossibility of saying all, the impossibility of being the phallic mother's lover, of possessing the (maternal) phallus. This impossibility means that either the mother is phallic (mysterious) and the child is a mere pawn; or the child possesses the mother, thereby discovering her incompleteness and winding up empty-handed. These two alternatives correspond in Freud's story of the little girl to the choice between the acceptance of femininity with its correlative passivity, its diminution of libido, and the blind denial of fact, the futile activity of the "masculinity complex," as reactions to the discovery of the mother's "castration." In the Sadean text these alternatives are universalized, presenting themselves equally to both sexes. From the feminine position, the subject admits that he does not have the potential/potency to fulfill his impossible desires. This is the position of Justine, the lucid victim who believes her fate is written by God (out of her power), as well as of any libertine who has "broken all restraints" and knows that, whatever he does, nature has circumscribed his possibilities so that he can do no more than serve her will. The second alternative is the masculine position, which is characterized by denial of the impossibility of having and being the phallus. This alternative is represented in Sade's text by those libertines of either sex who heap crime upon crime, always repeating the violation of the mother (the discovery of the mother's "castration"), deluded by the diversity of their crimes and their victims into believing that what is lacking

for their satisfaction is quantitative not qualitative. This is
Clairwil's position when she suggests replacing the impossible
crime with an abundance of possible crimes. The masculine
position means trying to prove that what one has (the penis
or clitoris, the castrated mother) is the phallus.

Sade's text bears the imprint of the intimate ambivalence
that constitutes the relation of the human subject to the
phallic mother/maternal phallus. In that relation the feminine as well as the masculine position can be filled by either
sex, both roles being equally unsatisfactory. Most of Sade's
characters oscillate between the two positions: alternating
between frustration/lucidity and hope/delusion. The phallic
mother is neither male nor female but the impossible merging
of all possibilities (of both sexes), thus equally impossible for
either sex to be or to have.

NOTES

1 See Claude Lévi-Strauss, *The Elementary Structures of Kinship*, trans.
James Harle Bell et al. (Boston: Beacon Press, 1969).
2 All references to *La Nouvelle Justine* and *L'Histoire de Juliette* are
taken from vols. xv–xxiv of the Marquis de Sade, *Œuvres complètes*
(Paris: Pauvert, 1968). All translations from Sade mine.
3 Sade, *Les 120 Journées de Sodome* (Paris: Pauvert, 1972), vol.
I, p. 45.
4 Gilbert Lély, *Vie de Sade* (Paris: Gallimard, 1958), vol. II,
p. 333.
5 Sigmund Freud, "Some psychical consequences of the anatomical distinction between the sexes," in *The Standard Edition of
the Complete Psychological Works*, ed. James Strachey (London:
Hogarth, 1953–74), vol. xix, pp. 248–58.
6 Freud, "Female sexuality," in *Standard Edition*, vol. xxi,
p. 235.
7 Jacques Lacan, "La signification du phallus," in *Ecrits* (Paris:
Seuil, 1966), p. 692.
8 Sade, *Aline et Valcour* (Paris: Union Générale d'Editions, 1971),
vol. II, p. 469.
9 Unless otherwise noted, references to the letters are taken from
Sade, *Lettres choisies* (Paris: Pauvert, 1963).
10 Paul Bourdin, *Correspondence inédite du Marquis de Sade, de ses*

proches et de ses familiers (Paris: Librairie de France, 1929), p. 98.

11 Letter of October 21, 1780, in Lély, *Vie de Sade*, p. 173.

12 Freud, *The Interpretation of Dreams*, in *Standard Edition*, vol. v, p. 448.

13 Sade, "Idées sur les romans," in *Les Crimes de l'amour* (Paris: Union Générale d'Editions, 1971), pp. 42–43.

CHAPTER 7

The encyclopedia of excess

Marcel Hénaff
(Translated by Allen S. Weiss)

If we hadn't said everything, analyzed everything, how would you want us to be able to find out what is suitable for you?

The 120 Days of Sodom

Violence bears within itself this dishevelled negation, which puts an end to all possibility of discourse.

(Georges Bataille, *L'Erotisme*)

THE ALL AND THE TOO MUCH

"To say everything" is the sign of a great audaciousness, an apparently boundless program, which Sadean discourse deems indispensable and definitive. This formula is disarmingly simple, yet nothing is more paradoxical if we pay close attention to it. In effect, two contradictory connotations are intermingled here: (a) that of *totality*: "to say everything" is the encyclopedic project of the circuit of signifiers, the collection of givens, the accumulation of arguments. In short, for this first point of view, "to say everything" would be the exhaustive and monumental task of literally saying everything, i.e. the Hegelian ambition; (b) that of *excess*. In this case, "to say everything" would be the demand to hide nothing, to uncover everything, in the sense of the claim (sometimes the threat), "I'm going to tell everything . . . "; or else it is the complicity between the Sadean character and his interlocutors, when he proposes to tell them the tale of his crimes: "I sense that I can tell you everything." The formula is that of breaking into, of lifting, censorship, bringing the repressed to light. "To say everything" is literally the Freudian formula, the fundamental rule of psychoanalysis as a technique for recognizing and avowing desire.

Thus, according to Sade, "to say everything" would be to will totality *and* excess simultaneously. This is precisely its challenge, since discourse has always been called upon to choose between these two terms. To will both simultaneously constitutes perhaps the fundamental aporia of discourse, insofar as the discourse of totality constitutes itself only by blinding itself to the prohibition which permits its closure and eliminates all remainder. The *all* is maintained only by banishing the *too much*: to confront and transgress this prohibition is the very movement of excess which breaks down the partition, blurs the limits and makes all totality impossible, indeed ridiculous.

Totality and excess: the situation is thus one of an "either/ or." We cannot normally hold to both of these claims at the same time without risking total discursive paralysis, or at best stuttering. One cannot simultaneously be on both sides of the prohibition within the same discourse.

And yet, it is precisely this aporia that the Sadean discourse proposes to sustain, by realizing what can be termed as encyclopedia of excess. This combines the two contradictory positions in a constant displacement between theory and narrative, between treatise and the scene in which the logical blockage of "either/or" is thwarted. To shift from the form of the treatise as well as from that of the simple narrative, or to pervert one form by the other, to produce this strange theoretical-narrative mixture, is a strategy to which we will return.

The encyclopedic endeavor was a passion of the eighteenth century, which saw a proliferation of dictionaries: dictionaries of ideas, languages, civilizations, arts, techniques. Not only scholars and specialists, but also most of the well-known writers and philosophers of the age (such as Voltaire, Diderot, D'Holbach, Rousseau, etc.) collaborated on these reports.

Sade adds yet one more dictionary to this list, the most

insane and most inadmissible: that of "perversions." Yet this dictionary does not purport to have either the title or the form of the others, and just barely maintains their texture. It is the parody of a dictionary, caught in a narrative fabric, carried away by a fiction which deprives it of all "scientific" pretense. This is to better designate what it puts into play: desire rather than knowledge, or desire within knowledge.

The work of Sade which best displays this project is clearly *The 120 Days of Sodom*. Sade himself states the two principles which preside over the organization of his text: (a) a repertory of the passions where each reader can find those of his choice; (b) the integration of this repertory within a narrative which causes each of the analyzed terms to appear in an actual situation, or in a plan to be realized later.

Repertory:

Many of the extravagances you are about to see illustrated will doubtless displease you, yes, I am well aware of it, but there are amongst them a few which will warm you to the point of costing you some fuck, and that, reader, is all we ask of you; if we have not said everything, analyzed everything, tax us not with partiality, for you cannot expect us to have guessed what suits you best. Rather, it is up to you to take what you please and leave the rest alone another reader will do the same, and little by little, everyone will find himself satisfied. (*120 Days*, p. 253; vol. XIII, p. 61)[1]

Narrative:

We have, moreover, blended these six hundred passions into the storytellers' narratives. That is one more thing whereof the reader were well to have foreknowledge; it would have been too monotonous to catalogue them one by one outside the body of the story. But as some reader not much learned in these matters might perhaps confuse the designated passions with the adventure or simple event in the narrator's life, each of these passions has been carefully distinguished by a marginal notation: a line, above which is the title that may be given the passion. This mark indicates the exact place where the account of the passions begins, and the end of the paragraph always indicates where it finishes. (*120 Days*, pp. 253–4; vol. XII, p. 61)

The care taken to preserve the effectiveness and the framework of a dictionary within the "body of the narrative" entails a painstaking didacticism, to the point of suggesting how the work should be used:

And now, friend-reader, you must prepare your heart and your mind for the most impure tale that has ever been told since our world began, a book the likes of which are met with neither amongst the ancients nor amongst us moderns. Fancy, now, that all pleasure-taking either sanctioned by good manners or enjoined by that fool you speak of incessantly, of whom you know nothing and whom you call Nature; fancy, I say, that all these modes of taking pleasure will be expressly excluded from this anthology, or that whenever peradventure you do indeed encounter them here, they will always be accompained by some crime or colored by some infamy. (*120 Days*, pp. 252–53; vol. XIII, pp. 60–61)

What follows is the description of the characters, in which the principal characteristics of age, social standing, general physical type, sexual preferences, specific interests, and so on are compiled in the form of a police file.

Within this synoptic presentation, as in its meticulous typographic disposition (the marginal notes and indentations), Sade is trying to make *120 Days* easy to use. And as with a dictionary, we can begin and end anywhere. What is important above all is to always know where we are, and never to be mistaken about the predicates. We know who's who, what each person is capable of, what each person desires, etc. Everything is circumscribed from the outset, and nothing is left ambiguous.

And yet this is a very strange dictionary, one which offers tales in place of definitions, and a logical classification based on gradations from the simple to the complex in place of an alphabetic classification. It is rather the simulacrum of a dictionary, since all that remains of a dictionary is the diagram, the formal schema, while the content is dispensed with.

But the narrative (this drama, as it were) is no less strange than the dictionary. It abandons all suspense by putting its cards on the table from the very beginning, and thus reveals its overall plan. In this regard we must consider the paradox of beginning a narrative with an *introduction* (where the characters' aims and their programs are presented.) An *introduction* is a preamble which pertains to the category of the *treatise* rather than that of the narrative, and where the object and method of a discourse are revealed. The traditional ruse of narrative, on the contrary, is to slip information into the interstices of the diagesis or to graft it onto the structure. This is principally the work of *indices*, *informants*,[2] and *description*.[3] Such information tends to melt into the narrative element to the point of being confused, entangled, of being effaced as information, producing an optimal "naturalization" of the narrative. The entry into the fiction must be immediate, and each staging of referential signs is gradually distributed within the narrative chain, and becomes invisible. The "author" must withdraw from the narrative to leave the "characters" all the privileges of reality.

Such are some of the elementary rules of the game which Sade is concerned with in *The 120 Days of Sodom*. For example, he replaces the art of implicit, oblique information with a didactic exposé, which immediately displays all of the givens. Or, he gives the reader numerous opportunities to intervene, which has the effect of marking off the fictional space, thus eliminating the effect of illusion:

Thus, there resulted an arrangement which, for the reader's convenience, we shall recapitulate. (*120 Days*, p. 193; vol. xiii, p. 3) I leave to the reader to fancy . . . (*120 Days*, p. 194; vol. xiii p. 4) do our best to portray each one of the four heroes . . . (*120 Days*, pp. 196–97; vol. xiii, p. 7).

We immediately know everything, and the reader, taken in hand, is invited to verify the information. We can always ask, however, if the didacticism (dictionaries, treatises, etc.) doesn't seriously risk ruining or paralyzing the narrative. Isn't it precisely because Sade was conscious of this threat that, rather paradoxically, he infused into the text of *The 120 Days of Sodom* an entire series of enigmatic clauses? These demands to wait and the premises of future revelations permit a diachronization of the exposé's all-too-massive synchronism, as well as the exploitation of that old hermeneutic ploy which demands good suspense.

But there is nothing to be gained by hurrying our story or by broaching subjects which can only receive adequate treatment in the sequel. (*120 Days*, p. 196; vol. XIII, p. 6)

Durcet . . . was quietly perpetrating infamies the proper time has not come to disclose. (*120 Days*, p. 334; vol. XIII, p. 138)

little Hébé returned weeping from the hurly-burly; there was even more to it than tears, but we dare not yet disclose just what it was had set her to trembling. A little patience, friend reader, and we shall soon hide nothing from your inquisitive gaze. (*120 Days*, p. 485; vol. XIII, p. 270)

Adelaide, Louison, and Franchon . . . moved into the salon; certain considerations oblige us to draw a curtain over what transpired there. (*120 Days*, p. 501; vol. XIII, p. 285)

Recourse to the hermeneutic argument of the enigma is so obvious that its manipulation is actually indiscreet and separate from the establishment of an indexical system which, in well-formed narrative montages, slides subtly into the diagesis. But here, on the contrary, the appeal to enigma is accompanied by an extremely ostentatious projection of the writer into the didactic "we" and the address to the reader. The demand to wait perhaps reveals a methodological imperative more than a narrative technique, and far from aiding a too-weak narrative, it doubtless pertains wholly to the category of the *treatise*. These incidental clauses, which are distributed along the textual line, operate less to arrange the revelation of a mystery or of a veiled truth than scrupulously to respect the logical gradation of the exposé, as we see in these other "enigmatic" statements:

We are in despair, for here we are once again forced by the design of our history to make a little detour: yes, we must for the time being omit describing those lubricious corrections, but our readers will not hold it against us; they appreciate our inability to give them complete satisfaction at the present moment; but they can be sure of it, their time will come. (*120 Days*, p. 350; vol. XIII, p. 148)

We regret to say that the sequence we originally established for the treatment of our matter obliges us to postpone yet a little longer the pleasure the reader will doubtless take in learning the details of this religious ceremony; but the appropriate moment for disclosing them will surely arrive, and probably fairly soon. (*120 Days*, p. 345; vol. XIII, p. 153)

To the extent that the program is fulfilled according to the order of the exposé – which is the very order of demonstration – the retained (rather than hidden) information is confided: "The further we advance, the more thoroughly we may inform the reader about certain facts we were obliged to no more than hint at in the earlier part of our story" (*120 Days*, p. 372; vol. XIII, p. 171).

The expiatory model as well as the tabular structure both subsist by simulating a code of these enigmatic formations. This is a dictionary *and* a written work, but *neither* one *nor* the other: the aporia of "either/or" is sketched out in the alternation of "and . . . and" and "neither/nor." The dictionary, like the treatise, pertains to the serious, solemn knowledge of scholarship, to the academy. A serious knowledge of the "passions" can be inscribed only in a normative and ultimately moralizing metaphysical discourse; a repertory of perversions can only take the dull and pretentious form of a medical discourse.

The dictionary, in its classical form, oversimplifies, neutralizes, and is incapable of letting us perceive the nuances which create the specificity of any given passion. It generalizes and renders harmless. But the dictionary also has an advantage: it *names*, and since its function is to create a repertory of names and to make their meanings explicit, it is given the right to inventory anything, even what may be classified as "scabrous." Science is permitted the status of perfect innocence to feed its acquisitive hunger; everything must be explored and labeled. Hence the dictionary's unique privilege, to be fully exploited.

Narrative, on the other hand, particularizes the "passions," and gives them a precise referent in which the signs of their specificity are staged. However, this staging traditionally does not name, it suggests. The more the passion approaches the forbidden, the more the narrative is metaphorically constructed. Hence the alternative: either the dictionary has the right to name, but remains incapable of particularizing its object, or the narrative realizes this particularization, but at the price of censorship in the naming of its object.

By simultaneously putting both into play, by short-circuiting their reciprocal positions, Sade is suddenly given the means to say everything. We must note, however, that the utilization of narrative form is not reduced to animating words and designations in order to forestall boredom, but responds rather to the more essential need of realizing that we cannot have a dictionary of pleasure (nor even a science, as Lacan claims). What is necessary is to write so that the body leaves its trace in language. This trace is brought about by the story, where the constantly reiterated event of pleasure is inscribed. This is an experience of the body which traverses and subsequently destroys all classifications by the fury of its adventure. This is why, for Sade, the *voyage* is an *a priori* element for the staging of desire.

Dictionary *and* narrative: this relationship (which is normally one of mutual exclusion, as is the case for all paradigmatic structures) inevitably tempts libertine thought to expect its perverse permutations. To disguise the dictionary as a narrative or to impose upon the narrative the dictionary's ordered rigor is to subvert one by the other, to compel them to exchange their status. The narrative can name things plainly, and the dictionary can stage them. We even find here the procedure which legitimizes incest: to confuse established differences, to accumulate contradictory predicates on the same subject, etc. The Sadean text realizes this *mixture*, this *monster* – the philosopher–adventurer, the academy–brothel, erudition–debauchery, the treatise–orgy. It is only by daring to say *too much* that it becomes really possible to say *everything*: there is an Encyclopedia of Excess.

JOURNEY AND EXHAUSTION: THE OBSESSION WITH REMAINS

"To say everything" is normally considered the mark of paranoia. But how can we reach a similar limit through perversion? This can be accomplished by substituting the meticulous *journey* of knowledge and its situations for an undifferentiated, generalized *synthesis*. It suffices to cut up, to subdivide, to repeat. The narrative body is displayed in the succession of sequences, their variations, the distribution of arguments and their repetition. Similarly, the libertine gaze cuts up and parcels out the desired body – and the inventory is thereby confused with dismemberment, an infinite unfolding.

The encyclopedic project, in the pre-Hegelian sense of the term, consists in this enumeration, this work of classification and recapitulation. On the level of knowledge, it is the equivalent of what the great maritime expeditions (of Bougainville, La Pérouse, etc.) represented on the level of our exploration of the planet: an inventory of the known world and the appropriation of the new world. All this ended up inscribed on patiently registered inventories. The *Book* ceased to be fantasized as a mysterious treasure chest containing the secret of all knowledge (a myth analogous to that of the philosopher's stone). It is henceforth represented as the indefinite *surface* of writing: recording acquired knowledge, inventorying real objects, creating an immensely developmental picture of knowledge.

The surfaces of the Book, the Earth, the Body, are thus skins – replete with folds and sites which must be traversed, inventoried, saturated, modified. Discourse, Voyage, and Pleasure all trace out the same gesture in different registers – a detailed, obstinate, fussy procedure, which is implicitly invoked as a fundamental materialist hypothesis, namely, that the world is finite and that a complete inventory is possible. There is no longer a reserved domain, there are no longer any prohibitions. To be deprived of any part of knowledge is to create a mystery, a taboo; it is to enthrone a god upon the void of ignorance, and thus to ruin all other knowledge. The stake is all or nothing in Sade's formula: "If you don't know everything you know nothing at all." This concerns the desiring body and the variations of pleasure – a repressed domain if ever there was one – which Sade daringly insists upon being the first to explore. And he knows that when everything has been said about desire and sexuality (the ultimate *terra incognita*), everything will truly have been said, and the catalogue will be saturated.

But to the extent that this picture is one of excess, the certainty of saturation can never be perfectly attained, and new excesses are always imaginable. The Sadean paradox is precisely to attempt a systematic description of what can be defined outside the system. And yet, to founder in an exhaustive inventory is to resign oneself to the unsaid, to renounce the possibility of really saying everything. This worry about missing an element, about leaving a blank space, unleashes an entire mechanism of repetition: redoing the same scenes, the same treatises, the same arguments. We observe, in fact, a veritably obsessional type of conjuring ritual, with its compulsion to backtrack and to verify that nothing whatsoever had been neglected, that nothing was forgotten. All this to control subsequent traces, plans, and outcomes. In short, it is a question of obtaining a complete repertory, a saturation *without remainder*, so that the *too much* can enter into the *all*.

Narrative fury and expiatory repetitions betray an enormous difficulty in Sade's mastering of totality and completing the journey. Is this the kind of encyclopedic pretension that is found in the dream of Absolute Knowledge, from the unfinished attempt of Novalis to Hegel's monumental *Encyclopedia* (monumental not because of the number of volumes or the quantity of information contained within them, but because of the purely architectonic and all-encompassing nature of its logic)? We might, in fact, presume the contrary, since for Hegel to say everything is not to exhaust the inventory, nor to traverse the immense territory of the known, nor to engage that surface on which everything is added, follows in sequence, is lost and found again. For Hegel, the Whole is said in each part, precisely by stating its development from the first moment to the ultimate form. This voyage is immobile; it is a metamorphosis of substance-becoming-subject, by means of which each stage of its development is established in memory, every moment is perfectly retained in depth, due to the constant work of the negative, which permits each surpassed form to be manifest as interiorized, i.e. as essence within the succeeding form.

The *Aufhebung* is thus an astonishing transformative machine that leaves no leftovers, accumulates without remainder, and produces without surprise, since the final result is already inscribed in the first moment and every event is included as a necessity of discourse. We are no longer on a journey, but in a deductive method.

For Sade, however, the *remainder* is not reduced, but maintained in its very difference. The impossibility of any negativity, and thus of dialectical assimilation (since there is no way of establishing contradiction), maintains the pure heterogeneity of every moment, a succession without internal unity or logical integration, a factitious accumulation and irreducible oneness. Consequently, the pleasure of the voyage, namely the element of *surprise*, is affirmed and preserved. This is an immediate and successive pleasure, renewable within the course of the voyage. This is all that is demanded by the libertine, who desires no interior metamorphosis and recognizes no subjectivity. Thus substance cannot become subject; it can only remain completely open to what the voyage offers. Bodies are not assimilated, cultures remain heterogeneous (the oldest and most primitive may in fact be ahead of or preferable to our own), desires are not transcended, and time remains a succession of separate instants. The unfolding of the *Book* reveals no inside: we are always outside, always on the surface. Infinity is only the illusion of immensity, and the inside only an effect of the density of surfaces.

THE MASTER OF DISCOURSE, THE ACCOMPLICE, AND THE OTHER

There is no Other of the Other.

Lacan

If the voyage is to be completed, it is initially necessary to leave no place for prohibitions, but especially to leave no possibility of contradiction – i.e. what can issue from a malevolent adversary, an "evil demon." Since Sade didn't have the astuteness (or the naivety) to rid himself of this at the very beginning by an artifice of method, he must consequently affront it until the very end of the journey. But who can this invisible, tormenting adversary be, if not the Master's Other? Yet, wouldn't this Other be the inverse of the Master, that is, his Slave, his Victim?

To say everything is, in effect, uniquely the Master's privilege, his linguistic *ius primæ noctis*. If all is said, discourse is without rejoinder, and speech is cut off from every opponent: when all is said, there is no longer anything left to be said, to be argued. At the end of the demonstration, the Master requires nothing but approbation. Such a foreclosure of contradiction puts the adversary in the position of victim, and eliminates the very right to speech.4 We should note that it is not that the victim *can* contradict the Master: even to *want* to contradict him is to bring upon oneself the status of victim, and thus to render oneself silent. The *Master lives alone, his being is independent*, without Other, and his discourse is completely exhausted: all the victims have been sacrificed, and the narrative is over. (Thus, for example, in *Juliette*, the ultimate, most resistant victim is Juliette, who presumes to maintain a discourse.) Thus, the only figure of the Other still imaginable is the one to whom the narrative and its demonstration are directed: the Reader. This turns the reader into an accomplice who shapes the entire apparatus of Sadean fiction. Such an accomplice is thereby elected into the Master's circle: the only possible place of reciprocity, by means of which every pretension to other discourses, which would be the discourse of the Other, is dismissed. The reader's complicity eliminates the ultimate risk of contradiction, and the conquest is thus complete. But this is not at all apparent; complicity is inescapable: thus when the chain of arguments and situations are completed, adherence necessarily follows (like truth for Spinoza.)5 The bodies of Readers, the Master's accomplices, are formed and engendered by the text, at the very end of the demonstration's unfolding. This is carried through by the narrative's great length, in which the victims' bodies ultimately disappear.

This relation to the reader marks the Sadean discourse with a constant oscillation between suspicion and seduction. The formal, tactical *suspicion* assumes, however, that the reader has not accepted the arguments advanced, and that the demonstrations must be offered again. This doubt is symbolized in the narrative by the interlocutor, to whom the treatise is addressed, and who pretends to ignore a doctrinal point, or to lack certainty about the value of a formulation, only in order to sustain discourse. On the other hand, there is *seduction* as well, which entails trapping readers in the movements of their own desire and making them recognize its investment in the entire discourse, and indeed, in every discourse. The relation between scene and treatise is thus not only a play of exchanges – a bit of sex for a bit of philosophy – it is also the very intertextual proof of the demonstration's libidinal impact. This poses the following axiom: "The clearer you think, the better you'll come."

It should be noted that the interpellation of the reader is a common tactic in eighteenth-century narrative, a tactic which clearly reveals its status as fiction – yet soon afterwards, realist narrative will accomplish the contrary. Sade seems to be following a very widespread tradition, although the use of this procedure in Sade acquires an added importance derived from a logic entirely specific to his work, which is to turn the reader into a Master, so that the Master can have no Other. There is no place for the Other since the Master occupies the entire narrative space.

The victims themselves pose no problem of alterity: forbidden to speak, cast outside the symbolic, they are, strictly speaking, nothing. In Sade, there are no dialectical Master–Slave relationships of the Hegelian type, because the Sadean Master is not constituted as such by means of a "struggle to the death," but rather by birth and fortune (either inherited or stolen). There is never a face-to-face confrontation, except with other Masters at the very interior of the power structure, and even these confrontations end in assassination or treason. The Master is born in and sustained by Discourse, while the victims, existing outside of discourse, cannot create any opposition. They remain without recourse and without mediation, since they are relegated to the silence of an anonymous mass incapable of revolt. The Master's domination is set forth as a matter of fact, coextensive with the vastness of an unanswerable Discourse. The only imaginable respondent, the reader, is likewise reduced by the narrative's form, its ruse.

The relation between writer and reader, between Master and Master, is not contractual, but rather *conspiratorial*. To read is already to conspire: thus to *say everything* does not define a wisdom, but a power, the power of which the reader – libertine and complicit by hypothesis and by conclusion – is invited to partake. To read is already to be among the elect.

THE UNAVOWABLE, THE OBSCENE, THE DETAIL

Oh, how beautiful corrupted nature is in her details!

Juliette

There is an encyclopedic Sadean project, but it is conceived of as a provocation, insofar as it is forbidden to speak about what is indicated for the mastery of Discourse itself. This is a strange mastery established in relation to what mastery normally excludes. To say everything that must be kept in silence creates a breach in legality. This play of transgression, the crime of *lèse-frontières*, entails the destruction of the last stronghold of the secret, the last possibility of prohibition. All must be said in order to leave no place for the ineffable. As long as what functions on the side of excess is not renounced, not only is everything not yet said, but in fact nothing at all is said, according to the principle that nothing can be known if everything is not known: "At Cythera Venus had more than one temple, you know; come ope the most arcane, come bugger me. Delcour, make haste . . . for we must leave no delight untasted, no horror uncommitted" (*Juliette*, p. 312; vol. VIII, p. 301).

This completeness of excess provokes a change in the nature of knowledge. There is no longer the simple knowledge of objects, but rather the experience of pleasure, which transforms the "normal" body into a libertine body. What is known in and through excess doesn't simply add to other types of knowledge, but radically overthrows them. It does this by exhibiting what their operations repress, namely violence and desire. To effect this revelation, to compel this avowal of the unavowable, is perhaps the most dangerous attempt and the least supportable aggression imaginable against the social order. As Freud explains in *Totem and Taboo*, society is founded upon a crime committed in common, but one of which we must remain ignorant. In effect, the constitution of community is achieved by repression, the anarchic violence characteristic of individual or group instincts. The renunciation of such violence is effected through *sacrifice*,[6] which mimics violence in order to exorcise and master it. Hence evil is designated, circumscribed, and vanquished. What is engendered by this renunciation is an order of the symbolic, a convention of exchange, a contractual system,[7] which makes possible something like a community. Every order of values, like every organization of knowledge, is based upon this compromise, which is also the inaugural prohibition. The order which proceeds from such renunciation keeps watch with a fierce vigilance, so that this sedated and domesticated monster does not awaken, so that the menace of chaos is contained at all costs. This chaos would surge from a free unleashing of the forces which, by means of sacrifice and contract, have already been successfully neutralized, short-circuited, placed outside of discourse.

Immediately indicated by all this is the political genesis of all knowledge, which obtains recognition only by presenting its contractual credentials. (This is precisely why academicism and sclerosis are not accidents, but rather signs of the inevitable fatigue of this structure; stupidity has no other history.) What we demand of knowledge is to not know, or more precisely to know nothing, of the instincts as long as they contain desire and violence, sex and blood – the murderous and fornicating beast – two related axes of chaos.

Sexuality will be incorporated into the system of differences and prohibitions that constitutes the *family*. Violence – principally murder – will be institutionalized and regulated within the structure of the *state*, which will transform such violence into the distinctive sign of its authority (i.e. the right to make war and the death penalty.) By having perceived all this rather clearly, Sade is able to gauge the inadmissible audacity of the crime that he will commit against the "fundamental mystery," and to pronounce the limits of the sayable:

And now, friend-reader, you must prepare your heart and your mind for the most impure tale that has ever been told since our world began, a book the likes of which are met with neither amongst the ancients nor amongst us moderns. Fancy, now, that all pleasure-taking either sanctioned by good manners or enjoined by that fool you speak of incessantly, of whom you know nothing and whom you call Nature; fancy, I say, that all these modes of taking pleasure will be expressly excluded from this anthology, or that whenever per adventure you do indeed encounter them here, they will always be accompanied by some crime or colored by some infamy. (*120 Days*, pp. 252–53; vol. XIII, pp. 60–1)

To bring to light what is unspeakably horrible is to make it enter into discourse, the form of which is related to a contract. Whence the paradox, the specifically Sadean wager: to say in masterly form precisely what mastery was established to oppose. In fact, the form as such is not contested, though it might very well have been. As an object inherited like a natural given, classical seventeenth-century French language leaves enunciation without any alternative. Thus the question is not whether or not to reject it, but rather how to make it say what contradicts it, what disavows it. In order to do this, however, the body of language must be inscribed with all the forbidden signifiers which classical language repressed: sex, blood, excrement, crimes, lies. But what Sade didn't realize is that language itself is the very scene of prohibition, the absolute form of the law. In the eighteenth century, discourse meant only the referent, and nature was directly given through language. We had to wait until Freud and Saussure for a new understanding of language as the seat of prohibition.

Aggression could not have any effect upon the signifier, which was at that time a blind spot. Classical language was ethereal, the milieu of the explicitness of discourse, the thick veil of its transparency. At the time, the only recourse available was in the lexical order: to write and rewrite dictionaries was the permanent strategy of the eighteenth century. One remade the world by changing definitions and imposing new ones. This is why Sade concerns himself with words: he attacks conventional meaning by deviating from respectable usage and by mixing given terms with forbidden, "vulgar" words. But there is never any thought of questioning the structure of language, since this structure was not even seen. The way to attack language was to inundate it with the very statements it was made to exclude. The obscene effect stems from the separation between traditional syntactic and rhetorical forms and the vice signified. This presupposes the existence of another society (with its political order and value system, its legal structures, etc.), which *must not* speak the language of honest citizens and *belles lettres*. It is precisely this implication that is felt to be intolerable, a collusion which is considered scandalous.

The enterprise of the political and literary intimidation of classical language aimed at making such a collusion unimaginable. Sade's unpardonable and unpardoned challenge was to make it possible by practicing it. This is why transgression in Sade assumes the order of *saying everything*; Sade's writing proves that the received language can materially say everything it is in fact not supposed to say. It is not enough to think this; one must dare to do it. Sade's hypothesis, his risk, is that there is no statement, however perverse it may be, that is ultimately unspeakable. The barrier is not on the side of the structure, but of the imagination, and it is the latter that must be freed. This is why enunciation must go to the limit, must scrupulously extend itself to the lowliest things, recover the smallest differences, cover and release every signified. In short, it must particularly consider all the *details*. This consideration is constant in all of Sade's narratives:

Noirceuil was impatient to find out how my liaison with Madame de Clairwil was progressing; the warmth where-with I spoke of her translated my gratitude. He wanted graphic particulars, I supplied them. (*Juliette*, p. 298; vol. VIII, p. 287)

each couple had ten minutes for solving the puzzle – then when the time had expired the dunces were flogged red and raw by our libertine who, as I dare say you very well imagine, derived quite as much pleasure from their mistakes as from their correct penetration of his wishes. (*Juliette*, p. 626; vol. IX, p. 35)

It is in *The 120 Days of Sodom* that the theory of this imperative of stating the details is most explicitly formulated, immediately after Duclos's first tale:

"Duclos," the Président interrupted at this point, "we have, I believe, advised you that your narrations must be decorated with the most numerous and searching details; the precise way and extent to which we may judge how the passion you describe relates to human manners and man's character is determined by your willingness to disguise no circumstance; and what is more, the least circumstance is apt to have an immense influence upon the procuring of that kind of sensory irritation we expect from your stories."

"Yes, my Lord," Duclos replied, "I have been advised to omit no detail and to enter into the most minute particulars whenever they serve to shed light upon the human personality, or upon the species of passion; have I neglected something in connection with this one?"

"You have," said the Président; "I have not the faintest notion of your second monk's prick, nor any idea of its discharge. In addition, did he frig your cunt, pray tell, and did he have you dandle his device? You see what I mean by neglected details." (*120 Days*, p. 271; vol. XIII, pp. 78–79)

Duclos then gives the information expected of her, which elicits the following remarks by one of the libertines: "'That's it, Duclos,' said Durcet, 'the Président was right; I could not visualize a thing on the basis of your first telling, but now I have your man well in view.'" *120 Days*, p. 272; vol. XIII, p. 79). The imagination is astonished by the real in its very details. Within the histories of debaucheries, where gestures and situations are on the whole foreseeable, the detail is the sign of the unforeseen. It is the trait which particularizes everything by pushing back the limits of saturation: it signals the inventive capacity of desire within the inventory of excess. Desire itself is invented by means of details. And if the details are stressed in the margins of discourse, as the very debris of discourse, they are rediscovered as what is excluded from the official scene of accepted generalities. Details are plotted in regard to the slippage and deficiency of these generalities. This is precisely why for the traditional composition the enunciation of details is related to the scabrous and the obscene, to the inavowability of pleasure. For the Sadean, "these details excite me to such an extent . . ." Such is the specifically libertine proof of the ambition to say everything, since this is precisely what traditional discourse resists.

Freud, for example, knew this very well when he made the principle of saying everything – *alles sagen* – the subject's rule of enunciation, and simultaneously made attention to detail the analyst's rule of listening. Now, these psychoanalytical matters are intelligible only if presented in *full and complete detail*, just as an analysis gets going only when the patient distinguishes the minute details from the abstractions which are their surrogate.[8] The detail is where *things happen*, where the censorship created by secondary formations is slackened and where the instincts ceaselessly create symptoms in a proliferation of bungled actions and slips of the tongue. Because, as with wit, it is enjoyed [*ca jouit*],[9] i.e. insofar as the unconscious speaks. As Freud explains in *Jokes and their Relation to the Unconscious*, it is only small details that indicate that wit, nevertheless, stems from the unconscious.

Analysis must go all the way and leave nothing outside enunciation. We do not regard an analysis as terminated until *all* the obscurities of the case are cleared up, the gaps in the patient's memory filled in, the precipitating causes of the repressions discovered.[10] We should note that Freud's opposition between substitutive abstractions and small details is noteworthy with regard to the Sadean economy of saying everything. For this economy, the first term adequately defines the level of contractual exchange, the order of what can be foreseen, and general normality – that is, the average type of behavior which results in neither excess nor expenditure. The second term defines the level of *singularity*, the limit of exchange, the production of unique differences, the absence of equivalence; in short, the upsurge of new figures of perversion which permits the possibility of pleasure as pure loss (due to the deprivation of all signs and structures of substitution).

In this regard Freud does speak about a "local economy," but this notion doesn't suffice. (Confined to the dominant homeostatic model of energy, he could hardly speak of it otherwise.) Rather, as concerns the cathexis of details, one should first find where this economy fails, and then find what causes the economy of desire to be expensive, even ruinous, insofar as such an economy recuperates nothing since it continually rids itself of "substitutive abstractions" and general equivalents, i.e. any concept of money or system of exchange. As Luce Irigary notes, this is a process of rupture: "The rule of *saying everything* puts inter-diction back into play: the unspeakable articulation which passes from the interior to the exterior of discourse."[11]

THE SECRET CHAMBER, OR HOW TO SPEAK THE UNSPEAKABLE

The crime is hidden, and what escapes us is the most frightful. In the night offered to our fear we are obliged to imagine the worst.

Georges Bataille, *Le Procès de Gilles de Rais*

Near the public pleasure rooms are the secret chambers where one can in seclusion surrender oneself to all the debaucheries of libertinage.

(*Juliette*, vol. VIII, p. 404)

There is, after all, no equivalent to solitary crimes.

(*Juliette*, p. 495; vol. VIII, p. 474)

In *The 120 Days of Sodom*, as in *Juliette*, everything that happens occurs within the narrative scene; everything that is visible must be sayable. This unreserved exposure, this boundless exposition, is precisely what defines the space of the obscene. This move is so radical that it ceases to operate upon its own limits. Because of this, Sade insists that the place of total exposition cannot be one of infinite excess. Every marked space defines an axiomatics and a combinatory system, a finite set of determinations, a saturable system. With the orgy, saturation is aimed at by a general demand for order. It is this order which permits the exhaustion of singular connections, the doubling of pleasure by language, and the total view of the spectacle.

Torture is presented as a means of reopening the system: the tearing apart of bodies disrupts the combinatory system, and entirely reconstructs the scene of leisure. A new, markedly different, and complex ensemble is put into play. Pleasures are henceforth connected to sufferings, and cries of pleasure are mixed with screams of pain. But it is especially the victims' bodies which enter a cycle of horrible metamorphoses, a fall towards the formlessness of an inorganic magma. Whipped to the quick, flayed alive, slashed, burnt, cut up, mutilated: the variations of their destruction define new combinations and thus new pleasures. A new space, surrounded by screams and inundated with blood, offers more radical – and thus more improbable, more chaotic – distributions. To accomplish this, it was necessary to open up bodies, mangle their forms, burst their skin, expose their organs and viscera. But once exposed, new surfaces are created, foundationless surfaces obscenely exhibited in unmediated nudity (where there is no more under the skin than on it). The erotic supplement occurs in the passage from above to below which produces frantic movements and unexpected figures upon the assaulted body. Torture thereby attains the goals of novel production: the creation of unprecedented cycles of possibilities, furnishing entirely new pleasures for sight, hearing, touch, and the imagination. This leads to the ultimate moment where orgasm coincides with the victim's last breath. The system is thus closed again, and all begins anew: torture extends the limits by multiplying perverse combinations. All of the nameable horrors – by whose excessive means all limits are shattered – are inscribed on the tortured body.

How can this be? Can the narration of the orgy pass beyond

the places and bodies which compose its very scene, without itself being suppressed as narrative? A thousand insanities, a thousand horrors, are possible, but remain unrecounted. And if the Sadean narrative is stretched out, prolonged, ceaselessly resumed, it is only to approximate the final sum. It is known in advance that the sum is finite: the trajectory is fixed. The narrative must be completed without the occurrence of a boundless transgression or an incommensurable madness. For if such madness were possible, it would have occurred at the outset, and the tale would not have taken place at all. The tale begins only by desiring what might suppress it and proceeds only by failure to attain the latter; it concludes by renouncing its desire. Narrative leisure is the voluptuous voyage through an ensemble which is perceived as finite. This finitude is, nevertheless, immense, wonderfully filled with surprises, with the unforeseen, with renewals: its formula is $n+1$, repeated indefinitely. Once again names, characters, and places suffice to create new stories, even if these are the same old gestures and thoughts already stated. All that is needed is to add details and variations $(n+1)$ to the name, and this permits a new combination. This is why it is always necessary to recommence the narrative, since even though the ensemble is theoretically finite, it is in fact never exhausted. We must find the painting's vanishing point, an opening in perspective, a point where the gaze is no longer spoken of and where the gesture is no longer recited. We must find something by means of which the ungraspableness of what remains unstated leaves the imagination – and thus desire – the possibility of infinite extension, without, however, threatening the pleasure offered by the tale. This vanishing point is precisely the *secret chamber*, that place where the horrors are no longer nameable:

So he and I, Braccisini, and Olympia removed into the secret sanctuary of the Princess's pleasures where further infamies were celebrated and, upon my honor, I blush at describing them to you. (*Juliette*, p. 744; vol. IX, p. 148)

I have never been able to discover what went on in those infernal closets (*Philosophy in the Bedroom*, p. 514; vol. XIII, p. 297)

And, together with Sophie and Michette, Durcet fled into his closet to discharge. I don't know how, but none the less in a manner which must not have suited Sophie, for she uttered a piercing scream and emerged from the sanctuary as red as a cockscomb. (*Philosophy in the Bedroom*, p. 525; vol. XIII, p. 306)

This place of horrors and secrets keeps our knowledge in suspense. It is the place of *remains*, where everything else takes place. It is beyond the bedroom; the bedroom is the place of the narrative, the treatise, of erotic practice, of the visible, of the scene which necessarily grasps the entirety of what is speakable. This chamber beyond the scene constitutes the narrative's most astonishing ruse, to draw attention to the absolute horrors, even if it initially marks the failure of the narrative to circumscribe these horrors. It is inscribed in the narrative "emptiness" where nomination abdicates its rights. We know that something took place, but we never know precisely what occurred; consequently we are compelled to imagine a reality more forceful than Discourse, a violence to which only silence can respond.

The victims' silence corresponds to this narrative "whiteness" or blankness. In general, the victims do not say very much, for two reasons. First, only the libertine, as Master, possesses language: in fact, it is this very privilege *in the text* which institutes mastery. Second, and as a corollary, only pleasure is enunciated, since it is exclusively the Master's privilege. The victim's suffering cannot be spoken; it can only be indicated, insofar as it stimulates pleasure. But its textual consistency is so thin that it perpetually fails in regard to the codes of verisimilitude.

The libertine enters the secret chamber alone with the victim, because if another libertine were to accompany him, he could – as a Master of language – bear witness to what occurred. In fact, according to the logic of the obscene which demands that everything be said, such testimony would be necessary since it would recount the other scene. What can be seen by a third party becomes speakable for everyone, and the limits of the speakable become precisely those of the excluded third party. This limit confirms that the strange passivity of the

Sadean victims is first of all due to their logical non-existence, to the confiscation of the symbolic inflicted upon them. And Sade could very well provide a "psychological" justification for this solitude:

> there are moments when, however agreeable the company of a person like in mind to ourselves, we nevertheless prefer solitude, thinking, perhaps, that we will be freer, that our fancy will enjoy a wider scope; for when alone one is dispensed of that kind of shame or bashfulness so hard to be rid of when with others; and there is, after all, no equivalent to solitary crimes. (*Juliette*, p. 495; vol. VIII, p. 474)

Yet the fact remains that this is determined by textual functions. The libertine is alone in the chamber because he is no longer the subject of narration, since he too is placed outside discourse: not falling short of it, like the victim, but beyond it. An indescribable violence begins with this rupture of limits: such definitive horrors transcend the familiar place of language.

We readers stand before the door which, in the text, metaphorizes the limits of the obscene. Whence the impossibility of saying everything, the impossibility of adding new combinations to those already utilized. The impossibility follows, therefore, of adding anything to the symbolic order which fully governs the Sadean rage against the body. This is aimed at shattering the closure and breaking through the prison of signs.

It is not surprising that, in the secret chamber, the only thing that is successfully inserted in the narrative to indicate this horror is the *scream*. The scream is the pre-symbolic use of the voice, the voice before language takes charge of it, the voice which escapes from the body, which is extorted from it like other secretions: sperm, shit, urine, farts, blood. Such is the voice reduced to its pure material flux. The scream unites two constant Sadean necessities: (a) the prediscursive, which invokes nature prior to humanity (indifferent, innocent, eternal nature); (b) the trans-discursive, which is attained in the victim's pulverized language, in the scandalous institution of the orgy and crime (violent and cruel nature, which becomes accessible only through violence and cruelty). The body reunites these two registers: led into the secret chamber, it can no longer speak or be spoken of. The scream, which is not yet language, indicates that language no longer occurs, that it is destroyed, that the narrative must be forsaken, and that within the fierce solitude of torture, the extreme violence inflicted upon the body is radically hidden from all forms of discursivity. The body is finally reduced to its "state of nature," to its most naked materiality, according to the schema of the French materialist philosopher Julien de La Mettrie: a mass of flesh and a network of nerves spread out on the skin, from which torture extracts the very last movements of life for the libertine's pleasure.

This scream doesn't affect the victims' silence, since it confirms and reinforces their exclusion from language. Their screams are not speech, but only a sonorous eruption, a gush of voice in the gush of blood.

In contrast to other orgies, what occurs in the secret chamber is never programmed, since what is programmable coincides with what can be narrated. Every program opens with this imperative: "Put some order in our orgies!", which is to say, let us produce an axiomatic and a narrative, and above all let us define the Law by introducing it into what it prohibits. The secret chamber, on the contrary, is the place of disorder, from which the libertines exit disheveled and delirious. It is the totally logical, insane, dissolute space beyond the narrative, the chaos of the body in the hole of discourse. This chamber announces the limit, if not the very failure, of Sadean transgression. In effect, the obscene, as well as aggression, is formulated as the challenge to "say everything." But how can one say within language what is narratively possible only by interrupting the narrative, only by excluding the narrativity coextensive with language? Language remains ordered or parodic, but delirium, conceived of as an absolute excess, is unspeakable: it is imaginable only at the limits of language.

This secret chamber thus constitutes a strange and essential symptom in Sade's text: strange insofar as it functions as a prohibition; essential insofar as it is the empty, non-narrated place which orchestrates the spoken, saturated places of pro-grammed orgies. The secret chamber even engenders these saturated places, by postulating their incessant repetition; hence it is perhaps the point at which the narrative is renewed and the stakes are raised. What is required to lead us into this secret chamber is a *statement* capable of recovering the *deed* inconceivably perpetrated therein. But in this case we would find ourselves in a bedroom at whose end a mysterious door would lead to yet another secret chamber. For once discourse enunciates the gesture, it places it in the order of the conceivable, in the combinatory of possibilities. To circumscribe the unspeakable horror is thus a frantic, futile endeavor, where the Sadean narrative fury encounters the following paradox. Even though disfigured, crushed and annihilated, *the body resists*. The very inaccessibility of the secret chamber thus becomes a sign of this resistance. But it is a resistance to discourse, and not the claim of the soul's invulnerability, as we find in Christian martyrs. Thus the secret chamber does not evoke an afterworld, a beyond. It is, rather, the positive existence of a backroom where the body's radical materiality is demonstrated: the skin and organs fall away from language. For even if the body's resistance suspends *speech*, it nonetheless summons forth another mode of signification. The secret chamber is somewhat like the object in Zen practice or in ancient Stoicism: it cannot be enunciated or described, but it can be *designated*. It thus entails an *anaphoric* dimension, which inscribes the body's very irreducibility and the eruption of gestures in the text, where the executioner's violence is annulled by the victims' silence.

Wittgenstein says it in this way in the *Tractatus*: "What can be shown cannot be said," and "What cannot be spoken must be passed over in silence." And as Bataille claims in *L'Erotisme*, "Violence fears within itself that disheveled Negation which puts an end to all possibility of discourse." What *remains* to be said?

THE CRIME OF WRITING

How can we have a writing that kills?

Bertholt Brecht

There is no longer anything to say within the order of the signified, that of the narrative enunciation. The discourse of excess has saturated its nominations, and the theater of crime has exhausted its tableaux. And yet the ruse – or the strength – of writing would be the following: if the ultimate crime cannot be spoken, it is necessary that speech itself be turned into a permanent crime. If language is the form of the law, if language is what constitutes all community, and if language is what such community in return produces and observes with the greatest vigilance, then any offense inflicted upon language becomes the very possibility of crime – its general matrix, its pure model. Such is the moral crime one attains by waiting, which Juliette recommends to Clairwil, who formulates this vow:

"I would like," Clairwil answered, "to find a crime which, even when I had left off doing it, would go on having perpetual effect, in such a way that so long as I lived, at every hour of the day and as I lay sleeping at night, I would be constantly the cause of a particular disorder, and that this disorder might broaden to the point where it brought about a corruption so universal or a disturbance so formal that even after my life was over I would survive in the everlasting continuation of my wickedness . . ." (*Juliette*, p. 525; vol. VIII, p. 503)

The *crime of writing* is certainly that by *saying everything*, Sade intends to make himself guilty. To say everything is the exhaustive attempt to name and stage the signifiers of debauchery, cruelty, and murder. This attempt produces the writing of the obscene as a double betrayal: the betrayal of the exclusionary codes of the language of communication by the use of words which connote the common people and especially the "rabble"; and the betrayal of the exclusionary codes of literary language by means of a radical rejection of metaphoric procedures and the conventions they sustain. As a betrayal of class and a betrayal of culture in a generalized corruption of language, to *say everything* is, strictly speaking, that crime which engenders all of the crimes that it pronounces. It is the Sadean crime *par excellence*. Nothing else remains.

NOTES

1 All references to Sade refer first to the English translation, then to the French edition of the *Oeuvres complètes* (Paris: Editions du Cercle du Livre Précieux, 1966–67). The English translations are from: *The 120 Days of Sodom and Other Writings*, trans. Austryn Wainhouse and Richard Seaver (New York: Grove Press, 1966); *Juliette*, trans. Austryn Wainhouse (New York: Grove Press, 1968); *Justine, Philosophy in the Bedroom, Eugénie de Franval and Other Writings*, trans. Richard Seaver and Austryn Wainhouse (New York: Grove Press, 1965).

2 See Roland Barthes, "Introduction à l'analyse structurale des récits," *Communications* 8 (1966), pp. 10–11.

3 See Gérard Genette, "Frontières du récit," *Communications* 8 (1966), p. 156.

4 This is why Deleuze, most pertinently, speaks of a "violence of demonstration" in regard to Sade. (See his *Présentation de Sacher-Masoch*, Paris: Minuit, 1967.)

5 Such necessity appears in the reasoning of "One more effort, Frenchmen, if you are to become republicians": "and let a considerable prize, to be bestowed by the Nation, be awarded to him who, having said and demonstrated everything upon this score [i.e., about God and religion], will leave to his countrymen no more than a scythe to mow the land clean of those phantoms" (*Philosophy in the Bedroom*, p. 306; vol. III, p. 489).

6 See René Girard, *La Violence et le sacré* (Paris: Grasset, 1972) and Julia Kristeva, *La Révolution du langage poétique* (Paris: Seuil, 1974).

7 See Marcel Mauss's claim: "Ultimately, there exists perhaps no sacrifice without something contractual about it." (Mauss, *Oeuvres complètes*, Paris: Minuit, 1968, vol. I, p. 305.)

8 Sigmund Freud, letter to Pfister (6 June 1910), in *Psychoanalysis and Faith: The Letters of Sigmund Freud and Oskar Pfister*, ed. Heinrichman and Ernst L. Freud, Eng. trans. by Eric Mosbacher (New York: Basic Books, 1963), p. 38.

9 There is a pun here on *jouir* meaning "rejoice in" and "enjoy sexually" (eds.).

10 Sigmund Freud, *Introductory Lectures on Psychoanalysis*, trans. James Strachey (New York: Norton, 1977), pp. 452–53.

11 See "Le sexe fait 'comme' signe," in *Langages* 17 (March 1970), p. 42.

CHAPTER 8

"Sex," or, the misfortunes of literature
Dalia Judovitz

Le réel c'est l'impossible.

Jacques Lacan

L'impossible, c'est la littérature.

Georges Bataille

"It is necessary," wrote Baudelaire, "to keep coming back to Sade, again and again."[1] Baudelaire's injunction has been quite prophetic, since contemporary critics keep on returning to Sade in order to assess his contribution to modernity. D. A. F. de Sade's novelistic work has been interpreted by critics since Bataille as a literature of transgression.[2] However, the limits which the Sadean text challenges are not those of sexuality alone. Rather, through his exhaustive exposition of sexuality Sade succeeds in expanding its meaning, not only to include perverse and even criminal modes of activity, but also to challenge all moral referents, and thus fundamentally to alter the very definition of the limits of thought.

As Michel Foucault suggests in his essay "A preface to transgression," Sade's transgressive gesture posits through the language of sexuality an ontological and theological challenge regarding man's definition and relation to God:

From the moment that Sade delivered its first words and marked out, in a single discourse, the boundaries of what suddenly became its kingdom, the language of sexuality has lifted us into the night where God is absent, where all our actions are addressed to this absence in a profanation which at once identifies it, dissipates it, exhausts itself in it, and restores it to the empty purity of its transgression.[3]

Sade's extensive exploration of the boundaries of sexuality is interpreted by Foucault as the prototype of all transgressive gestures, since it stages the challenge of the limits of philosophy and religion. Based on Georges Bataille and Pierre Klossowski, Foucault's interpretation of the role of sexuality underlines the liminal character of Sadean thought, presenting him as the closure of classical thought based on representation. Foucault suggests that Sadean discourse is the last discourse that undertakes "representation," that is to say, defines its order through an exhaustive nomenclature and totalizing categorization.[4]

However, the encyclopedic character of representation in Sade's work threatens through its excessive display to foreclose and thus to destroy the boundaries of classical representation. The question thus arises whether it is sufficient, or even adequate, to classify Sade's novelistic and philosophical works in terms of "transgression." This study will show that while embodying the principles of the Enlightenment – the search for totalizing categories and a universal order – Sade's representation of reason and humanity is in fact a parody of the ideology of the Enlightenment. His ostensible encyclopedic ambition to "say everything" and to "show everything" results both in the saturation of the classical order of representation and in its actual violation, through the production of an excess that challenges the notion of order itself. Everything that up to Sade constitutes the exterior of reason – evil, crime, monstrosity, and sexual perversion – is brought within its domain, thereby redefining the positive connotations which his contemporaries associated with reason. The very premises of eighteenth-century thought are systematically exposed and debased by Sade, so that the underpinnings of its logical foundations are pitted through parody against themselves. Sade's work thus emerges less as a literature of scandal than as the scandal of literature, insofar as his reflections on representation embody and stage the confrontation of thought with its limits. Sade's demythologization of reason, as the substratum of representation, involves (as this study will show) the violent expansion of its logical and systematic properties, so that thought itself becomes the figurative victim of the excesses of literary and philosophical parody.

THE MISFORTUNES OF LITERATURE

In his *Reflections on the Novel*, Sade defines the novel (*roman*) as follows: "We give the name 'novel' to any work of imagination fashioned from the most uncommon adventures which men experience in the course of their lives" (p. 97).[5] Despite the somewhat Aristotelian tone of this pronouncement, which had been previously applied to the mechanisms of tragedy intended to evoke fear and pity, Sade's comments later in his pamphlet indicate that this statement should be taken "literally." That is to say, Sade's novels will deal with adventures so uncommon that their implausibility will threaten the very definition of the novel. In the *Poetics*, Aristotle designates misfortune as an accident inspired by a character flaw or weakness (*hamartia*), intended to inspire sympathy and catharsis.[6] Whereas for Sade, misfortune becomes a rule in itself – an ultimate challenge to any possible identification on the part of the reader. Since vice will reap the rewards of virtue, the process of identification with the character in a cathartic sense is precluded. The Sadean anti-novel thus presents its reader with a paradoxical dilemma. On the one hand, these works refuse mimesis as a principle of imitation and identification that guides the reader's relation to the text. On the other hand, the Sadean anti-novel will rely on a new concept of imitation. Rather than pretending to copy reality, his novels parody the very conventions that structure novelistic "reality."

This strategy for appealing to identification on the part of the reader, while simultaneously rejecting mimetic conventions, can be seen in Sade's warning to his readers. Attacking other authors that make "vice seem attractive," Sade explains in *Reflections on the Novel* how the violence of his novelistic representations excludes all possible identification:

I have no wish to make vice seem attractive. Unlike Crébillon and Dorat, I have not set myself the dangerous goal of enticing women to love characters who deceive them; on the contrary, I want them to loathe these characters. 'Tis the only way one can avoid being duped by them. And, in order to succeed in that purpose, I painted that hero who treads the path of vice with features so frightful that they will most assuredly not inspire either pity or love. In so doing, I dare say I am become more moral than those who believe they have licence to embellish them. (pp. 115–16)

Sade's works defy the reader's expectations, since they refuse claims that rely on the traditional conception of the novel as a vehicle for imitation and as a model for truth. While Sade recognizes that the moral referent of classical novels is merely a subterfuge for presenting images that violate it, his condemnation cannot be construed literally as a moral claim. Although Sade suggests that he is "more moral" than his contemporaries, his ostensible "moral" intention is immediately put into question by his disclaimer at the end of the essay that he is the author of the scandalous *Justine*. By challenging his own authenticity as the author of *Justine*, Sade undermines any simplistic inference regarding the authoritative and direct referential relation of the author and his text. His comment at the end of his treatise on the novel sets off the question of the identity of the author and reduces it to a parody of the authorial persona.

Sade's parody of his own authorial persona is made explicit in an attack on one of the critics of his *The Crimes of Love*, a man called Villeterque. Sade brutally admonishes his critic by accusing him of falsely identifying the author with the fictional characters:

Loathsome ignoramus: have you not yet learned that every character in any dramatic work must employ a language in keeping with his character, and that, when he does, 'tis the fictional character who is speaking and not the author? and that, in such an instance, 'tis indeed common that the character inspired by the role he is playing, says things completely contrary to what the author may say when he himself is speaking?[7]

Sade's critique of Villeterque as a bad reader, who persists in conflating author and character, exposes the myth that underlies literature, as a mirror of the identity of the author.

Rather than interpreting the author as a naive referent for the literary work, Sade suggests that the author himself may be nothing more than a fictional character, that is an invention or a convention through which the literary work is made intelligible. He taunts Villeterque by flaunting the one thing that he and his characters agree about:

Ah, Monsieur Villeterque, what a fool you are! This is one truth concerning which both I and my characters will always be in complete agreement whenever we have the occasion to exchange views regarding your prosaic existence. (*SV*, p. 128)

By affirming his explicit complicity with his fictional characters, Sade underlines his refusal to be simply assimilated to his work. In so doing, he disrupts the mimetic relation between the author and the work, by having his characters mime him as comical mouthpieces that reiterate his putative claims. By both disengaging himself from his characters and enlisting their support through a perverse play with the notion of mimesis, Sade succeeds in distinguishing himself from what he calls Villeterque's "*mirror*-authors" (*SV*, p. 129). Sade's attack on Villeterque and his camp of "mimetic" authors represents his own complex position as a parodist, who uses imitation only to destroy it as a category which has any referential relation to "reality." His response does not merely address Villeterque, but functions as a warning to all future critics who may persist in naively identifying him with his characters, and who will search for clues to his authorial identity by identifying the author with the literary work.

In *The Misfortunes of Virtue*, Sade systematically enacts his critique of the classical novel through strategies that disrupt identification with both mimetic and moral referents. In the preface, Sade forewarns the reader that the aim of the novel is to depict the misfortunes of virtue, rather than its rewards. By suspending moral claims, he challenges the limits of novelistic verisimilitude and plausibility. *The Misfortunes of Virtue* presents the reader with an implausible plot: that of the relentless, exaggerated, and caricature-like description of the heroine's misfortunes.[8] The heroine, Justine/Sophie (who can hardly be called such since she is nothing more than a compendium of banal moral maxims), is shown to be suffering from her unsuccessful attempts to reconcile her own beliefs and her worldly experiences. Her misfortunes are profoundly literary: they represent the encounter with a classical discourse, a discourse of normative morality and good faith, and its violation through its explosive clashes with other types of discourse representing various institutions – noble, scientific, religious, and mercantile.

The discomfort of the reader in face of the erotic victimization of the heroine takes on a surreal, almost dream-like character. As Blanchot has noted, Sade's eroticism paradoxically derives its brutal reality and exaggerated freedom from its fictional nature:

Sade's eroticism is a dream eroticism, since it expresses itself exclusively in fiction; but the more this eroticism is imagined, the more it requires a fiction from which dream is excluded, a fiction wherein debauchery can be enacted and lived . . .[9]

Blanchot's observation regarding the deliberate fictional staging of eroticism in Sade's novels is helpful towards elucidating the reader's complicitous relation to fiction. The paradox, as Blanchot suggests, is that Sade uses fiction in such an exaggerated fashion as to challenge its limits and consequently to abolish, through fiction, the reader's sense of novelistic reality.

The reader's effort to identify with the protagonists of the novel is thwarted from the novel's inception. *The Misfortunes of Virtue* introduces two heroines, the sisters Juliette and Justine, who are remarkably different. They each represent in a caricature-like fashion the obverse of the other. Juliette is presented as the character who, though virtuous, learns that virtue has no real currency in the social world. She proceeds to sell the physical equivalent of her virtue, many times over, thereby parodying and debasing it as counterfeit money. She considers virtue as a mere sign, a convention that can be traded in the social domain in order to generate power, pleasure, and security. Her activities document her remarkable education from victim to master and passage from pleasure to crime, since her behavior shuns both the notion of social contract and that of a universal moral referent.

At the other end of the spectrum, Justine represents the epitome of virtue, a virtue that is so proud of itself that it invites violation. The reader is trapped, since s/he cannot identify with either character without a sense of moral complicity with one or the other side – vice or virtue. This problem is exacerbated by the fact that although the story focuses entirely on the misfortunes of Justine (alias, virtue) the character is further removed from the reader through a linguistic displacement. Justine's real name is Sophie (wisdom, in Greek), a name all the more ironic since the heroine displays her magnificent virtue very unwisely, inviting violation and destruction. By compulsively upholding an ideal standard of behavior, Justine/Sophie invites transgression. The desiring structure of the text is constituted around the adventures of virtue, the narration of its consistent violation. The reader is thus freed from identification with the discourse of victimization, and made aware of the complicity involved in the act of reading.

Justine's encounter with Bressac in *The Misfortunes of Virtue* emblematizes both her status as erotic victim and the reader's complicitous position as victim of novelistic conventions (*IV*, p. 75). Hidden behind a bush, the heroine witnesses the verbal and physical exchanges between the aristocrat Bressac and his valet. Doubling the position of the reader, Justine, as a female voyeur, discovers that the act of witnessing the discourse and act of sodomy involves complicity. Despite her sense of moral condemnation, she is literally drawn into the scene, since, having been discovered by Bressac, she is tied to a tree and threatened with flagellation and sodomy. Thus from the very beginnings of the novel, Sade demonstrates that there can be no exterior or privileged position for Sophie or, for that matter, the reader as a voyeur to the scene. Having been "drawn" into the scene, both Justine and the reader discover that they risk being marked by this experience. By identifying with the heroine, the reader becomes a victim as well, since the act of reading, governed by the mimetic relation of reader and text, implies the risk of being marked by the punitive logic of the text. The physical violence unleashed by the text is thus directed not merely towards the heroine, but rather at the traditional conventions that govern the classical novel.

In other words, the reader may discover, like Justine, that the act of representation involves an inescapable complicity. The consistent violence unleashed upon the body of the heroine becomes the index of violence endemic to classical representation in general. The act of marking Justine's body, through sexual, perverse, and punitive acts, traces upon the body the script of the social and political ideology which the heroine consciously attempts to contain through her virtue. Just as characters such as Bressac and Du Buisson attempt to stamp their own demystified social ideology upon their victim, their frustration with her ideas will culminate in Justine's being falsely branded as a thief. This unjust punishment, however, is logically consistent with the heroine's structural position in the novel, since her victimization is due to her unconscious assimilation of popular ideology, her metaphorical "thievery" of a popular ideal of virtue. As an unconscious exponent of popular ideology, Justine persists in refusing either to reflect or learn from her misadventures, or to admit to being marked by competing negative ideologies. This refusal to examine the social and physical implications of ideology leads to the more and more violent tone of the novel as it attempts to literalize ideology and to implicate Justine unwittingly in more heinous crimes, such as murder and arson. Notwithstanding the heroine's ostensible innocence, her observance of virtue becomes the site of violence against the other, since the unreflected nature of this observance can be manipulated all the more effectively. Passing from the position of spectator to that of unsuspecting actor, Justine is shown to be playing the role of the victim whose innocence becomes the stage for a trial of complicity.

The trajectory of the unfortunate adventures of the heroine Justine (alias Sophie) involves successive encounters with several types of institutions: a noble or feudal model (Bressac); a scientific or experimental model (Rodin); a Christian religious model (the convent of Sainte-Marie des Bois) and at the end, a false double of the noble and mercantile model (Dalville's château), which simulates the codes of both institutions in order to function as a "factory" for the production of false currency. Marcel Hénaff has shown that the economy of Sadean libertinage is a consumer economy that operates by reference to these three major models: feudal, monastic, and mercantile.[10] However, each of these social institutions has ceased to function in a traditional sense. Neither the castle, nor the monastery, nor the factory function as normal sites of production. Instead their social, religious, or economic role has been subverted, since they have been appropriated and perverted for either sexual or monetary ends. Although sexuality appears to be the shared subtext of all these social institutions, since it represents their principles of social exchange or consumer economy, this perception is soon qualified. The last example in the book, that of Dalville's château where he abuses his subjects both as laborers and as sexual objects, demonstrates that their status as autonomous subjects is totally in question, since the perversion of the social order is equated with the production of false currency. Thus the sexual referent, although universal, is no more privileged than any of the other terms of the novel, since it can also be subject to an economy of simulation. Just as money can be counterfeited and thus function within the social domain, so can sexuality be reified, objectified, and perverted from its legitimate reproductive functions. Social institutions whose previous aims involved the cumulative interest of social production or reproduction are demystified as purveyors of expenditure – that is to say, waste.

To these central models of social exchange we may also add the production of knowledge, whose ideological underpinnings are elucidated by Sade in his parody of scientific discourse. The methodology of scientific knowledge, particularly the experimental method, is caricatured in order to reveal that science, like religion, relies on a set of beliefs that blinds the observer/believer to the scandalous implications of the method. Sophie's encounter with the surgeon Rodin, a researcher who practices vivisection of the sexual organs, reveals the fact that even medical discourse relies on a concept of knowledge whose methods imply the reduction of subjects to objects, that is, the pleasure principle of manipulation and power. Medical knowledge is equated with Dalville's counterfeit money, to the extent that both rely on sexuality only as a means to something else. In the first case sexuality makes possible the discovery of new ideas; in the second case, sexuality is a vehicle for the production of false currency which stands in for the ideas. Within this economy of total simulation, neither sexuality nor ideas can function legitimately. As simulated products of an economy of waste which dispenses with the subject, both sexuality and money are exchanged arbitrarily, thereby wreaking havoc on notions of both social production and reproduction.

The superimposition of these different institutional codes within the same context has profound effects on the concept of the individual as a social and private entity. To begin with, the social and the private become indistinguishable within the socialized context of the convent. There is no room either for privacy or, ultimately, for interiority. This can be seen in the advice offered by Omphale to Justine, who tells her that there are no excuses in regard to the law: one cannot apologize by saying that one should not be punished for the breaking a law because one did not know it. As Omphale explains, one must either be instructed by one's companions or guess everything by oneself; without any forewarning one is held responsible and punished for everything (*IV*, p. 123). Omphale's warning is very clear: ignorance is no excuse in the eyes of the law. Consequently, in the Sadean text there is no space, public or private, that escapes the script of the law, since the individual (even at the most private moments) is still within the confines of the social scenario. Justine's useless efforts to retain her personal identity within the context of the perverted convent of Ste. Marie des Bois represent Sade's radical critique of the humanist interpretation of man as an autonomous individual entity. Even the body, which is the index of the personal, is victimized in such a way as to transgress the concept of the body as a private property. It is not by accident that the Sadean body has often been compared to a machine, since its impersonal and mechanical character best represents the technical inscription of ideology upon the body. This is why the protagonists in Sade demonstrate a lack of self-consciousness in the psychological sense, or, from a theological perspective, a lack of spiritual interiority. Sade parodies St. Paul's dictum in Romans that the law is not the letter but the spirit. In his works, there is only the law as the letter and no spirit.

In *The Misfortunes of Virtue*, Justine's refusal to recognize the function of the law as an emblem of the social symbolic leads to her ultimate destruction, ironically by nature rather than by society. This ironic ending, which we shall examine later in more detail, reflects Sade's exploration and final assimilation of the natural to the social. Justine/Sophie's death by a thunderbolt, which is her "unjust punishment" in the world of the novel, reflects her complicitous relation to popular ideology: her identification with the order of representation based on conventional moral principles. She represents the bad reader, the reader who mistakes the material and signifying levels of the text. In the novel, it is exactly her conceit regarding a certain way that representation behaves, or its exemplarity, which is constantly tested and negated. Despite the overtly sadistic victimization of the heroine and, by extension, the traditional reader, it becomes clear, following Foucault's observation, that the "object of sadism" in the novel is not ultimately the heroine, but "everything that might have been said" – that is, conventional discourse.[11] Insofar as the heroine herself is a representation of the reader, it is her bad faith as a reader and good faith as a character that constitute the plot of the text and the texture of her misfortunes.

FROM THE BEDROOM TO THE DEATHBED OF PHILOSOPHY

If *The Misfortunes of Virtue* represents a heroine whose misfortunes derive from her inability to learn from her experiences, *Philosophy in the Bedroom* presents the counter-scenario of a

heroine whose erotic education leads to the facile equation
of eroticism with perversion and crime. The title of the
novel *Philosophy in the Bedroom* encapsulates the paradoxical
content of the work, its effort to combine eroticism and
philosophy. However, despite the overt affiliations of this
novel to other erotic novels in the eighteenth century and
to the materialist philosophy of D'Holbach and Helvétius,
it soon becomes clear that neither eroticism nor philosophy
is treated in a traditional way.[12] As the following analysis
will show, Sade is not simply using philosophy as a pretext
for the presentation of erotic scenes, or vice versa. Rather,
his exploration of perverse sexuality and crime corresponds to
and reflects his effort to destroy the foundations of rationalist
thought. Perversion, understood in these terms, takes the
sexual referent as its point of departure in order to take to
task theoretical thought itself.

The dialogue form of *Philosophy in the Bedroom* and its theatrical character present problems for the reader. The narrative
level, or what is told, is enacted and staged for the reader
while at the same time providing theoretical justification. As
Sollers has noted, word, gesture, and thought are brought
together within a global theatre which is the "writing of the
inadmissible."[13] The problem for the reader is that the identification with the erotic scene as the stage of desire is constantly
interrupted by philosophical disquisitions which threaten to
mislead the reader into a criminal relation to the text. The
violation of the traditional norms that govern the relation
between reader and novel, novel and reality, corresponds to
the perverse representation of sexuality and reason. As Michel
Tort observes: "We find a correspondence in Sade's work
between the theoretical law of maximizing perverse deviation,
and a theory of the evolution of novelistic forms and their
necessary exhaustion."[14] This correspondance in Sade's work
between a theory of perversity and the use of deviant novelistic
forms will be the springboard for our discussion of the status of
representation and its philosophical conditions. In reading the
novel more closely, we shall demonstrate that the perversity is
not merely an incidental aspect of the novel, but rather that

it reflects Sade's theory of representation and his critique of classical reason.

Despite the overt erotic and licentious content of *Philosophy in the Bedroom*, the reader quickly becomes aware of the fact that both the erotic body and the nature of pleasure are being redefined. The problem is that the incessant couplings and scramblings of body parts defy not only our conventional notion of sexuality but also, more importantly, the autonomy of the body as the bearer and purveyor of pleasure. Eugénie's initiation to sexuality by her two "teachers," Mme de Saint-Ange and Dolmancé (who are brother and sister), rapidly progresses into perverse activities. The conventions that define both the anatomy and the functions of the "natural" body are wilfully ignored in order to redefine the body and the pleasures traditionally associated with it. Mme de Saint-Ange's explanation as to why there are so many mirrors in her bedroom clarifies the status of the libertine body in the novel:

By repeating our attitudes and postures in a thousand different ways, they infinitely multiply those same pleasures for the persons seated here upon this ottoman. Thus everything is visible, no part of the body can remain hidden: everything must be seen; these images are so many groups disposed around those enchained by love, so many delicious tableaux where lewdness waxes drunk and which soon drive it to its climax. (*PB*, p. 203)

Mme de Saint-Ange's reply elucidates the status of sexuality in the novel. Pleasure is no longer based on the natural body, nor on its conventional associations. Rather the natural body is supplemented here by the pleasures incited by its replication through images. The limits of the natural body are extended through mirrors whose reflections generate an infinitely fragmented and deformed representation of sexuality. The effort to make the body totally visible, so that nothing may remain hidden, results in the multiplication of the body as "delicious tableaux." These "mirror" images of the body redefine pleasure as a perverse excess generated through representation. The "pleasure principle" governing the Sadean text no longer affirms the autonomy of the conventional body, but rather its deviation and multiplication through perverse representations. Perversion is no longer the expression of particular forms of deviation, but emerges as a general attitude towards representation.

In the novel, the body is no longer presented according to classical conventions, asking to be deciphered, decoded, or interpreted. As Hénaff observes, the body in Sade exhibits no symptoms, it is not enigmatic, and knows no content other than that of its libertine context. The sexual expenditure of the body requires a language proper to expenditure – that of use value, not the referential language of communication or interpretation. The body is defined purely by its functionality, and as such is reduced to a machine (recalling De la Mettrie), but a machine that exists only as a hook-up to other machines. Given this purely functional interpretation of the body, it is not surprising that cruelty may become equated with and supersede pleasure. As Dolmancé explains:

it is purely a question of exposing our nervous system to the most violent possible shock; now there is no doubt that we are much more keenly affected by pain than by pleasure: the reverberations that result in us when the sensation of pain is produced in others will essentially be of a more vigorous character . . . (PB, p. 252)

Pain is described in terms of its shock value, recalling Sade's description, in his *Reflections on the Novel*, as to why he chose to write about subjects that inspire shock and terror. Following Sade's perverse logic, the representation of pain "reverberates" or mirrors sensation more effectively than pleasure. Cruelty can in fact be experienced purely as a mental representation that generates physical effects: "Look, Madame, do you see it? Do you see this libertine discharge *mentally*, without anyone having touched her?" (PB, p. 288). The body here becomes incidental, since the imagination can represent events whose shock value exceeds that of reality. Instead of investing sexuality in the body in a material sense, Sade suggests that the materiality of sexuality is in the order of representation. By positing cruelty as a new kind of pleasure principle, Sade perversely undermines the mind–body dualism, in order to challenge the limits of both reason and the natural body through representation.

Having undermined the hierarchical separation of the mind and the body and demonstrated their interchangeability as organs of pleasure, Sade proceeds to question further the identity of the body. In *Philosophy in the Bedroom*, the body is presented as an undifferentiated entity, whose orifices are indistinguishable by reference to pleasure:

For no one will wish to maintain that all the parts of the body do not *resemble* each other, that there are some which are pure, and others defiled; but, as it is unthinkable that such nonsense be advanced seriously . . . (*PB*, pp. 325–26; emphasis added)

The traditional distinctions and hierarchies that describe the body are abolished, in order to define the body through the principle of resemblance. The cultural conventions that valorize certain parts of the body in order to exclude others are denounced, so that the entire body may become the purveyor of pleasure. By affirming the functional resemblance of all the parts of the body, Sade is scrambling its conventional definition, in order to constitute the libertine body through perversion and parody. Not content to question the identity of the body, Sade goes on to ask what man is, and why he occupies a privileged place in the world:

What is man? and what difference is there between him and other plants, between him and all the other animals of the world? None, obviously . . . Since the parallels are so exact that the inquiring eye of philosophy is absolutely unable to perceive any grounds for discrimination [*dissemblance*], there is just as much evil in killing animals as men, or just as little, and whatever be the distinctions we make, they will be found to stem from our pride's prejudices, than which, unhappily, nothing is more absurd. (*PB*, pp. 329–30)

By refusing to acknowledge a philosophical basis for man's distinctive place in the hierarchy of natural beings, Sade destroys man's foundational position. His argument, that man resembles all the other natural beings so closely that even philosophy is unable to establish any fundamental difference between them, threatens all moral distinctions. The resemblance between men and animals endangers man's identity (or self-resemblance): his preservation and immunity

from crime. Sade's overt refusal to appeal to reason as the
distinguishing trait that separates men from animals reflects
his philosophical position rejecting transcendental categories
based on foundational difference.[15] As such, it represents both
an attack on and a dismissal of the Cartesian definition of man.
Sade's effort to assimilate man to animal reflects his concept
of nature, which is both undifferentiated and indifferent. By
denying man's privileged position in nature, Sade reopens the
question of man's definition and relation to nature.

Sade's gesture represents an explicit attack on the theological foundation of man made in the likeness of God.
For the libertine is a new kind of (wo)man, whose likeness
has been rendered incoherent by the incessant scrambling
of all the different parts. The libertine does not resemble
"man" as a universal type, lacking the internal coherence
that defines the identity of the classical subject. Rather, the
libertine resembles him or herself excessively, since identity
is constituted through a play of simulations. The libertine's
identity is conceived as a copy with no prototype, a subject that
knows no originary or foundational moment. Consequently,
Sade's definition of "man" differs radically from the criteria
used during the Enlightenment. By questioning the specificity
and the sovereignty of man, as a being different from other
natural beings, Sade challenges the humanist interpretation of
man, espoused by tradition from St. Augustine and Montaigne
to Diderot and Rousseau.

The Sadean critique of traditional humanism is based on
his concept of nature, which is no longer simply an object for
contemplation or manipulation, but rather a new source for
poetic inspiration. Sade's elaboration of libertine philosophy is
grounded in an understanding of nature, which is free of moral
connotations: nature is described as possessing no inherent
distinctions in its organization. Vice and virtue are represented
by Dolmancé as being equal in respect to nature: "one single
motor is operative in this universe, and that motor is Nature.
The miracles – rather, the physical effects – of this mother of
the human race, differently interpreted by men, have been dei-
fied by them under a thousand forms, each more extraordinary

than the other . . ." (*PB*, p. 360). This lack of difference or distinguishing traits in nature impairs man's effort to establish moral distinctions, as well as uphold his sovereign status. The problem is that nature is both "motor" and "mother," that is to say, an originary principle which generates the effect of difference while resembling itself. The notion of difference only comes into play as men attempt to interpret nature, and thereby disrupt, through difference, the governing principle of resemblance. The space of nature is presented in terms of the excess generated through resemblance, thereby equating it with the space of parody.[16] Considered from this perspective, culture is no longer conceived as the obverse of nature, but rather as a mirror of its already perverse principles. Given this interpretation of nature, it is not surprising that Sade attacks the laws which affirm the preservation of humanity, through either marriage or the interdiction of crime.

Having redefined nature as an undifferentiated principle, and thereby affirmed the arbitrary character of human conventions, Sade proceeds in *Philosophy in the Bedroom* to parody the law of incest, the very principle that separates nature from culture. His preposterous effort to valorize incest must be understood as the logical result of his attempt *ad absurdum* to describe nature in a new way. By hypothesizing the undifferentiated and indifferent character of nature, Sade frees himself to make the most absurd fictional claims. This is because the notion of "natural law" is for him merely a projection of man-made fictions. In his pseudo-revolutionary pamphlet, "One more effort, Frenchmen, if you are to become Republicans" (which constitutes a dominant section of *Philosophy in the Bedroom*), Dolmancé outrageously contends that incest is the law of all republican governments based on fraternity (*PB*, p. 242). Sade's bitterly ironic claim represents his violent attempt to parody revolutionary rhetoric. As an exponent of fraternity, Sade is haunted by his own precarious position as a victim who only accidentally escaped being guillotined during the Terror.[17] By interpreting the notion of fraternity literally as incest, Sade parodies and reveals the violent underpinnings of the discourse of liberty.

Dolmancé goes on to explain why incest may become the
new law of the revolutionary state: "If, in a word, love is born
of *resemblance*, where may it be more perfect than between
brother and sister, between father and daughter?" (*PB*, p.
236, emphasis added). Sade redefines the principle of erotic
love as no longer being based on sexual or cultural difference.
By positing *resemblance* as the principle of love, Sade perversely
arrives at incest as the necessary conclusion of his social and
philosophical parody. Filial and fraternal love is privileged,
since, as Sade explains elsewhere, an incestuous marriage
provides "double reason to love."[18] His use of this phrase
suggests that the scandal of incest is tied to the duplication,
and hence deregulation, of heretofore socially incompatible
categories. Thus both eroticism and writing share a similar
fate in Sade's work: as discourses of resemblance, their true
referent is the order of representation itself. But representation
here no longer means the imitation of reality according to
convention, but rather its systematic destruction through the
deviant movement engendered by parody.

The outrage perpetrated by Sade's incestuous discourse
undermines the notion of nature by substituting for it the fictitious space of parody. Josué Harari suggests that "the crime
of writing" exceeds the limits of the real, since the premedi-
tated character of Sade's incestuous narrative transforms the
relation between theory and practice by valorizing fiction.[19]
The originality of Sadean discourse resides less in its efforts to
transgress the real than in its success in redefining literature
itself as a deviant, and even criminal, activity. By equating
writing with perversity and crime, Sade redefines nature as
the referent of his authorial project. Thus his obsession with
incest reflects an effort to rethink nature in terms of his theory
of representation, which is based on resemblance. If incest
is a privileged term in this investigation, this is because it
embodies the very scandal of representation. Incest is the
index of a social, and hence a linguistic, crisis: it represents
the capacity to combine unassimilable social categories and
thus generate fictitious predicates.

This attempt to violate the natural social order by mixing

and scrambling social and linguistic categories can be seen in *Juliette*, where Noirceuil presents his ultimate fantasy of perverse marriage. He wants to marry twice on the same day, impersonating both roles, man and woman, while imitated by Juliette, who, transvested as a man, would marry another woman:

It is a most extraordinary caprice I have been dwelling on for a very long time, Juliette. . . . I should like to marry . . . twice, and upon the same day . . . at noon, in masculine attire, I wish to take a bardash for my wife. There is still more . . . I wish to have a woman do the same as I; and what other woman but you could participate in this Fantasy? You, dressed as a man, must wed a tribade at the same ceremony at which I, guised as a woman, become the wife of a man; next, dressed as a woman, you will wed another tribade wearing masculine clothing, at the very moment I, having resumed my ordinary attire, go to the altar to become united in holy matrimony with a catamite disguised as a girl."[20]

Sade's scenario represents the ultimate perversion of nature, since the false replication of gender roles generates the ultimate incest fantasy, that of a marriage of the like where man and woman both marry their own sex. Hénaff comments on this scene by noting Sade's desire to permutate and exhaust all possible sexual positions.[21] However, this first type of chiasmus, of saturation in an encyclopedic sense, is accompanied by an even more radical gesture. For the desire for totality is accompanied by the production of an excess *beyond* totality. Noirceuil's demand to be imitated by Juliette, as he imitates himself as a man, creates an excess of signification which can no longer be accommodated in the order of representation.[22] Marriage as the social union of difference, as an exogamous relation, is doubly reenacted on the same day, each time with the same sexual partners. This fantasy of mimicry becomes the figurative index of incest as a space of pure parody. The free circulation of all the predicates of sexuality, their arbitrary accumulation and expenditure, de-essentializes both gender and the moral values attached to it. The sexual referent of the Sadean text thus emerges as pure simulacrum: a copy without a real referent, that is, the principle of parody itself.

Unlike the materialist thinkers of his day, Helvétius and D'Holbach, Sade does not simply revert to a naturalistic ideology.[23] He does not valorize nature as a new idol; on the contrary, he attempts to negate it and defile it, and yet nature eludes him.[24] Since Sade views even crime and evil as part of the workings of nature, the efforts to negate nature further confirm her principles. Nature thus represents a philosophical and moral scandal, since man can adopt neither an exterior nor a sovereign position in relation to it. The crisis that nature presents for the characters, as well as the author, is a crisis that can be resolved only by challenging the notion of representation itself. Given the fact that nature is a perverse representation, Sade's solution is to copy it and infinitely perpetuate it:

yes, I abhor Nature; and I detest her because I know her well. Aware of her frightful secret, I have fallen back on myself and I have felt . . . I have experienced a kind of pleasure in copying her foul deeds . . . Should I love such a mother? No; but I will imitate her, all the while detesting her, I shall copy her, as she wishes, but I shall curse her unceasingly . . .[25]

Almani's comment in *Juliette* summarizes Sade's dilemma as an author who, forced to copy nature, uses imitation as a form of denunciation. This copy, like any other representation, resembles nature and deviates from it at the same time. By presenting the task of copying nature as a burden, Sade parodies Boileau's injunction in *L'Art poétique*: "Imitate nature, only nature is true." Whereas for Boileau nature signifies a perfect ideal, for Sade it signifies crime and evil, hence the burden of its representation. Rather than defining the task of the writer in terms of verisimilitude (*vraisemblance*), understood as the appearance of truth in fidelity to nature, Sade defies the conventions of novelistic plausibility. His "fidelity" to nature is no longer based on idealization; rather it represents his perverse interpretation of literature. While claiming to copy nature, Sade chooses to depict its most deviant manifestations, thereby revealing that the "truth" of nature is in the order of parody.

Sade's perverse pleasure as an author replicating images

of nature echoes Mme de Saint-Ange's description of the libertine's pleasure at seeing the body multiplied through reflections. For both, perversion is the figure of the excess generated through *re-presentation*, understood as the copy of a prior or pre-given presentation. By simulating nature through parody, Sade opens up the exploration of a new novelistic space, where the principle of fiction is elevated to a new "reality" which exceeds the constraints of the dichotomy of both nature and culture.[26] Rather than accepting the traditional division between theory and practice, Sade stages the contamination of philosophy through the writing of fiction. By elaborating a theory of representation based on parody, Sade mockingly stages the hypostasis of erotic and criminal pleasure: the coincidence of the "bedroom" and the "death-bed" of philosophy.

THE IMPOSSIBLE AS LITERATURE

Having outlined the most salient aspects of Sade's theory of representation, we shall now return to the question of why transgression is an inadequate term to describe Sade's writings. If we go back to Foucault's formulation, in his "Preface to transgression," it becomes clearer why this term fails to account for the liminal character of Sade's work:

Transgression does not seek to oppose one thing to another, nor does it achieve its purpose through mockery or by upsetting the solidity of foundations; . . . Transgression is neither violence in a divided world (in an ethical world) nor a victory over limits (in a dialectical or revolutionary world); and exactly for this reason its role is to measure the excessive distance that it opens at the heart of the limit and to trace the flashing line that causes the limit to arise.[27]

Foucault correctly emphasizes the fact that transgression must be dissociated from its negative ethical and dialectical associations, and thus from an oppositional logic. However, he situates the domain of transgression outside both parody and the question of philosophical foundations. His formulation is both a critique and an elaboration of Klossowski's and Bataille's philosophical recovery of transgression into an anti-theology, by affirming Nietzsche's and Blanchot's "'yes' of contestation."

By not considering the bitterly ironic and caricature-like character of Sade's representations of transgression, the philosophical readings of Sade foreclose the interrogation of its literary character. Foucault's interpretation of transgression as a gesture beyond "mockery" or parody implies that transgression as a philosophical gesture may exceed the limits of literature, while inevitably tracing out its impossible and excessive outline. The problem is that the encyclopedic aspects of Sadean discourse are bracketed in Sade's work by the foreclosure of classical representation, not merely by extending its limits (its transgressive function), but by actually short-circuiting its codes and discourses (its parodic function). Consequently, the excess produced in the order of representation through parody results in the abolition of difference and the unassimilable deferral within representation of the possibility of constituting a foundational order.

Sade's complicitous relation to nature and to his own position as writer-victim is made explicit in *Reflections on the Novel*. In one of the most celebrated passages of this work, he elucidates the status of the writer in relation to nature by claiming that as the "son" and "lover of nature" the writer must become her incestuous lover:

O you who wish to venture upon this difficult and thorny career, bear ever in mind that the novelist is the child of Nature, that she has created him to be her painter; if he does not become his mother's lover the moment she gives birth to him, let him never write, for we shall never read him. But if he feels that burning need to portray everything, if, with fear and trembling he probes into the bosom of Nature, in search of his art and for models to discover, if he possesses the fever of talent and the enthusiasm of genius, let him follow the hand that leads him; once having divined man, he will paint him. (*RN*, pp. 110–11)

This comment allows us to bring together our reflections on both representation and nature. Briefly, Sade's description of the novelist as the true man of nature involves the fundamental task of representing nature. However, this relation of depiction (*peindre*) is interpreted by Sade according to the logic of parody as an incestuous relationship, a relation of crime and complicity. As nature's lover and son, he situates the novelistic project in the cultural space, where the imitation of nature is perverted through the deployment of a scandalous filiation. The task of the author, according to Sade, is not simply to replicate nature, but to imitate its sublime excesses. The act of writing is tied to the production of excess in the domain of representation, which because of its parodic nature disrupts irrevocably the conventional formulation of novelistic mimesis. The attempt to mimic nature, by being truly faithful to her designs, leads to the complicitous identification of the hand of nature with that of the author. While appearing to follow Nature ("the hand that leads him"), the hand of the author incestuously traces out the criminal excesses of literature.

A similar incident appears at the end of *Philosophy in the Bedroom*, where Eugénie's apprenticeship culminates in the attempt to violate the maternal body by becoming the putative lover of nature. Eugénie's perverse education in *Philosophy in the Bedroom* results in her rewriting her natural origins through the violation of her mother's body. Her figurative incest with her mother, which is accompanied by the sewing up of the latter's genitals with a red thread (a gesture doubled by Dolmancé's sewing up of her anus) enacts in a fantastic and violent sense Sade's definition of the novelist as the lover of nature.[28] The equation of the gesture of writing (as a stand-in for culture) reifies and displaces the maternal body (as a site for natural reproduction). Eugénie's violent marking of her mother's body is already the repetition of the marks of flagellation administered by her libertine father. Eugénie's violent emergence into the symbolic order can be seen as the doubling of paternal violence and the inscription of its patriarchal legacy upon the maternal body. However, this equation of culture and violence also becomes the site for the reinscription of the opposition of nature and culture, since by denaturing nature Eugénie, like the Sadean author, redefines the project of writing as a criminal gesture whose violence disrupts the function of nature as origin and generator of categories.

Eugénie's suture of the maternal body excludes it from a natural system of social reproduction and exchange that describes female sexuality. The mother's body is saturated by totality, generating an excess beyond totality. Thus the gesture of simulation produces an incalculable excess, that of the play of representation itself. The violence of this operation upon the mother, described in clinical terms, mimics the violence of the act of writing. As a simulacrum of nature, the maternal body becomes at the same time the site of transgression of the order of nature, which it ostensibly copies. Eugénie's sewing needle and red thread figure, through this process of disfiguration, the position of the writer in Sade, whose pen has become a sewing-needle. Thus writing embodies through this violent patchwork the doubly gendered hand of a feminine nature and masculine culture.

The ending of *The Misfortunes of Virtue* presents yet another scenario of writing as a criminal activity. The arbitrary destruction of Justine, just as she is beginning to enjoy the fruits of virtue, once again functions as a sign of the perverse complicity of the novelist and nature. It is as if her sense of destiny as a victim invites and prescribes her final violation: her death by a lightning bolt at the hands of nature. Justine's grotesque destruction and erasure from the world of the novel etches upon her body the disfiguring material trace of nature, which she had always refused to acknowledge: "Lightning had entered by the right breast, it burned the chest, and came out through her mouth, disfiguring her face so much that it inspired horror" (*IV*, p. 184). The final disfiguration of Justine by the lightning bolt, the mark of the arbitrary character of Nature, summarizes Sade's effort to present historical being by equating it with natural contingency. Passing through the right breast and coming out through the mouth, writing emerges as a process of figuration that reproduces the body through disfiguration. Having functioned as a mere mouthpiece for values that did not come from the heart, Justine's caricatural existence is erased by the hand of the author, mimic and lover of nature. The perverse fidelity of the author, as the incestuous lover of nature, becomes transfigured in the act of writing presented undecidably as the hand of both nature and man. This undecidability reveals something fundamental about the function of representation in Sade: the refusal to found a stable principle for representation. Through the expenditure of mimesis, as an endless play of simulations, the Sadean text represents itself as a copy with no original, as pure parody. In *The Misfortunes of Virtue*, this undecidability is put to an end only when all representation stops: when the author puts down his or her pen and/or sewing-needle.

In conclusion, we are left to ponder Sade's peculiar position in the history of literature. In so doing we turn to Sollers's provocative question regarding the paradoxical legacy of the Sadean text for modernity: "How is it that Sade is at once prohibited and accepted, prohibited as fiction (as writing) and accepted as reality; forbidden as general reading and accepted as psychological and physiological reference?"[29] For Sollers, the fact is at issue that "we have not truly yet decided to read Sade," meaning that conventional readings are unable to account for the fact that in his writings, nature is the fiction of culture. Sollers's question summarizes in a radical fashion the objections that this study has raised to reading Sade as a transgressive author. Even if we regard the space of transgression as a positive space of contestation, the fact remains that such readings uphold sexuality as the ultimate referent of the contestation of the real. By maintaining the distinction between fiction and reality, without understanding how Sade erodes their mutual boundaries through parody, the transgressive readings reinforce the paradox of the Sadean text being banned as fiction, while at the same time being upheld as the referent of our psychological and physiological reality.

Can Sade's literary representation of sexuality be banned, while sexuality itself is given a "extra-literary" status? As this study has demonstrated, the Sadean project, as reflected in both his novelistic practice and his philosophical reflections, can be better understood as a discourse of parody, whose strategic imitation of previous literary and philosophical conventions upsets the very traditions that it simulates. The sexual referent in the Sadean text has no more privilege than the nature it ostensibly replicates. The sexual fortunes or misfortunes of the Sadean heroines are profoundly literary. The eroticism of the Sadean text is not defined by the choice of objects it chooses to represent, be they the body, perversity or crime. Rather, eroticism is a reflection of Sade's interpretation of writing as a complicitous, perverse, and at times even criminal gesture. As Simone de Beauvoir has pertinently noted: "It was not murder that fullfilled Sade's erotic nature: it was literature."[30]

NOTES

1 Charles Baudelaire, "Projects et notes diverses," in *Oeuvres complètes* (Paris: Seuil, 1968), p. 705 (my translation).

2 For Georges Bataille's writings on Sade, see chapter 1, this volume; "L'homme souverain de Sade" and "Sade et l'homme normal," in *L'Erotisme* (Paris: Minuit, 1957) and "Sade" in *La Littérature et le mal* (Paris: Gallimard, 1957); also see Pierre Klossowski, *Sade mon prochain* (Paris: Seuil, 1967); Maurice Blanchot, *Lautréamont et Sade* (Paris: Union Générale d'Editions, 1967). For a general account of these three major contributors, see Jane Gallop, *Intersections: A Reading of Sade with Bataille, Blanchot, and Klossowski* (Lincoln: University of Nebraska Press, 1981).

3 Michel Foucault, "A Preface to Transgression," in *Language, Counter-Memory, Practice*, intro. and trans. Donald F. Bouchard and Sherry Simon (Ithaca: Cornell University Press, 1977), p. 31.

4 See Foucault's comments on representation in *Les Mots et les choses* (Paris: Gallimard, 1966), pp. 60–91.

5 All references to these works will be to the following translations: *Reflections on the Novel*, henceforth abbreviated as *RN*, is from The Marquis de Sade, *The 120 Days of Sodom and Other Writings*, trans. Austryn Wainhouse and Richard Seaver (New York: Grove Press, 1966); *Philosophy in the Bedroom*, abbreviated *PB*, is from The Marquis de Sade, *Justine, Philosophy in the Bedroom and Other Writings*, trans. Richard Seaver and Austryn Wainhouse (New York: Grove Press, 1965).

6 Aristotle observes that "Fear and pity can be caused by the spectacle or by the plot structure itself": from *The Poetics*, in *On Poetry and Style*, trans. G. M. A. Grube (New York: Bobbs

and Merrill, 1979), p. 26. Aristotle's partiality for plot as the favored vehicle for eliciting emotion is parodied by Sade's exaggerated plots.

7 Villeterque's review of *Les Crimes de l'Amour* first appeared in *Le Journal des Arts, des Sciences, et de la Littérature* 90 (October 22, 1800), pp. 281–84; reprinted in The Marquis de Sade, *The 120 Days of Sodom and Other Writings*, pp. 117–19, as "Villeterque's Review of *Les Crimes de l'Amour*." Sade's response appears in the same volume, pp. 121–29, as "The author of *Les Crimes de l'Amour* to Villeterque hack writer"; henceforth abbreviated as *SV*.

8 All the references to *The Misfortunes of Virtue* are to the commonly available paperback edition of *Les Infortunes de la vertu* (Paris: Garnier-Flammarion, 1969), abbreviated as *IV* (my translations).

9 Maurice Blanchot, "Sade," a reprint of a section of *Lautréamont et Sade* in The Marquis de Sade, *Justine, Philosophy in the Bedroom, and Other Writings*, p. 57.

10 Marcel Hénaff, *Sade: L'invention du corps libertin* (Paris: Presses Universitaires de France, 1978), p. 205. Instead of an industrial model, I have chosen to use here a mercantile one, which describes concepts of social exchange and production more adequately.

11 Michel Foucault, "Language to infinity," in *Language, Counter-Memory, Practice*, p. 62.

12 For a general analysis of the writings and trends of thought of the Enlightenment, see Daniel Mornet, *La Pensée française au XVIIIe siècle* (Paris: Colin, 1965).

13 Philippe Sollers, "Sade dans le texte," *Tel Quel* 28 (1967), p. 44; my translation.

14 Michel Tort, "L'effet Sade," *Tel Quel* 28 (1967), p. 78.

15 Sade's critique of the notion of foundational difference anticipates Martin Heidegger's definition of "ontological difference," understood as the "differentiation of beings and Being," in *Nietzsche*, vol. IV: *Nihilism*, trans. Frank A. Capuzzi and ed. David F. Krell (San Francisco: Harper & Row, 1982), pp. 153–55.

16 Jean Fabre suggests that Sade's concept of Nature founds a new tradition that must be distinguished from the classical interpretations of Nature; *Idées sur le roman: de Madame de Lafayette au Marquis de Sade* (Paris: Klincksieck, 1979), p. 187.

17 For an interpretation of Sade's writing as escape from physical detention, see Béatrice Didier, *Sade: une écriture du désir* (Paris: Denoël-Gonthier, 1976).

18 See *Eugénie de Franval* in *Justine, Philosophy in the Bedroom, and Other Writings*, p. 119.

19 For an analysis of incest and its relation to poetic practice in Sade's works, see Josué V. Harari, *Scenarios of the Imaginary* (Ithaca and London: Cornell University Press, 1987), pp. 172–87.

20 The Marquis de Sade, *Oeuvres complètes* (Paris: Pauvert, 1956–70), vol. IX, p. 569; *Juliette*, p. 1175.

21 Hénaff, *Sade*, pp. 44–48.

22 Cf. Barthes's comment that the crime of incest involves a transgression of semantic rules by creating homonymy: it makes "one signified receive simultaneously several signifiers that are traditionally distinct." This leads him to conclude that transgression is merely a linguistic ploy, one of naming outside lexical divisions: the "act *contra-naturum* is exhausted in an utterance of counter-language": *Sade, Fourier, Loyola* (Paris: Seuil, 1971), pp. 137–38.

23 For a discussion of Sade's interpretation of Nature in relation to D'Holbach and Helvétius see Pierre Naville, "Sade et la philosophie," in *Oeuvres complètes*, vol. XI.

24 Blanchot suggests that Sade's struggle with nature represents a more advanced dialectical stage than his struggle with God, since by showing that the notion of nothingness or non-being belongs to the world, "one cannot conceive of the world's non-being except from within a totality, which is still the world": in The Marquis de Sade, *Justine, Philosophy in the Bedroom, and Other Writings*, p. 63.

25 Cited by Pierre Klossowski, "Nature as destructive principle," in *120 Days of Sodom*, pp. 72–73.

26 Cf. Barthes, who distinguishes the conventions of the social and realistic novel from the conventions of the Sadean novel by describing the latter as the "repeated production of a practice (and not of an historical 'picture')": *Sade, Fourier* ... p. 131.

27 Foucault, *Language, Counter-Memory, Practice*, p. 35.

28 Barthes describes this gesture of sewing in Sade as follows: "To sew is finally to remake a world without sewing, to return from the divinely cut-up body – whose cut-up state is the source of all Sadean pleasure – to the abjection of the smooth body, the total body": *Sade, Fourier* ..., p. 169.

29 "Sade dans le texte," p. 38.

30 "Must we burn Sade?," in The Marquis de Sade, *The 120 Days of Sodom and Other Writings*, p. 33.

CHAPTER 9

Structures of exchange, acts of transgression

Allen S. Weiss

> Copulation and mirrors are abominable. For one of those gnostics, the visible universe was an illusion or (more precisely) a sophism. Mirrors and fatherhood are abominable because they multiply and disseminate that universe.
>
> Jorge Luis Borges, *Tlön, Uqbar, Orbis Tertius*

Numerous modes of contemporary theory hold that thought, and the structure of subjectivity itself, are functions of the dominant conditions of expressibility. This stance implies that the structure of subjectivity is not a function of psychic topology, but rather one of linguistic/poetic tropology. Following Nietzsche, Foucault writes that the purpose of genealogy is "to reveal the heterogeneous systems which, masked by the self, inhibit the formation of any form of identity."[1] The self is a fiction acting as a form of identity; the heterogeneous systems are the various plays of tropes and figures that simultaneously form the fictive self and undermine its ultimate possibility as stable form. The central problem of hermeneutics thus becomes the description of the manner in which the self is formed and maintained by the figurative structures of expression. In asking "What does that mean?" one must necessarily demand "Who is speaking?"; and in asking "Who is speaking?" one must necessarily demand "How was it said?" One might go so far as to claim that the personal voice suffuses all texts: one must discover the tropes and figures that dissimulate it. Conversely, the subject of any text or enunciation is maintained by the figural/tropic structure of the discourse: again, we must reveal and examine these tropes and figures in order to realize the tentative, and ultimately narrative, structure of all discourse of "Truth."

I wish to investigate one such rhetorical structure: the *chiasm*. In traditional rhetoric, the chiasm (*chiasmus*) is formed by the inversion of syntactical elements in the second of two juxtaposed clauses. This AB/BA structure thus determines the form of reversal, making it an exemplary figure of mimesis. The chiasm reveals a figure in the form of a mirror, which explains the fascination that it holds for many writers. Jean-François Lyotard, writing on Merleau-Ponty, claims that the chiasm is, "the figure constitutive of the sensible, the figure constitutive of figures."[2] It is the figure of sensibility because of the reversible structure of the "flesh"; the figure of figures because of the exchangeable economy of signs. Yet while the privileged use of the chiasm to express the structure of subjectivity and intersubjectivity must be investigated, so too must we investigate the manner in which the placement of the chiasm within different textual systems determines different models of subjectivity. The discovery of a figure or trope as the organizational principle of a textual system (or as the constitutive aspect of a model of subjectivity) must itself be understood only as yet another figure, and not as a foundation. Deconstruction, or genealogy, does not lead to foundational structures; it only provides the means of uncovering varied series of tropes and figures. It might be said that the foundation of meaning is to be found in the sum total of the differences among all possible expressions within a system, among all possible figures, and never as any single given figure.

In *Juliette*, Sade presents the following phantasm of the libertine character Noirceuil:

It is a most extraordinary fantasy I have been dwelling upon for a very long time, Juliette, and I have been awaiting your return with impatience, having in all the world nobody but you with whom I could satisfy it. I should like to marry . . . I should like to get married, not once, but twice, and upon the same day: at ten o'clock in the morning, I wish, dressed as a woman, to wed a man; at noon, in masculine attire, I wish to take a bardash for my wife. There is still more ... I wish to have a woman imitate me; and what other woman but you could participate in this fantasy? You, dressed as a man, must wed a tribade at the same mass at which I, guised as a woman, become the wife of a man; next, dressed as a woman, you will wed another tribade wearing masculine clothing, at the very moment I, having resumed the attire of my sex, will marry a bardash dressed as a girl.[3]

Noirceuil's fantasy presents a complex set of chiasms, the peculiar structures of which should be examined. While the structure of marriage, as a joining of alterity, is not precisely a chiasmatic structure, Sade wishes to extirpate all possibility of a radical alterity, since alterity undermines the structures of mastery. Hence marriage is presented by Sade only in terms of the master. In these ceremonies there are only imitations of Noirceuil, i.e. a multiplication of possibilities by chiasm. The structure of these ceremonies may be schematized as follows:

	Appearance	*Reality*
First mass: (10 a.m.)	Two men marry two women.	Noirceuil, dressed as a woman, marries a man; and Juliette, dressed as a man, marries a tribade. Thus a man marries a man and a woman marries a woman.
Second mass: (Noon)	Two men marry two women.	Noirceuil, dressed as a man, marries a homosexual dressed as a woman; and Juliette, dressed as a woman, marries a tribade dressed as a man. Thus a man marries a man and a woman marries a woman.

The chiasms formed are as follows: (1) Noirceuil dressed as a woman is a reversal of sex roles (as is a homosexual man dressed as a woman); (2) Noirceuil marrying a man reverses the classical structure of matrimony; (3) Juliette dressed as a man is a reversal of sex roles (as is a lesbian dressed as a man); (4) Juliette marrying a woman is a reversal of the classical structure of matrimony; (5) homosexuality and lesbianism reverse "normative" sexual identities (and tribadism, a lesbian practice of imitating heterosexual intercourse, is an ironic form of this reversal); (6) Juliette imitating Noirceuil is a reversal of roles and identities within this fantasy; (7) the two marriages are reversals of each other; (8) there is a manifest reversal of appearance and reality. Every relation within this scene may be construed as chiasmatic. It must be stressed that in no case is a "normal" male/female marriage arranged, and the structures of the reversals are always determined according to Noirceuil's, i.e. the Master's, role. Even Juliette, the "protagonist" of the story, only imitates Noirceuil, hence undoing her identity in the series of scenes through which she passes.

Such "marriages" are certainly not matters of contractual reciprocity, nor of the implied emotional reciprocity of love; they are not at all structures of exchange, but rather modes of formalizing and imitating domination through the permutation and multiplication of attributes and connections. This task, aiming at absolute mastery, exemplifies the Sadean task, and structures the entire Sadean text. As Marcel Hénaff claims, in his study *Sade: L'invention du corps libertin*: "to extend the catalogue is to permutate all of the elements without restriction. Logic is not abandoned: it is made unlimited without reserve. The catalogue is the theater of the unlimited exchange of roles and positions."[4]

Sade aims at the closure of the system, but at a very specific closure, in which there is always a permutational center of power and mastery. Yet even so, the Master too may become victim, within a new and ultimate form of chiasm. A complete possibility of permutation and reversal entails: the closure is structural, not existential. Mastery is a function, almost literally, of manipulation: to organize is to control. In any case, for Sade, totality achieves the extrapolation of multiplicity to closure, eliminating difference by including all possibilities. This technique of expression (and presumed action) empties symbolism of all efficacy, since all possible figurative stances become (or may become) actualized. There is no more "as if," no more latency or ambiguity. Hence the ultimate redundancy of the chiasmatic relations in the previous passage about the marriage: no more is expressed, or acted out, than Noirceuil already knows or desires. No more is symbolized than already exists for Noirceuil. There is no reciprocity at the intersubjective level between the partners of the marriages: there is only pure theatricality, the pure staging of Noirceuil's fantasy. Intersubjectivity is suppressed by pure domination, and this suppression of intersubjectivity, at its limit, inaugurates the possibility of the suppression of subjectivity itself.

Sade expresses his denial of the usual reciprocal implications of the chiasmatic relation in the following quotation from *Philosophy in the Bedroom*, about the use of mirrors, which are the physical instantiations *par excellence* of the chiasm:

Eugénie: Oh dear God! the delicious niche! But why all these mirrors?

Mme de Saint-Ange: By repeating our attitudes and postures in a thousand different ways, they infinitely multiply those same pleasures for the persons seated here upon this ottoman. Thus everything is visible, no part of the body can remain hidden: everything must be seen; these images are so many groups disposed around those enchained by love, so many delicious tableaux wherewith lewdness waxes drunk and which soon drive it to its climax.[5]

This use of mirrors does not express a relation of narcissism or reciprocity, but rather multiplies effects so that all is visible and controllable. This too implies an attempt at closure by exhausting all possibilities. As Hénaff (following Gérard Genette) suggests, the mirror is no longer, as it was for the baroque sensibility, "the privileged instrument of metamorphoses of an unstable, evanescent subject, uncertain of its identity."[6] Rather, for Sade the mirror becomes an instrument for the elimination of subjectivity, an elimination predicated upon a completely exterior control. For Sade, the mirror doesn't complicate the organization of subjectivity, but simply exhibits the stances, positions, and postures of the body. It assures that nothing remains hidden: for Sade this serves the same purposes of power and control as does

Jeremy Bentham's functionally similar *Panopticon*, which is understood by Foucault to be the very architectural figure of control, a control founded upon the minutiæ of observation and confinement.7 The Sadean specular closure parallels the architectural enclosure of the Sadean château.

The baroque mirror serves to create; the Sadean mirror serves to catalogue. The baroque mirror creates distortions which express the interior life; the Sadean mirror empties all interiority into the catalogue of possible stances. Expression becomes no more than position. And the completion of this task is achieved by the all-seeing Master: the mirror permits not only the sight of the other, but also the sight of the entire scene, with nothing hidden, not even the Master. The Master sees everything and says everything; in the Sadean universe these are sufficient conditions for knowing everything. This anti-ontotheological stance entails the replacement of metaphysics by a mechanics, i.e. by a model of manipulation. The actual "philosophy" of *Philosophy in the Bedroom* is just another form of logorrhea as ordering and staging: it is a philosophy of the imperative. What was once transcendent or taboo now becomes a part of the scene. Thus, as Roland Barthes claims, "We better understand upon what and toward what Sade's erotic combinatory rests and tends: its origin and its sanctions are rhetorical."8 This claim may be extended to Sade's entire ontology.

The chiasmatic structure of the mirror operates just like the chiasmatic structure of the marriages: not as a model of intersubjective reciprocity, but as an organization of discourse which eliminates subjectivity itself by eliminating all depth, all latency, and all auto-figuration, except that of the Master. Subjectivity is replaced by subjugation.

Foucault is correct in writing that "The precise object of 'sadism' is not the other, nor his body, nor his sovereignty: it is everything that might have been said."9 Such sadism entails precisely the control of the symbolic by means of its elimination in the literal, by denying the symbolic as openess to difference, to the Other. Hence the monotony of Sade's texts. The Sadean text is structuralist methodology become nightmare. It is subjectivity undone by the presumption of totality. The mirror, the chiasm, does not afford the foundation of subjectivity or sociability by presenting the self as a semblance of the other, as is the case for Lacan.[10] Rather, such use of the chiasm denies all structures of exchange by leaving nothing to be exchanged within a complete presentation of the scene and a complete control of language and the body. Sade reduces the diacritical relations of the chiasm to the reductionist relations of analogy (in which the first term, that of the Master, determines all subsequent relations.) The Sadean text is one of systematics, closure, and semiotic constraint, not one of rupture or transgression.

The chiasm is a central figure in Merleau-Ponty's final work, *The Visible and the Invisible*. For Merleau-Ponty the chiasm is, as Jean-François Lyotard suggests, the figure of sensibility, and consequently the figure of subjectivity and intersubjectivity. The foundation of the chiasm (which is reversibility)[11] maintains the separation, the "fragmentation of being . . . (two eyes, two ears: the possibility for discrimination, for the use of the diacritical), it is the advent of difference (on the ground of resemblance . . .)."[12] Within this mode of fragmentation is the touching/touched phenomenon, constitutive of both subjectivity and intersubjectivity, since "each of the two beings is an archetype for the other."[13] This archetypal relation of the flesh is the chiasm. For Merleau-Ponty, subjectivity is not a positivist phenomenon, but a diacritical phenomenon; the subject is not an entity, but an open field of compossibilities within the flesh, founded upon resemblances within an originary differentiation.

Sade's marriage scene is a chiasmatic model of reduction to a central structure of mastery; Merleau-Ponty's model of the chiasm as the form of intersubjectivity effects just the opposite. Merleau-Ponty writes that the chiasm

forms its unity across incompossibilities such as that of my world and the world of the other – By reason of this mediation through reversal, this chiasm, there is not simply a for-Oneself for-the-Other antithesis, there is Being as containing all that, first as sensible

Being, and then as Being without restriction . . . Chiasm, instead of the For the Other: that means that there is not only a me–other rivalry, but a co-functioning. We function as one unique body.[14]

For Merleau-Ponty, the self and the other are incompossibilities which live through different worlds (in the Heideggerian sense of the worldhood-of-the-world). Yet these incompossibilities of alterity are ultimately lived as compossibilities within the same flesh, which subtends the cultural world and sustains it. What Merleau-Ponty criticized as the "for-Oneself for-the-Other antithesis" amounts to the antithesis between Master and victim in the Sadean text, where Master and victim are not "archetypes for the other," but rather of completely different ontological orders. The Sadean Master always considers the multiplication of bodies, and aims at eliminating consideration of the "for-the-Other" by manifesting a pure "for-Oneself." Needless to say, for Sade there is no intersubjective functioning as "one unique body," and there is ultimately no incompossibility within the controlled permutations and combinations of the Sadean, sadistic scene. Even the Master/victim antithesis is not an incompossibility, since there is always the possibility of the Master becoming a victim.

In Merleau-Ponty, the being of flesh is "Being without restriction."[15] This does not imply the Sadean catalogue of permutations without restriction, what Hénaff (following Bataille) referred to as a logic without reserve. For Merleau-Ponty, the lack of restriction of the flesh implies that the flesh is a "being in latency."[16] This is precisely the latency, the ambiguity, that we have seen eliminated from the Sadean personnage and the Sadean scene, an elimination effected by destroying the symbolic function by manifesting an unlimited catalogue of events. Conversely, for Merleau-Ponty the latency and ambiguity of the flesh are constituted according to "the occult trading of the metaphor – where what counts is no longer the manifest meaning of each word and of each image, but the lateral relations, the kinships that are implicated in their transfers and their exchanges."[17]

While Sadean mastery is a function of the dissolution of

the symbolic function and of the manifestation of an unrestricted scopophilia, the Merleau-Pontian flesh is a function of the latencies, invisibilities, and depths of meaning implicit in polysymbolism. "Overdetermination (= circularity, chiasm)."[18] Such polysymbolism or overdetermination structures the phenomenological horizon which is the very ontological foundation of freedom. While Sade may have used Ockham's razor, Merleau-Ponty was concerned with a poetic multiplication of effects.

Merleau-Ponty describes the flesh as a "mirror phenomenon," utilizing the same metaphor as Sade to express its chiasmatic relationship:

... man is the mirror for man. The mirror itself is the instrument of a universal magic that changes things into a spectacle, spectacles into things, myself into another, and another into myself. Artists have often mused upon mirrors because beneath this "mechanical trick," they recognized, just as they did in the case of the trick of perspective, the metamorphosis of seeing and seen which defines both our flesh and the painter's vocation.[19]

The chiasmatic "mirror" phenomenon entails the "fission of appearance and Being."[20] The metaphysical doubling of the chiasmatic fission has also been expressed by the doubling of appearance and reality in the Sadean marriage scene. Yet Sadean discourse ultimately reduces the metaphysical to the physical, indeed to the corporeal, with the intent of consolidating mastery. Merleau-Ponty, on the other hand, maintains the transcendent as the horizon of the corporeal, with the intent of inaugurating the very possibility of freedom.

It is true for both Sade and Merleau-Ponty that, as Merleau-Ponty writes: "Speaking subject: it is the subject of a praxis."[21] Yet for Sade such praxis is the mechanics of manipulation, of domination, within which there is a duplication of speech and scene, a mastery of the scene through speech. This duplication is possible only through absolute mastery (or infinite imagination). But for Merleau-Ponty, praxis aims at the instantiation of freedom and the ultimate dissolution of mastery, after which not even as "Truth" can there be an absolute adequation of word and deed. The

Merleau-Pontian task deconstructs the alliances of power and discourse; the Sadean task consolidates power through discourse.

Finally, it must be said that the results of Sade's and Merleau-Ponty's texts are, in an ironic sense, identical: they both achieve the deconstruction of subjectivity. Sade's texts accomplish this by the reduction of the subject to an infinitely interchangeable figure in a totalizing scheme of pure mastery and possession. Merleau-Ponty, on the other hand, recognized the dissolution of subjectivity as the function of an originary difference where "what there is to be grasped is a dispossession."[22] Thus for Merleau-Ponty there can be no totalizing philosophy, only an indirect ontology.

Tropes and figures objectify: they simultaneously afford a measure of difference and identity and subordinate the subject to a determination, a fixation, of attributes.

Merleau-Ponty: "Overdetermination (= circularity, chiasm) = any entity can be accentuated as an emblem of Being."[23] This claim may be amended to state that any figure can be accentuated as emblematic of the subject. Hence the polysymbolism of signs parallels the polymorphism of the flesh. This implies the efficacy of the baroque model of subjectivity suggested by Genette and Hénaff, a model contested by Sade. Hénaff: "In short, if a baroque character exists which traverses all figures, it is quite simply the soul."[24] Here the function of hermeneutics is not to determine how the subject utilizes figures, but conversely to establish how figures organize forms of subjectivity. Lyotard suggests that "All theory of metaphor is a theory of the soul, the subject."[25] And Foucault, following Nietzsche, claims that "The purpose of history, guided by genealogy, is not to discover the roots of our identity but to commit itself to its dissipation."[26]

What remains after this deconstruction, after this dissipation of subjectivity into an endless and foundationless series of tropes and figures? One possibility is a "logic of events" such as Foucault and Deleuze wish to develop. Such a logic refers to a "cæsura which fragments the moment and disperses the subject into a plurality of possible positions and functions."27 According to classical rhetoric, which is foundationally ontotheological, such functions of the subject endlessly attempt the expression of an absolute signified; the signifier is merely a function of the signified, where the signified is an absolute value. But in the post-structuralist rhetoric of a logic of events, the signified is always a function of the signifier; the signified is never anything else than another signifier. All signifieds are only figures and tropes. Value is nothing more than the determination, donation, and manipulation of attributes. This is precisely what Roland Barthes claims that Sade discovered: "Sade always chooses the discourse over the referent; he always sides with semiosis rather than mimesis."28

Yet it is never enough to determine what a trope or figure reveals: one must also seek what it conceals. Lyotard is thus correct in claiming, apropos of Merleau-Ponty's notion of the body as a chiasmatic structure of the flesh, that

It is not the body that disturbs language, it is something else that disturbs both language and the body. To accept the body as the location of events is to endorse the defensive displacement, the vast rationalization produced by the Platonic-Christian tradition with the intent of concealing desire.29

According to Lyotard's reading, Merleau-Ponty's theory of the body dissimulates the libido. Yet it is equally true that the libido is always cathected, that is to say, always bound to figurative systems. Such figures and tropes serve equally as the blockage *and* the expression of the libido. The discovery that the subject is a function of figuration serves to dissimulate the fact that these very same figures, the figures of subjectivity itself, serve to dissimulate the libido and desire. Might there be an ontological blind spot in our representations of subjectivity, or perhaps in subjectivity itself? Might this blind spot be none other than the body, or the libido? And yet, even if both Sade and Merleau-Ponty achieve a *de facto* deconstruction of subjectivity, this should not be taken to imply that there is an epistemological or ethical equivalence between their works. Within hermeneutic or literary systems where the body is given an ontological primacy or established as a paradigm of meaning, symbolic possibilities are determined by diverse modes of corporeal articulation or disarticulation. In this sense, Sade and Merleau-Ponty supplement each other; they are the matching but obverse sides of this "deconstruction" *avant la lettre*. Sade (in the context of the eighteenth century Enlightenment sublimated into the Revolution and racked by the Terror) disclosed the libido through a literary semiosis, and worked that libido into the destruction of the body. Merleau-Ponty (in the context of a post-war phenomenology, and disillusioned by the loss of the Communist political utopia) investigated how language is imbued with the body, and expressed that corporeal primacy, that "flesh," in such a way as to protect it from the ravages of libidinal impulses. Sade's disarticulation of the body is a precursor of the modernist theorization of the libido; Merleau-Ponty's articulation of thought as body is a culmination of the modernist theorization of language. And both were predecessors of the postmodernist juxtaposition of a disarticulated language and a diversified body – marked by gender, race, class, nationality – which problematizes any possible holistic, universalizing discourse. As post-modernist criticism insists, the critical point within any epistemology is the hinge between local and universal – or at least universalizing – systems. Already, the notions of an "anti-aesthetic" or an "anti-Oedipus" – radical, contentious, and destabilizing as they may be – are but local systems of thought within our larger, but still local, system of Western ecumenical pretentions. The question, at each moment of every discourse, is where and how the speaker and reader are situated within these systems.

Philosophical systems, much less tropes and figures, always define only a dimension of the imaginary, and never Being or subjectivity in totality. Thus, in the end, our most explicit interpretations, just like our most secret thoughts, will be held suspect. Not because of what they mean, but because of what they are: figures of ourselves.

NOTES

1 Michel Foucault, "Nietzsche, Genealogy, History," in *Language, Counter-Memory, Practice*, trans. Donald F. Bouchard (Ithaca: Cornell University Press, 1977), p. 162.

2 Jean-François Lyotard, *Discours/figure* (Paris: Klincksieck, 1974), p. 289.

3 The Marquis de Sade, *Juliette*, trans. Austryn Wainhouse (New York: Grove Press, 1968), p. 1175; my corrections to the translation are based on *Histoire de Juliette, Oeuvres complètes*, vol. IX (Paris: Cercle du Livre Précieux, 1966), p. 569.

4 Marcel Hénaff, *Sade: L'invention du corps libertin* (Paris: Presses Universitaires de France, 1978), p. 126.

5 The Marquis de Sade, *Philosophy in the Bedroom*, trans. Richard Seaver and Ausryn Wainhouse (New York: Grove Press, 1966), pp. 202–3.

6 Hénaff, *Sade*, p. 127; cf. also Gérard Genette's *Figures I* (Paris: Seuil, 1966), *passim*.

7 Michel Foucault, *Discipline and Punish*, trans. Alan Sheridan (New York: Vintage, 1979), *passim*, esp. pp. 195–228. One should also note here the psychoanalytic insights into the relation between sadism and the scopic drives.

8 Roland Barthes, *Sade, Fourier, Loyola*, trans. Richard Miller (New York: Hill and Wang, 1976), p. 32.

9 Michel Foucault, "Language to Infinity," in *Language*, p. 62.

10 Jacques Lacan, "Le stade du miroir comme formateur de la fonction du je," in *Ecrits* I (Paris: Seuil, 1966), pp. 89–97.

11 Maurice Merleau-Ponty, *The Visible and the Invisible*, trans. Alphonso Lingis (Evanston: Northwestern University Press, 1960), p. 217.

12 Ibid., p. 217.

13 Ibid., p. 137.

14 Ibid., p. 215.

15 Ibid.

16 Ibid., p. 136.

17 Ibid., p. 125.

18 Ibid., p. 270.

19 Maurice Merleau-Ponty, "Eye and Mind," in *The Primacy of Perception*, trans. Carleton Dallery (Evanston: Northwestern University Press, 1964), p. 168.

20 Ibid., p. 256.

21 *The Visible and the Invisible*, p. 201.

22 Ibid., p. 266.

23 Ibid., p. 270.
24 Hénaff, *Sade*, p. 128.
25 Lyotard, *Discours/figure*, p. 257.
26 Foucault, "Nietzsche", p. 162; cf. the writings of Pierre Klossowski, especially his novel *Roberte ce soir* and *Nietzsche et le cercle vicieux*, which have as their central themes the problem of the dissolution of subjectivity after the death of God. Nietzsche and Sade were the inspiration for these works, which in turn inspired Foucault.
27 Foucault, "What is an Author?" in *Language*, p. 130n.
28 Barthes, *Sade, Fourier* . . ., p. 37.
29 Lyotard, *Discours/figure*, p. 22.

CHAPTER 10

Gender and narrative possibilities

Nancy K. Miller

The fortunes of *Juliette* are always solitary. And they are
endless.

Michel Foucault, *Les Mots et les choses*

Within the critical canon on *Juliette*, it is generally acknowledged that the heroine's trajectory demonstrates the characteristics of a *Bildungsroman*. And Juliette's passage from innocence
to sophistication, ignorance to knowledge, apprenticeship to
mastery, can indeed be classified as the story of an education – even a spiritual one, for the eschatological intersects
the scatalogical at every point.[1] It has also been observed,
however, that the *Bildungsroman* is a "male affair," "a male
form because women have tended to be viewed traditionally
as static, rather than dynamic, as instances of femaleness considered essential rather than existential."[2] The typical subject
of the genre is a sensitive young man, who, upon moving
from a sheltered environment to the challenges of the world,
loses an original innocence as he achieves a measure of social
integration and *savoir-vivre*. Although radically transformed by
her exposure to life as experience, Juliette represents a double
exception to that formula: she does not perform in the world
as the reader is likely to know it, and she is a *female* apprentice.
Thus, reading Juliette's *apprentissage* as an intertext, say, to
Wilhelm Meister's reveals, on one level, a text whose specificity
lies in a relation of variance with an ideal (generic) model.[3]
But there is a further methodological consideration: how is the
semiosis of apprenticeship generated when the feminine sign
must be articulated within a system of signification in which it

has no place? The answer lies in a characteristic trait of Sadean *écriture*: reversal. Juliette's *Bildung* – her self-development – is achieved by a reversal of the valorization assigned to the cultural and literary conventions encoding femaleness, the positively marked status of daughter, wife, mother. The novel thus builds upon the stages of emancipation from the familial, on the denegation of bourgeois femininity.

Beautiful, wealthy, and convent-educated, Juliette is an ideal daughter perfectly equipped to circulate in society as an object of legitimate and sanctioned exchange. The untimely loss of both parents puts an end to such great expectations: of a life of leisure and procreation under the ægis of a prosperous husband. (Orphans have no title to privilege.) Undaunted, Juliette determines to pursue her interrupted schooling: "To be sure, I had a rigorous apprenticeship to undergo; these often painful first steps were to complete the corruption of my morals" (*Juliette*, p.103).[4] The educative principle of Juliette's text entails the unlearning of official scholastic values; and her training program is designed to eradicate any lingering traces of moral prejudice by completion of the requirements as established in the catalogue of sexual offerings. A university of perversity, perhaps, but academe prevails – at the very least in the form of hierarchy – until the end.

Juliette learns quickly, for she is highly motivated from the start:

Endowed with the most energetic temperament, I had, starting at the age of nine, accustomed my fingers to respond to whatever desires arose in my mind, and from that period onward I aspired to nothing but the happiness of finding the occasion for instruction and to launch myself into a career the gates unto which my native forwardness had already flung wide, and with such agreeable effects. (p. 4)

She performs the permutations of sexual exercises with astonishing skill, and advances so rapidly, in fact, that after her first indoctrination the reader may well wonder how the remaining volumes can be structured convincingly upon a developmental premise. But, as Barthes has pointed out, "For the libertines, the educative project has another breadth . . . The mastery that is sought here is that of philosophy: the education is not of such or such a character, *it is of the reader*.⁵ The reader of Juliette — or to be more precise, the *narrataire*⁶ (the reader as inscribed) — is reminded constantly by the pervasive educational code and by footnotes that a lesson is to be learned:

Hot-blooded and lewdly disposed ladies, these are words to the wise, hark attentively to them: they are addressed not only to Juliette but to yourselves also; if your intelligence is in any sense comparable to hers, you'll not fail to extract great benefit from them. (p. 340, note)

So offer us your thanks, mesdames, and endeavor to outshine our heroines, we ask no more of you; for your instruction, your sensations, and your happiness are in verity the sole objects for whose sake some wearisome efforts are undertaken; and if you damned us in *Justine*, our hope is that *Juliette* will earn us your blessings. (p. 489, note)

The exhortation to emulate, to imitate the process as set forth, creates the impression of development, both ongoing and potential, even if, in a cooler moment, the measurement of change proves to be a rhetorical device: hyperbole. (The paradox is only apparent, persuasion being the *telos* of rhetoric.) In addition to these formal indices, moreover, it seems to me that the sense of progression that is indeed decipherable in an otherwise heterogeneous mass of sexual exploits, derives, as I said earlier, from the particularly valorized program which is the enfranchisement of the individual from the family: all the more striking because undertaken by a woman. In both cases, it is a case of generic *topoi*.⁷

That liberation should pass through the family to go beyond it is not itself surprising within the Sadean system, where in order for a libertine to "faire ses preuves," he or she must break the bonds of "natural" kinship. Since the family, as a matrix formed by the ties of blood and sanctified by societal rules, is a mediating term between nature and culture, it provides an ideal arena in which to do battle. But Juliette is an orphan, and thus, one would expect, exempt by definition from the family principle. Her text, nevertheless, is opened, closed, and punctuated by references to the family as though absence could be assured only by the reiterated denial of presence. Juliette's sister Justine, for example, is named and dismissed in the first paragraph, and the reader is invited to remember her presumably only as a point of reference, the contrapuntal reminder of another kind of destiny. And yet Justine will reappear at crucial moments in the narrative with a good deal more impact than a simple index of polarity.

In the same way, Juliette's original and desultory account of her parents' demise will be recapitulated with new significance when she gives her history to Noirceuil. For she will learn in the course of the first "savante dissertation" pronounced for her benefit that Noirceuil is nothing less than "the murderer of your parents." The revelation leads to a declaration of love from Juliette: "'Monster,'" I repeated, 'thou art an abomination, I love thee'" (p. 149). Such admiration wins Juliette admission to Noirceuil's school of crime, and, guided by a mentor and lover, she blossoms: the apprentice dedicates herself to pleasing the master, seeking to model her soul upon his. "As for the submission you request of me, it shall be entire; dispose of me, I am yours; a woman, I know my place and that dependence is my lot" (p. 207). Noirceuil, however, clarifies their relationship: "I would have you a woman and a slave unto me and my friends; a despot unto everyone else . . . and I here and now swear that I shall avail you of the means" (ibid.). Juliette is thus granted freedom to perform – sexually and criminally – but that freedom is mediated by a higher authority. The supremacy of the couple is maintained, and within that couple, the male prerogative supported by power in the world.

Despite the mutual fondness at the heart of their union, it is deemed expedient for Juliette to take up residence with Noirceuil's friend, the Minister, Saint-Fond. Because of the latter's extraordinary fortune, Juliette finds herself (at age seventeen) mistress of the interior, the ultimate "maîtresse de maison." Juliette is given "all France" to devastate with crime and a premium for domestic originality. But again there is a restriction: "Henceforth upon entering this place, and while you are here, your condition will be that of a common whore;

and at all other times you will be one of the greatest ladies in the kingdom" (p. 236). Two sets of oppositional criteria are relevant: spatio-social: inside/outside (the message, moreover, is delivered in a "cabinet secret"); and gender-determined mastery: female slave/male master: "Wherever I am, my Lord, I shall be your slave, your admirer eternally, and the very soul of your most exquisite pleasures" (p. 236). That this relationship of authority is fundamental to the apprenticeship model can be clearly shown by adopting a Greimasian perspective according to which Noirceuil's role – and Saint-Fond's to a lesser degree – is that of the *Destinateur*:

In an exemplary apprenticeship narrative, this role is played by the father – or by someone who appears *like the father* – of the hero-subject. The father tends increasingly to assume the role of the helper, since one of his functions is to facilitate the hero's apprenticeship – be it to communicate essential knowledge, or, more fundamentally, to encourage him in his quest.[8]

The importance of this father-figure status as exemplified by Noirceuil will be elaborated upon at the end of our analysis. At this point, what is pertinent is the articulation of the *significant* and *formative* power role in *masculine* terms.

In the world of *Bildung*, hyperbolized by a Sadean dynamic, the *status* is never *quo*. Juliette requests a role model to emulate, and at the same time a tutee of her own: "I'd like to share my knowledge with another; I keenly sense my need of instruction, I no less keenly desire to educate someone: I must have a teacher, yes, and I must have a pupil too" (p. 263). The educational principle is thus reinscribed, but with a crucial nuance: Juliette attains the rank of instructor within a *female* hierarchy. Again, within the egalitarian atmosphere of sexual utopia, difference pertains. Clairwil, handpicked by Noirceuil for the position, refines Juliette's techniques, and introduces her to "La Société des Amis du Crime." Noirceuil, for his part, no longer maintains membership:

"In the days when men were in the majority there," he replied, "I never missed a single one; but I have given up going since everything has fallen into the hands of a sex whose authority I dislike. Saint-Fond felt the same way and dropped out shortly after I did. But that is not particularly relevant," Noirceuil continued; "if those orgies amuse you, and since Clairwil enjoys them, there is no reason why you shouldn't join in: everything vicious must be given a fair try, and only virtue is thoroughly boring." (p. 498)

So with Clairwil as her model (and Noirceuil's fiancée as her experimental subject), Juliette continues to progress, although total approval is withheld for what Clairwil considers Juliette's inability to act in cold blood.

Juliette is soon given a perfect opportunity to demon-strate her improvement. Her *real* father, Bernole, unexpectedly appears, seeking to enlist his daughter as a mediator vis-à-vis Saint-Fond. The canonical recognition scene, complete with documents and identifying birthmark, motivates an excla-mation from Justine, who, we are reminded, is present at the gathering in which Juliette is holding forth. Justine is censured for her filial piety and returned to a silence that she maintains until the very end of the novel, where she reappears, only to be condemned to death. The familial component of this sequence is thus reinforced, and the pause created by Justine's intervention functions as a marker, a juncture in the text, isolating this particular *épreuve* as a narrative unit. Unlike her sister, Juliette is indifferent to the discovery of her real father and the difficulty of his situation: "of that there could be no question, but to it Nature incited in me no response at all, none. It was with sheer indifference I stared at the person standing in front of me" (p. 466). After consultation with Noirceuil and Saint-Fond, Juliette revises her initial impulse to dismiss the importune progenitor and determines instead to seduce and kill him – to prove that the efforts to reform her soul have not been fruitless. The plot is carried out with the father caught *in flagrante delicto*, in a posture of unambiguous compromise. Juliette shoots her father, while participating fully in the concomitant orgy. If the subversion of the family were not clear enough, a pregnancy (Juliette's first) results from these incestuous relations, followed by a remarkable, painless, and cosmetic abortion. Thus the family is truncated, as it were, at both ends of the tree. The convergence of taboos redundantly confirms the symbolic nature of Juliette's progress in liberation.⁹

Clairwil, however, is still not satisfied with Juliette's evolution and in particular chides Juliette for not seeing that every man is a member of "a sex bitterly at war with your own," and that consequently, she must never miss "an opportunity for avenging the insults women have endured" (p. 527). Curiously, like Rousseau's Claire D'Orbe, Clairwil is a female-identified woman, while Juliette, like Julie, consistently embraces male identification – hence the Father.¹⁰ But I am anticipating. At this stage of her adventures, Juliette is introduced by Clairwil to yet another (female) mentor, Durand, through whom Juliette becomes a sorceress's apprentice. Durand initiates Juliette into the art of poison – since Medea, the archetypal female art. Equally important, she foretells the conditions of Juliette's fall from favor: "When vice doth cease woe shall betide" (p. 531). Indeed, immediately following this exchange, and at the very center of the novel, Juliette reveals, by an involuntary shudder, a moral compunction that Saint-Fond deems to be fatal. His power turns against her. By violating the terms of their contract she has abrogated her right to (paternal) protection and is forced to fend for herself. Within six months, however, married to the Comte de Lorsange, Juliette has a new domestic arrangement and can start making plans again. Notably, despite the anti-procreative stance maintained by Juliette and her fellow libertines throughout the novel, Juliette decides to have a child: "The measure was essential: I had to consolidate my claims to the fortune of the man who had given me his name. I could not do this without a child – but was it fathered by my virtuous husband . . . ?" (p. 561). As one might expect, for Juliette conjugality is no more compelling than filiality. Indeed, when she learns that Saint-Fond is searching for her, she rapidly disposes of her "tender spouse" (with Durand's poison), leaves her daughter Marianne with a curate friend and lover, and sets out to seek fortune and pleasure on her own, this being made possible only by her new status as a rich widow.

Thus travels follow apprenticeship: Juliette develops her

own style, and is vastly successful as a practitioner of the crimes of love. But she at last decides to return home seven years later, and, towards the novel's close, to rejoin Noirceuil and her daughter in Paris.[11] Upon seeing Marianne, she finds her pretty, but explains (in terms identical to those used in describing her reaction to the discovery of her true father) that Nature – in this case the maternal function – was *mute*: "I am obliged to say that in embracing Marianne I feel absolutely nothing stir in me but the pulsations of lubricity" (p. 1152). Juliette looks forward only to guiding Marianne's nubility – to apprenticeship: "There's a pretty subject for educating." We would seem to have here a Sadean premise for a familial continuum, but any vestiges of the nuclear family are destroyed in the last orgy recounted by Juliette. Noirceuil is determined to "have" Marianne. Juliette's reaction reveals the traces of motherly distress. But pity for the victim, albeit her child, is short-lived. Seeing Noirceuil demolish his own two sons, Juliette concurs with his desire; and, after a momentary reluctance, gets caught up in the activity: when Noirceuil throws Marianne into a roaring fire, Juliette helps him with a poker. The murder of Juliette's daughter is the last fully described episode. By its position in the text, and its obvious symbolic connotations, it marks the culmination of Juliette's progress, her emancipation from the role structure of the family. Noirceuil and Juliette spend the night following this crime together in mutual congratulation and harmony. Noirceuil, confirming his earlier assertion, "you are indispensable to my existence; I like committing crimes with nobody but you," pays Juliette the ultimate compliment, inviting her to spend the rest of her life with him: "Then let us live in crime forever; and may nothing in all Nature ever succeed in converting us to different principles" (pp. 1153, 1187).

But the novel is not yet purged of the familial. And it is the author who intervenes to tie up the threads of the narrative. In an inevitable repetition of her previous history, Justine's tears, stimulated by the "scandalous details" of Juliette's text, cause her to be cast out of the comfort of the château into the elements. Conveniently, Justine, perennial orphan of the storm, is struck down by a thunderbolt. Interpreting the disaster as divine intervention, the libertines abuse the corpse with Juliette's excited encouragement: "This most recent episode more than ever firms me in the career I have pursued up until now" (p. 1191). And precisely, this episode reconfirms the desecration of the familial as the thematic component structuring the test of Juliette's quest for emancipation. Ungrateful daughter, unnatural mother, unloving wife, unsisterly sister, Juliette defies all semantic expectations: she chooses to orphan herself, thus creating a neologism, making a normally passive verb active. And by widowing herself, she further subverts linguistic patterns, flaunting the need for protection proverbially ascribed to "widows and orphans."

The extent to which the semantic investment of normative structure is subverted here can be easily summarized by a model of socio-sexual relations adapted from Lévi-Strauss and elaborated by Greimas and Rastier (see p. 222). Whatever the investment of the model, it is a question, in the case of nature as in that of culture, of social values, and not of the rejection of nature outside meaning.[12]

In this perspective, the permitted and matrimonial relations of culture are prescribed and opposed to the forbidden, *abnormal* relations of Nature. In traditional French society, the first category is exemplified by conjugal love, the second, incest and homosexuality. Obviously, in such a society, the first set of roles $(C_1, \bar{C}_2)$ is privileged and positively valorized, the second $(\bar{C}_1, C_2)$ marked with the negative sign of transgression. In the fictional universe of the eighteenth-century novel, these relations of positivity to negativity are respected; that is to say, transgression is punished. But to measure fully the distance separating the Sadean universe from the most libertine of bourgeois fiction, it must be noted that the "normal" non-forbidden relation of *male* adultery lies within the category of "permitted" relations, whereas *female* adultery belongs to the category of "unacceptable" relations. Thus if we were to compare *Les Liaisons dangereuses*, for example, with *Les Prospérités du vice*

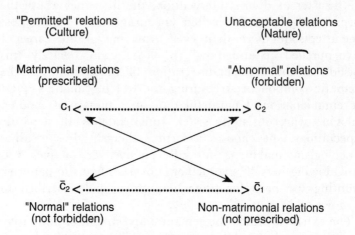

"Permitted" relations   Unacceptable relations
      (Culture)   (Nature)

Matrimonial relations   "Abnormal" relations
    (prescribed)   (forbidden)

c_1 c_2

$\bar{c}_2$ $\bar{c}_1$

  "Normal" relations   Non-matrimonial relations
   (not forbidden)   (not prescribed)

Note: In traditional French society, for example, we have the following
equivalences:

- c_1 conjugal love;
- c_2 incest, homosexuality;
- $\bar{c}_1$ adultery by the man (over and above conjugal love);
- $\bar{c}_2$ adultery by the woman (over and above homosexuality, etc.)

(texts often compared because of the similarities between the
two major female figures, Madame de Merteuil and Juliette),
Merteuil ($\bar{C}_1$) and Juliette (C_2) would both be labeled
as "unacceptable." For they defy the founding cultural constraints of both *pater* and *familias*: Merteuil by usurping male
prerogatives, Juliette by incest and homosexuality.[13] Despite
the fact, however, that Merteuil does not occupy the place of
supreme violation, the maximum of abhorrent activity (as
does Juliette), she is nonetheless the character most severely
punished in a scenario of sexual promiscuity. Prévan and
Valmont, for example, her homologues in adultery, are (in
the case of the former) applauded, and (in that of the latter)

allowed to die – gallantly – by the sword, whereas Merteuil is stripped of prestige, fortune, family, servants, friends, and allies. And that is not all: she is given the punishment befitting a monster. An eye is destroyed ("l'œil crevé"): symbolic sexual mutilation. Juliette, on the contrary, is consistently rewarded for her progress in transgression. Every crime affords her new respect – particularly in the eyes of the supreme arbiter of value, Noirceuil. The further she goes in her daring, the further she is integrated into the universe within which she functions. The novel concludes with her ascension. Society cannot eject Juliette as it can Merteuil because Juliette is beyond its reach. Once Juliette has delivered herself of *internalized* oppression, she is free of opposition.[14]

Thus, Juliette realizes the full potential of the apprenticeship program. On the one hand, she fulfills the criterion of the genre that at the end the "hero . . . has ripened via a series of amorous exploits ranging from the sensual to the sublime" (Miles, "The Pícaro's Journey," p. 984). On the other, her *Bildung* culminates with the assimilation of Sadean philosophy in the microcosm of the Sadean world, as defined early in her formation by Noirceuil: "Nor ought you to view familial ties as more sacred than these others, they are all equally fictitious. It is not true that you owe anything to the being out of whom you emerged; still less true that you are obliged to have any feeling whatever for a being that were to emerge from you. . . . Upon what rational basis can consanguinity establish duties?" (p. 193). Indeed, in her particular praxis, she has achieved – or so it would seem – personal liberation from the constraints of a role that would bind her to the bourgeois family.

But as the story draws to a close, a messenger arrives to deliver a letter announcing Noirceuil's summons to the Court, where he is to assume the reins of government: the outside world merges with the inner sanctum. Noirceuil then invites Juliette and her old friend Durand – unexpectedly arrived in the midst of these happy few – to accompany him to the Capital, while naming his male friends to high and official positions. Once again, the inside/outside differentiation pertains. Juliette will resume her role as super-mistress to Noirceuil's supreme administration: "As soon as Ulysses appeared, Circe once again became a woman, and the daughter of the Sun gave herself up to the Hero" (Tourné, "Le mythe," p. 86). It is in this sense that the ending recreates a familial situation: power roles based on gender distinctions. When the last *blood* relation is eliminated, a socially homologous relationship is substituted: the (extended) Sadean family reproduces the Freudian triangle.

Juliette, an orphan who chose to orphan herself, returns to the rule of the Father – of Noirceuil, but finally of the Author, who has the last word.[15] Her text is not autonomous; however subversive, it remains sub-text. Juliette had wished the story of her life to be entitled *Les Prospérités du vice*. That is, of course, the narrative we have. But the author tells us that our heroine, "unique in her kind," lived for another ten glorious years, and died "without having left any record of the events of her life." Continuing the fiction of his status as scribe, he adds, "so it is that no writer will be able to chronicle it for the public" (p. 1193). However, since "genuine *Bildung* involves a restructuring of recollections often analogous to the creative process itself" (Miles, "The pícaro's journey," p. 984), this deprivation, surely, is Juliette's and not the author's. Ultimately, her *Bildung* proves to be as volatile as her word. Oral history is not art; a voice is not a signature.

There is nothing fundamentally inconsistent here. It is in the logic of the idiolect. Noirceuil had celebrated the symbol of his power in the following manner: "this tool is my god, let it be one unto thee, Juliette: extol it, worship it, this despotic engine, show it every reverence" (p. 185). From the phallus to the pen and the word, culture transcodes for us. In the Sadean hierarchy, "the master is he who speaks, who *disposes of language in its entirely*" (Barthes, *Sade, Fourier . . .*, p. 36, my emphasis). In the final pages of the novel, it is precisely this *problématique* of mastery in language that is at stake. Juliette does not contest her restricted status, as will, for example, Emma Bovary: "What she envies in men is not so much the chance of travelling, but the possibility of writing; what she lacks in order to write are neither the words, nor the pen, but the phallus."[16] Nonetheless, in the final analysis, the feminine sign, "the speechless sign in the world of Law" (Sollers, "Sade dans le texte," p. 65), the world of the Father and culture, even in Sade's text, is mediated by masculine discourse.[17] So that whether, in the posterity of prosperity, in the euphoria of "happily ever after," Juliette bypassed the binary rule of the Father, we will never know. Her sign is silence; she is written.

NOTES

1 That this is, moreover, a narrative cliché of the period is well documented by Ronald Brissenden, in his excellent and illuminating article, "*La Philosophie dans le boudoir*, or, a young lady's entrance into the world," *Studies in Eighteenth-Century Culture* 2 (*Irrationalism in the Eighteenth Century*) (1972), pp. 113–42. On the coincidence of the erotic and the spiritual, see also Bary Ivker's remarks in "Towards a definition of libertinism in 18th-century French fiction," *Studies on Voltaire and the Eighteenth Century* 72 (1970), p. 231.

2 Ellen Morgan, "Human becoming: form and focus in the neo-feminist novel," is S.K. Cornillon, ed., *Images of Women in Fiction: Feminist Perspectives* (Bowling Green: Popular Press, 1972), p. 184.

3 I take as definition of genre Michael Riffaterre's, as elaborated in "Système d'un genre descriptif," *Poétique* 9 (1972), p. 16: "The perception of a genre is analogous to that of the cliché ... the reader reads it and recalls having read it elsewhere ... It is a phantom form which exists only in the mind of the reader; still it is only a standard of measurement by which he tests the real works. In short, a structure of which the texts are the variants."

4 All quoted references are drawn from The Marquis de Sade, *Juliette*, trans. Austryn Wainhouse (New York: Grove Press, 1968).

5 *Sade, Fourier, Loyola* (Paris: Seuil, 1971), p. 30. My emphasis.

6 For an analysis of the implications of this term, as used by Gerald Prince, see his article, "Introduction à l'étude du narrataire," *Poétique* 14 (1973), pp. 178–96. It is perhaps worth noting that Sade's (more exactly, the Author's) footnotes are directed specifically at a female *narrataire* when the matter in hand

bears on Juliette's behavior as *woman*; general (anthropological, historical) comments are not gender oriented.

7   I would like to maintain a distinction between genre – a problem of abstraction that lends itself to formalizations – and conventions. While it is true that many aspects of Juliette's progress renew clichés of libertine fiction (cf. Brissenden's work), I am more interested in disengaging structures which point to what T. Todorov has called "the relays by which the work is set in relation to the universe of literature." See his *Introduction à la littérature fantastique* (Paris: Seuil, 1970), p. 12. In this sense, I found an article by David Miles to be most useful: "The pícaro's journey to the confessional: the changing image of the hero in the German Bildungsroman," *PMLA* 89, no. 5 (Oct. 1974), pp. 980–82.

8   Susan Suleiman, "Pour une poétique du roman à thèse: l'exemple de Nizan," *Critique* 330 (Nov. 1974), p. 1006.

9   Brissenden cites the analogous scene in *La Philosophie dans le boudoir*, Eugénie's mutilation of her mother, and comments on its "Electral ... structure" ("*La Philosophie ...*", pp. 131–2).

10 Philippe Sollers notes the analogues, Julie/Juliette, Claire/Clairwil, to emphasize a more generalized intertextual relation: "L'histoire littéraire est donc à son tour démasquée." "Sade dans le texte," in *L' Ecriture et l'expérience des limites* (Paris: Seuil, 1968), p. 60.

11 Having opted to follow the thread of linearity and thematic progression, I do not discuss Juliette's activities abroad; they are constructed on the principle of hyperbole and repetition and deserve a separate study. For an analysis of the problem of libertine education in its temporal aspect, see Jean-Jacques Brochier's comments in "La circularité de l'espace," in Jean Fabre, ed., *Le Marquis de Sade* (Paris: Armand Colin, 1968), p. 173.

12 A. J. Greimas and François Rastier, "The interaction of semiotic constraints," in *Yale French Studies* 41 (1968), pp. 93–94.

13 Merteuil's behavior is condemned as transgression of the fundamental code of eighteenth century society, i.e. (public) male sexual activity (+) vs. (public) female sexual *in*-activity (+). Thus, Prévan's reputation is based on vaunted sexual aggression, Merteuil's upon its apparent absence; Prévan is thought to be irresistible, Merteuil, invincible. As a result of the information disclosed at the end of the novel (Merteuil's expression of desire in the form of *advances*), Prévan is reinstated and Merteuil destroyed.

14 This distinction is indeed crucial: "And there, where Laclos's Merteuil discovers a difficult balance between being and appearance, concerned to be herself but also to preserve her reputation, the Sadean heroine, without masks, unafraid of opinion, without restraint, *unconditionally* accepts the richness of her nature." Maurice Tourné, "Les mythes de la femme," in *Europe* (Oct. 1972), p. 80. But I take exception to the *"unconditional"* (italics mine) of Tourné's analysis. Femaleness is itself a *condition* of freedom. See n. 15.

15 "Juliette's submission to Noirceuil-Sade is thus, first of all, that of the character to its author: it is also that of a woman to her partner, *and, finally, as an equal in the conquest of freedom"* (Tourné, "Les mythes," p. 87, my emphasis). The juxtaposition of the terms *submission* and *freedom* poses a serious problem of interpretation, and suggests the famous Orwellian formula that some are more equal than others. As Catherine Claude rightly points out in "Une lecture de femme," *Europe* (Oct. 1972), pp. 64–70, Sade's presentation of male–female relations, in which maleness reigns supreme, should be a caution to those who would promote him as a revolutionary. From this viewpoint, there should be nothing surprising in the final reinscription of the writer as Father, and the return of the family.

16 Naomi Schor, "Pour une thématique restreinte: écriture, parole et différence dans *Madame Bovary*," *Littérature* 22 (May 1976), pp. 30–46.

17 Thus, I must finally disagree with Barthes, despite his great powers of seduction: "Juliette, proud and free in the world, sweet and submissive in pleasure, is enormously seductive; but what seduces me is the Juliette of the page, *the narrator who is made into the subject of discourse*, not the subject of reality" (*Sade, Fourier . . ., p.* 42, my emphasis). The subject of *parole*, however, is not the subject of *écriture*: Juliette's voice is narrated.

Sade's literary space

Lawrence Schehr

To understand Sade as a novelist, to read Sade as a practitioner of the genre of the eighteenth-century novel, we must begin to sift through and classify the multiple messages sent and formed around the author's name. Marcelin Pleynet has noted that "Sade" as a proper noun is generally excluded in our minds in favor of a common noun, "sadism," and an adjective, "sadistic." [1] He further points out (p. 31) that this exclusion serves to deny Sade the literary dimension that is his due. Sade's name is never purely a proper noun: it is always pronounced in inverted commas. We thus hint at a larger-than-life human being: "the Marquis de Sade." Or we turn the name into adjectives and common nouns (sadistic, sadist, sadism, sado-masochism) and thereby mark a signifying praxis, psychoanalysis and not literature. To understand Sade's difference as a novelist, to see what in his writing is truly different from the writing of Rousseau or Laclos, the captivity of the text to his improperly used name must come to an end. To speak schematically: in the first part of this essay I would like to try to consider the novels as texts henceforth independent of their author and thereby exempted from the connotations attached to the author's name, and specifically from the two versions of Sade we have come to accept: Sade the pervert and Sade the liberator. At the same time, I would like to distinguish between what I perceive as narrative material as such and the myth of Sade that has provided a cornerstone for psychoanalytical theory.

First of all, we need to consider the implications of reading Sade the pervert. His scandalous texts, which, after all, are novels, have traditionally been conflated with the myth of the scandalous Marquis, just as he was and is confused with them: it has been convenient to exile him and his writings by identifying him with the excesses of his own fictional creations. And his works have been consigned, even as they still are today, to some sort of vicarious, paraliterary position. Even though they are clearly eighteenth-century novels, they are usually refused status as such, at least institutionally. The myth of Sade – the Sadean text seen as an equivalent to the sadistic text – does not allow them to be included in a corpus whose addressee is the "gentle reader" so often apostrophized by authors. They have not ceased to exist, but have rather doggedly continued, surfacing now and again, never belonging and never being wholly excluded (as are, for example, the "forgotten" novels of the eighteenth or nineteenth centuries that only resurface in dissertations). Despite the fact that the differences between Sade's novels and other eighteenth-century novels relate to content and not to form, Sade's texts are seldom included, even in these formalist times, in overviews of the eighteenth-century novel. It is as if the excess of the contents blinded us to seeing the similarities of form.

Certainly, the eighteenth century saw a danger in all novels; there was a widely held belief that novels corrupt. As Jean-Jacques Rousseau points out in the preface to *La Nouvelle Héloïse*: "A chaste girl never read novels . . . One who, despite the title, dares read even a page of one, is a lost girl."[2] What keeps Sade in this position of having written dangerous texts, when all others have become acceptable? Sade, for one, did not see his work as different from that of other novelists. In fact, in his essay entitled *Reflections on the Novel*, the language he uses to describe their works, whether he likes them or not, resembles the language used in his own.[3] Rétif de la Bretonne "floods the public" (108; 14); the novels of Richardson and Fielding are "vigorous" (106; 12); Crébillon's novels "indulged vice and strayed from virtue" (105; 11); the English novelists show us man as he might be, "subjected to the modifying influences of vice" (106; 12). And quoting Diderot, Sade notes that the good novel, having "witnessed virtue overwhelmed by vice"

(106; 12), has "smitten our hearts" (106; 13). Following the advice of many other writers, Sade forbids potential novelists to distance themselves from verisimilitude (111; 17). And at the end of this essay that serves as a preface to a collection of stories (*Les Crimes de l'amour*), Sade echoes Rousseau's famous warning:

Unlike Crébillon and Dorat, I have not set myself the dangerous goal of enticing women to love characters who deceive them; on the contrary, I want them to loathe these characters. 'Tis the only way whereby one can avoid being duped by them. (pp. 115–16; p. 22).

And true to form, not only for Sade but for novelists in general who distance themselves from their works by saying that the manuscript was anonymous, a found document, or a "pure" fiction, Sade concludes with a lie: "[L]et no one ascribe to me the authorship of *J*......: I have never written any such works and I surely never shall" (116; 22).

We recognize formal similarities; we remark the perceived danger of the genre as a whole; but Sade is still banished to the library's *enfer*. Yet he remains somehow present as part of the whole library, though he is always marginalized, an observation that has been made by numerous critics. As Angela Carter notes:

It is fair to say that, when pornography serves – as with very rare exceptions it always does – to reinforce the prevailing system of values and ideas in a given society, it is tolerated; and when it does not, it is banned. (This already suggests there are more reasons than those of public decency for the banning of the work of Sade for almost two hundred years; only at the time of the French Revolution and at the present day have his books been available to the general public.)4

Marcelin Pleynet notes ("Sade," p. 26) that despite the more or less regular republication of *Justine* and *Juliette*, they were distributed "sous le manteau," that is to say "under wraps" or "under the counter" or "in a plain brown-paper bag." And though the academic world is frequently more liberal than the norm-makers *extra muros*, one might still venture to say that even when Sade is taught, his name remains in inverted commas: teaching Sade, putting Sade on comprehensive exams or the *agrégation*, involves a political and rhetorical gesture not found in putting Voltaire, Diderot, or Rousseau on the same examinations.

Still, this liminality has served Sade well. For even now, if he is still figuratively banished from the eighteenth-century collections or canon, he is reborn as a central figure of a certain modern paraliterary tradition. Neither inside nor outside the literary, but perhaps defining it liminally, this tradition finds its exponents in the work of Pierre Klossowski, Georges Bataille, and Maurice Blanchot.[5] The Sade who had once been banished is replaced by a new configuration of Sade, who is seen as the liberator of human sexuality, *l'honnête homme* in a revisionist mode, ultimately a Sade who, in telling the truth of our fantasms, belongs to the *sciences humaines* and not to literature. In their works, these three authors create Sade as their own predecessor. Such a rhetorical move is a double justification or self-authorization for the paraliterary endeavors of Blanchot: Sade provides a hybrid form for a fictional writing seemingly unlimited by generic constraint. Sade serves especially as a pretext for the works of Bataille and Klossowski, authors who justify their own liminal positions by revising the canon (if not the corpus) to include a heterogeneous and "heterological" liminality, and, in so doing, by giving themselves an illustrious forebear as well.

Were this position of liminality the only one in which Sade were pigeonholed, it would be a relatively easy matter to redeem him: that is to say, to exchange the Sade of liberation for a modern or even a postmodern Sade. For, oddly enough, if Sade has not yet been included in the literary canon, Blanchot, Bataille, and Klossowski have been, at least to some extent. Sade can therefore be included as a truly modern writer; his works are considered to be pre-twentieth-century narratives instead of eighteenth-century novels.[6] In fact, with the institutional acceptance of Bataille, Blanchot, and Klossowski, Sade can even be considered as a precursor to postmodernism! Sade's difference is recuperated in this syncopated chronology.

The similarity of his forms to those of Diderot, Laclos, or Rousseau is whitewashed: we no longer see Sade as an eighteenth-century writer using contemporary novelistic forms. Playing on the threshold of exclusion, these writers have created another myth of Sade, the Sade of liberation, the Sade as forebear or predecessor, what we might call a precursor.

But either fortunately or unfortunately, Sade is in another position, and this time it is central and not liminal; this is the Sade of sadism. The term was originally Krafft-Ebing's, but it was Freud who discovered it, included it in the world, and put it on the map. It was Freud who consecrated Sade in the form of sadism in his 1905 study, *Three Essays on the Theory of Sexuality*. Freud makes a fair exchange: by liberating Sade from exile and making him a cynosure, Freud exchanges sadism for Sade. The perversion is consecrated, and the subject, text, and author are all excluded:

> The most common and the most significant of all the perversions – the desire to inflict pain upon the sexual object, and its reverse – received from Krafft-Ebing the names of "sadism" and "masochism" for its active and passive forms respectively. Other writers . . . have preferred the narrower form "algolagnia." This emphasizes the pleasure in *pain*, the cruelty; whereas the names chosen by Krafft-Ebing bring into prominence the pleasure in any form of humiliation or subjection.[7]

Freud's comment is telling: somehow the literary allusion of Krafft-Ebing's terms, as opposed to the scientific language of Greek roots, has connotations of humiliation. While Freud is not suggesting that literature is somehow humiliating, or literary illusions are somehow less valuable (for they provided him a wealth of examples), it is clear that Sade's text does come into play for him, but that it is simultaneously repressed *as text*. Still, the use of the term "sadism" brings into prominence the literary nature of the text as well as its author. For Freud, what Sade talks about is true: it is as if Sade's narrative were itself the narrative of a fantasy or even of a real scene. But Freud omits the "literariness" of the Sadean text: the fact that there are constraints placed on it quite different from those involved in the recounting of a dream or fantasy by a patient to an analyst. Freud omits, or elides, the parameters and paradigms that make fiction what it is, and moreover, that might eventually put into question the "truth" framed by that fictional framework. The difference here is that Sophocles is, and always has been, canonical, whereas Sade and Sacher-Masoch are not. Sophocles survives under the onslaught of psychoanalysis; Sade does not. To find Sade and his text, then, we must look under the Freudian or post-Freudian palimpsest and, at least for now, exclude "sadism" and pretend that it does not yet exist, textually speaking. To find the literary Sade, we must reverse the implications of having initially excluded this literary Sade and replaced him with the Sade of liberation or some modern or postmodern Sade, who were themselves responses to this initial exclusion of the Sadean text and not simply of the Sadean text as literature.

This movement is similar to what Jacques Derrida describes in *Of Grammatology* as a triple violence: the first violence is in the act of naming and in giving names that it will be forbidden to pronounce; the second violence consists of removing this first name and of instituting the moral order. The third violence, possible but not always realized, is "evil, war, indiscretion, rape."[8] Thus, within the literary-historical horizon of Sade's text, the first violence would be Sade's own acts of naming what he names in any one of a hundred orgies and "sadistic" scenes in the novels. The second violence would be the repression of that naming in the name of morality and the redefinition of that morality as liberation or as psychoanalysis. Reversing upon itself, the third violence repeats the first to show the "evil, war, indiscretion, rape" within the novelistic as functions of the novelistic.

The question then is one of reading texts; and, more accurately, it is one of defining a position for Sade as a literary event that is not made liminal for extratextual reasons or for moral ones; nor is it coopted by or into another discipline. The field of inquiry has already been marked off through a questioning of the apophatic position described or denied both by literary history and acceptable inquiry (psychoanalysis).

"Apophatic" is the precise word: Sade's position is literally one that language has moved away from. For all the endless pages of description in the novels, Sade's text remains silent, even for the most revolutionary of readers. No truth value has been accorded to his textual stance and rhetoric, whereas the contents, as metaphor or abstraction, have been accorded a very high truth value. Even Roland Barthes, who reads Sade as literature and not as psychoanalysis or liberation, refuses to allow anything more than a pure semiotic position, ultimately a sterile one. Even he does not allow Sade to speak for himself, but fits him into some sort of poststructuralist mold in a move reminiscent of Claude Lévi-Strauss's own version of the Oedipus myth.[9]

For us, then, it is an easy matter to reverse polarities, without affecting the position of the textual elements, since they have not been touched: Sade's position shall henceforth, as if by fiat, be viewed as a phatic one, not an apophatic one. The text can/may speak. Sade can/may speak; the position remains to be defined. This path is most easily followed with the aid of an exemplary Sadean novel, *Juliette, ou les prospérités du vice*. Sade's own heritage is in the subtitle: the prosperities of vice, the means by which his and her fortune was secured. Her heritage is there as well, as text:

"Oh, my friends!" cried Juliette, wild from joy, "will he be wrong, the author who someday writes the story of my life, if he titles it *The Prosperities of Vice*? Make haste, Durand, tell us your wonderful tale, and be persuaded, let me say it at once, that 'tis I who beg you never again to leave us so long as you live."[10]

Telling the tale immortalizes the action and makes it prosper in its repetition of the event through writing. Of course, this text of prosperity is given in an act of closure which is itself impossible, for it predicts what we have already read. The impossible act of writing is accomplished here by Sade as he shifts the text to the third person from Juliette's twelve-hundred-page first-person narrative. Through this shift, the impossibility is demonstrated of writing *jouissance* as Sade conceives of it. The writing fulfills the text by repeating it and by inscribing the space of its production into the literary space. But it also negates that *jouissance* by showing that there is an unbridgeable difference between the *jouissance* and its writing. Juliette is not complete until she has her last orgasm, tantamount to death throes. The ultimate fulfillment and act of closure is impossible as a *locus loquendi*; it must be written. For the truly impossible moment, in fact the moment that maintains Sade's liminality, is not the sexual excess but a formal constraint: the text must occur *in articulo mortis*. But we only realize that this truly impossible moment exists at the end of our reading. Before that, we assume as we must that the text bridges the difference between itself and *jouissance*.

There is, as well, the necessity of feigning re-presentation through language in order to recuperate some authorial position:

> Unique in her kind, that woman died without having left any record of the events which distinguished the latter part of her life, and so it is that no writer will be able to chronicle it for the public. Those who might care to attempt its reconstruction will do little else than offer us their dreams in the place of realities, and between the two the difference is immense in the eyes of persons of taste and particularly in the eyes of those who have found the reading of this work of some interest.[11] (p. 1193)

In the essay *Reflections on the Novel* discussed above, Sade uses similar rhetoric to describe the so-called imitators of Jean-Jacques Rousseau. For Sade, there can be no *suite* for his work or for the author of *La Nouvelle Héloïse*:

> [W]e can safely assert that this sublime book will never be bettered; may that truth cause the pen to fall from the hands of that legion of ephemeral writers who, for the past thirty years, have continued to pour out poor imitations of that immortal original . . . (p. 105; p. 11)

Intradiegetically as well, as the ironic and parodic reversal of Rousseau's Julie in *La Nouvelle Héloïse* Juliette is, through censure and censorship, in an apophatic position. As a young girl reared in a convent, Juliette theoretically has no right to speak: she is a part of a social hierarchy where only "les hommes de qualité" have the right to speak with authority and impunity, which, in such a society, means the right to speak at all. Saint-Preux's impropriety in writing to Julie sets the whole improper communicational model in motion. The first three letters, all from Saint-Preux to Julie, underscore the impropriety of the writing. Julie answers, but she is already lost, even though she answers to say that "a virtuous heart should know how to overcome itself or be quiet."[12] The position of Julie or of Saint-Preux in *La Nouvelle Héloïse* or Juliette or even Sade, is technically a silent one, in fact, a mute one. They receive language and follow: they are receptacles for language, receivers not senders.

What makes *Juliette* a departure from *La Nouvelle Héloïse*, and from other novels written earlier in the century, is its distribution of the space of writing. We can separate the novelistic writing in France in the eighteenth century into two broad categories that justify narrative through moral grounds. On the one hand, there are the novels of the *honnête homme*, such as the long work of Prévost, whose *Manon Lescaut* is an authorized excerpt from a longer work entitled *Mémoires d'un homme de qualité*. Others authorized to write globally are those who have arrived or survived; such is the case for Marivaux's novels, *La Vie de Marianne* and *Le Paysan parvenu*. And one could even add moral tales like *La Religieuse* to this category, since the heroine's purity survives though she does not. On the other hand, there are novels that do not at all seem to be justified by the system: not only Sade's texts, but also, for example, *Les Liaisons dangereuses*, because its characters are anything but moral, and *La Nouvelle Héloïse*, because Saint-Preux is an inappropriate interloper, as well as all the scabrous and carnivalesque novels of the eighteenth century. The carnivalesque dialogism of a text like Le Sage's *Le Diable boiteux* or the extreme heteroglossia of Diderot's *Les Bijoux indiscrets* or Crébillon Fils's *Le Sopha* continues a pattern of the dialogical novel that Bakhtin sees as central to the novelistic tradition: we laugh, and in laughing we cannot censure.[13]

Two versions of this space exist prior to Sade's novels, two kinds of space of writing that correspond to versions of monological and dialogical space, without the universal continuity implied in the concept of the omniscient narrator of later praxis. One version of the space is univocal but not omniscient. In this space of writing seen in Crébillon Fils's *Le Sopha* and Diderot's *Les Bijoux indiscrets*, the space of enunciation is locally knowledgable and displaceable, but there is no global knowledge. Thus in Crébillon's novel, a sofa tells of where it has been and of its peregrinations through various households.[14] The displacement of the sofa is the excuse for the mastery of various local spaces through writing. In Diderot's novel, *Les Bijoux indiscrets*, the author uses a device like Gyges' ring to have women's genitalia talk.[15] But since the ring can have only one bearer at any given moment, it is passed from hand to hand just as Crébillon's sofa moves from location to location. And significantly, when it is a question of creating a truly pornotopic space of writing, evenly filled and and not polarized, Diderot modestly or wisely switches tongues and writes scabrous tales in English, Latin, Italian.[16]

The other version of the space of writing is that of the epistolary novel and corresponds to a plurivocal dialogical space. Each voice within the epistolary novel masters a local space but never exceeds that position. The space can be relatively large or small, depending on the mastery or innocence of the writer.[17] Madame de Merteuil's pen is wide-ranging; she can even occupy a metaliterary position at times, since she has mastered the space of writing by having read *Le Sopha*.[18] The space of writing of Julie in Rousseau's novel starts out minimally, but spreads as she develops within the "pathetic sentimentality" of the novel. There is also at least one example of a hybrid between these two forms of local writing, found, not surprisingly in *Les Liaisons dangereuses* (p. 99): in a famous scene in Letter 47, Valmont writes a letter to Madame de Tourvel by using the naked back of Emilie as a writing desk.

Laclos finds various ways to distend the space of writing and to make the pornotopia present as a locus of speech and writing in this scene. But Emilie is no Sadean victim, nor is the space that Laclos thereby defines a general one.

Sade breaks with his predecessors by generalizing the space of Emilie's back: it becomes the desk for writing, the scene for torture, and the locus of *jouissance* for the celebrant. This generalized space can be seen most emblematically in the various orgy scenes in *Juliette* and, of course, in *The 120 Days of Sodom* as the paradigm that informs the text as a whole. In this radical move, Sade empowers Juliette, who does speak (and at times interminably) to fill the entire space of the novel with language.[19] Sade has not only created a generalized pornotopia for the scene of writing but has also reversed the moral categorization of narrative: Juliette is always in a position of narrative authority, even from the start. Whereas Justine, ostensibly and somewhat less scandalously, can tell her story as a moral object lesson, the same claim cannot be made for Juliette. It is not a question of evolution, that is, gradual accession to an authorized position of enunciation as in a *Bildungsroman*, for Juliette's authority results from her actions; external authority is and has always been rejected.[20] It is rather a question of revolution.

Sade scandalously allows a theoretically non-viable communicator and agent to be a subject of action and of enunciation. It is not at all a situation where she is passed the scepter of authority after education, as is the case, for example, in *La Vie de Marianne*. Marianne can recursively tell the story of her life after she has become a *dame de qualité*. *Juliette* is in part an ironic parody of Marivaux's novel just as it parodies Rousseau's. But it is not merely a reversal, as Juliette is constantly arrogating to herself power and the authority to act and speak without entering into a social contract with everyone else. Were Juliette simply akin to Marianne, or even Madame de Merteuil in *Les Liaisons dangereuses*, or Moll Flanders, the story would have been less scandalous; but there is no entry into an act of inscription that validates the assumption of authority. Even the social contract of the *Société des Amis du Crime* is rather a covenant that refuses the yielding of freedom and sets about breaking social contracts with the other: "No condemnation by a court of law, no public disgrace, no defamation of character will disqualify a candidate for admission into the Sodality"

(p. 421).[21] And when it is in fact a question of writing a social contract, even in a perverse form, which is an agreement on a common language as well as being a social agreement, Juliette refuses to do so:

> "Very well. If ever Raimonde meets with a tragic and unaccountable end, let the blame fall nowhere but upon me. And now," Durand continued, "I demand that you put a paper into this girl's keeping, which authorizes her to denounce me as your assassin in the event you perish in some unhappy way at any moment during the course of our relations."
>
> "No, I object to such precautions, I entrust myself to you . . ." (p. 1036)[22]

There is an investment of desire – that of the author – in this creation of a parodic version of Rousseau's Julie in Juliette: a desire for her to do, or more precisely for her to say, what has been refused him. More than any of his other novels, more than any of the didactic monologues or dialogues, Juliette, both as novel and protagonist, is the idealized locus of enunciation and action for the author. Neither for Sade nor for Juliette is this action what we know or understand as sadism; it is the action of writing, the production and the inscription of the text. Both as novel and as character, Juliette is the fulfillment of desire (that is, textual desire) and the means of overcoming any difference between desire and its accomplishment. As the accomplishment of desire, the text itself bridges the difference between the subject of enunciation and the subject of action. Grammatically, the text thus recuperates all *énoncé* into enunciation, in a deixis that absolutely relates all textual events to the subject of enunciation. Even in the form of a tense like the *passé simple* – theoretically radically different from the subject of enunciation and even in the shape of a grammatically non-existent form such as "je foutis" (I fucked) – this is not different from the moment of enunciation that is the form for the *énoncé*: "I put my hand to her cunt, it was still warm, I frigged her; donning a dildo, I fucked her."[23]

The text is thus the recuperation or reappropriation of difference, so that text and desire appear identical, an identity only challenged by the end of the novel; in other words, the text serves to accomplish desire absolutely, and it is therefore perceived somehow as presence. Though reached through the back door, the Sadean position of enunciation ultimately does not seem to differ from that of white mythology, which seeks presentification in the act of representation.[24] For Sade, it takes the form of a representation of the total and absolute accomplishment of an act of desire. All that was necessary in order to evince a reproduction (thus refused by Sade) or simulacrum of white mythology was to give Sade the floor, *lui donner la parole* and make his a phatic position. But for this giving, there must be a taking or reception, different from the text that already has *la parole*. The Sadean text, for all its profound similarity with tradition, was not and is still not in the same position; its position is one of difference, even as it denies difference. Despite our tentative inclusion of Sade in a revised standard version of the canon, it or he continues to shock, that is, to express a difference. And the difference from tradition is already inscribed within the text as it stands, before it is excluded from the corpus. The phatic position is always and already (mis)appropriated, desire is given as accomplished and not, as in standard white mythology, as a movement or troping towards being accomplished. Somehow the text refuses, not to say denies, inclusion. Oddly enough, for this "erotic text" what is not given is the concomitant fiction. Sade's text refuses what is given and comes to stand as supplementary writing, in the place of an irrecuperable absence; and it refuses the re-reversal into fiction through some phallogocentric discourse of power, that is, the act of inscription. His text does not act to make present as much as it presents the already accomplished act of desire.

And if one makes a brief comparison between the position of enunciation of Sade's text and that of the other eighteenth-century novels already discussed, another radical difference becomes apparent. Both Crébillon's *Le Sopha* and Diderot's *Les Bijoux indiscrets* have a position authorized by a substitute phallus; they can only talk because a phallus has been "there." But in *Juliette*, Sade's position differs scandalously; there is no intrinsic connection between the phallus and the logos.

Here it is a question of something else, something already there, not supplementary, not given; something parenthetically, occasionally glimpsed in other works.[25] But this scandal is sustained only in Sade's work. It is a position of enunciation different from, not to say prior to, the phallic one. It could be called a *choric* space, the position of a space, a receptacle, a receiver, even an enzymatic locus on which the substrate comes to rest: "the flows of sperm," *foutre* in general, both as a noun and as a verb, and from which the substrate leaves as text.[26] The choric position needs no fecundating phallic logos for there to be text. The phallic position distinguishes and differentiates; it separates subject from object, subject from verb. Sade's position is in general not ungrammatical, but with its indiscriminate use of *foutre* as verb, noun, and interjection, it undoes any possible difference that a phallic text would make or have with such a key word.

The space of writing of *Juliette* is that of the *chora* discussed in the *Timæus*:

... existing place (*tes choras æi*), which admits not of destruction, and provides room for all things that have birth ... for when we regard this we dimly dream and affirm that it is somehow necessary (*anagkaion*) that all events should exist in some *spot* and occupying some *place* (*kai katechon choran tina*).[27]

All dissolves into this receptacle, home and birthplace of a different issue than the common one. Phallus and uterus (womb) are equally rejected by Sade in favor of the choric or Socratic asshole (*cul*) for which the male member, as Sade would say, is no longer the privileged phallus, but rather the temporary conduit for *les flots de sperme*, atomized and in suspension to be united as text in *le cul de Juliette*, not by some phallic power, but by *jouissance*. *Jouissance* itself serves as the ring of Gyges that makes all space penetrable to the discourse of narration. Rather than being the phallus or its substitute, the male organ, or even the clitoris, is now only the substitute *chora*, the temporary but unfertile receptacle for the atomized text, holding the *foutre*, indiscriminately male or female in origin, that will be united fruitfully to produce the novel. All events, truth, fictions, and roles, pass through that portal. What will come out is not procreation but creation; not reproduction, but production:

My friends, it is time I tell you a little about myself, and above all describe my opulence, fruit of the most determinedly dissolute living [*débauches*], in order that you will be able to contrast it with the state of indigence and adversity [*infortune*] wherein my sister, who had chosen good behavior, was languishing already. Your outlook and philosophy will suggest to you what conclusions are to be drawn from these comparisons. (409; vol. VIII, p. 393)

And in the form of Juliette's ego-ideal, the all-powerful and insatiable Catherine the Great, it is never clearer or more succinct. The phallus gives only death and writing; the choric *cul* produces the fulfillment of desire: "'The swelling [*bandant*] prick you are holding in your hand [*que vous empoignez*], Princess,' was my reply, 'is ready to sign her death warrant in your ass'" (876 vol. IX, p. 279).

Thus there exists a textual reason for the refusal of procreation that is not simply a reversal of the natural or normal world, as given in the status of the *Société des Amis du Crime*:

... propagation being utterly alien to its spirit and aims; true libertinage abhors progeniture; and the Sodality therefore disfavors it: female Members will denounce men given to this mania and if the latter prove incorrigible, they also will be invited to prepare their withdrawal from the Sodality. (p. 423; vol. VIII, p. 406)

It is the women then who have the ultimate power, since it is they who must refuse the procreative functions of male and female genitalia. Most fundamentally then, it is another mode of perception, another mode of enunciation, that is, another kind of birth, that of a text, something far more important, far more permanent than the ephemeral issue of one's loins. It is a birth by midwifery; there is always a third present as the physical or observing auxiliary for *jouissance*. Without this third, Juliette is inevitably silent when no one is present apart from a single lover; the other may discourse, but Juliette is usually mute, and does not produce actions that would otherwise immediately be translated into text. And, given the equipotentiality and the non-polarization of choric space, Juliette can, when necessary, be her own midwife for textual production, as long as others are present to fill the generalized choric space. This space is not simply the specificity of *le cul de Juliette*, but also the disseminated, undifferentiated space of lubricity, the orgy-room, where, even in the wildest, most ecstatic moments, Juliette always speaks coherently. Even in the re-telling of these moments, where she thus reaccomplishes her own *jouissance*, words never fail her. Being unnatural, this means of text production is a kind of bastard reasoning (*hapton logismo tini notho*), as Plato says in the same passage on the chora. The question of legitimately produced text is inevitably undercut by the eternal and perpetual *jouissance* of didactic *foutre*: Cordelli "socratizes" Juliette's *cul* (p. 1048).[28]

The choric impulse, the choric locus of enunciation, is a *refusal* of the voice of the phallogocentric universe, the voice which is proposed as a coming to full presence, in the form of a *recuperation* of presence through writing. At the same time, it is a refusal of the simultaneous act of repression of writing *as* writing. As the Pope says: "In these matters Nature is silent; the voice that thunders inside us belongs to the prejudice which with a little effort and determination we can quell forever" (p. 780).[29] For Sade, then, the Pope is, in his own way the ironic dissociation of phallus and logos, as are in general the abundant priests and brothers and especially those who receive confession, so plentiful in Sade's texts. The voice, be it *logos* or *phoné*, is only that of prejudice: pre-decision, phallic imposition of an arbitrary position of authority, given as the authoritative, original one. No longer a discourse of power, the male voice, the voice of power and authority, given as origin of institution and individual, dissolves into the disseminated *foutre* to be absorbed, as Sade says, to be taken into the choric receptacle. Juliette: "Sodomized by the Pope, the body of Jesus Christ nested in one's ass, oh, my friends! what rare delight [*quelles délices*]. It seemed to me I had never in all my life tasted quite the like" (p. 802; vol. IX, p. 206). Hers is a discourse of fulfillment and of plenitude. For it to work, there must be a maximization of input, the largest flow of *foutre* possible. Every orifice must be filled: hands, mouth, rear, armpits, and vagina, the last being the various or substitute *cul*, desacralized space that can be filled with the non-differentiated *foutre* of the *flots de sperme*. The *con* is another *cul* and not a locus of conception.³⁰ Hence, too, at least textually, if not sadistically, the need for maximized flow, be it blood, shit, urine, or *foutre* in general: all flows into the receptacle, understood specifically as the *cul*, and generally as a decentered or deplaced cloacal receptacle: "a deluge of wines, spirits, shit, fuck [*foutre*], and bits of human flesh" (p. 922; vol. IX, p. 324). All flows in not to reproduce, but to produce the logorrhea.

But there is also a question of deferral which amounts to a question of continuation: how long can the flow of *foutre* or of language continue? The *fouteur*, deprived of his or her *foutre* and not replenished, is already dead for Sade: *la petite mort* is death just the same. It is only those who can make the moment of production last who survive, for a time at least: those who discourse – Delbène, Noirceuil, Clairwil – and those who textualize the *foutre* – Juliette, and of course, Sade himself. But the choric receptacle cannot, quite clearly, just contain; the isolated monad that cannot pour *foutre* or text is as good as dead:

So saying, he secures her hands upon a butcher's block, embuggers her, and I cleave off her hands while he is operating; the blood is staunched, the stumps bandaged [*les plaies se bandent*]. . . . Immediately, fucking uninterruptedly, the barbarian orders his victim to open her mouth and stick forth her tongue: I seize it with tongs, I sever it at the root; I gouge out the remaining eye. . . . Noirceuil discharges.
. . . he drove the point of a knife successively into each of her ears. (pp. 1183–84; vol. IX, pp. 577–8)

The French continues: "[Noirceuil] la prive promptement du seul organe qui lui reste"; she is quickly deprived of her only remaining sense organ. If the ear, passive organ though it be, can be used as a receptacle, it too must be filled and closed; this is the antithesis of the Annunciation, the anti-message of the flesh made word. The monad is *foutu* in both the literal and figurative senses of the word, just as the one who is spent. The only one who can survive is the one who can process, the one who can produce.

This scene posits an ironic and pathetic figure opposed to Juliette. Not coincidentally, this scene of total closure comes at the end of the book, right before Juliette's own announcement of her own textualization. The closed monad is opposed to Juliette who can transform the torrents of liquid – blood, *foutre*, shit – into text. Not exactly the substance of the Eucharist, but rather, water into wine, wine into blood, and blood into text. Juliette's closure is other; she cannot be finished by action, but must be transformed textually. Finally, "s'écrie Juliette," the text becomes a third-person narrative; it produces a closure to the story:

> Thus did Madame de Lorsange conclude the story of her adventures, whose scandalous details had more than once wrung bitterest tears from the interesting Justine. Otherwise stirred were the Chevalier and the Marquis; the straining and full-colored pricks [*les vits nerveux*] they brought to light proved how different were the sentiments that animated them [*les avaient animés*]. (p. 1189; vol. IX, p. 582)

This narrative closure brings to an end the entirety of this phase of Sade's novelistic production, which includes both *Justine* and *Juliette*. In order to end the action, Justine must also finally die; in her death the death of the monad just described is itself rhetoricized. And Justine, who is the good and virtuous observer, the endless listener, and the vicarious reader, is finally reversed through a thunderclap [*un éclat de foudre*] which is as good as saying that she is finally killed by *un éclat de foutre*:

> Justine is shown the door; not only is she not given as much as a penny, she is sent forth stripped of the little that remained to her. Bewildered, humiliated by such ingratitude and so many abominations, but too content to escape what could have been worse still, the child of woe, murmuring thanks to God, totters past the château gates and down the lane leading to the highroad. . . . Scarcely does she reach it when a flash of lightning breaks from the heavens, and she is struck down, smitten by a thunderbolt that pierces her through [*Elle y est à peine arrivée, qu'un éclat de foudre la renverse, en la traversant de part en part.*] (p. 1190; vol. IX, p. 583)

As far as literary production is concerned, the act of closure of the text is a jockeying of positions of first and third persons,

between the *je* and the *elle*.[31] This is the necessary means for
Sade to accomplish his aim, fulfill his goal, *combler son désir*,
through text. For this fulfillment to occur, the phallic reasserts
itself as omnipotent, over what resisted (in *Justine*) and what
was other (in *Juliette*): "greatest success crowned our heroes
for the next ten years. At the end of that space, the death
of Madame de Lorsange caused her to disappear from the
world's scene just as it is customary that all brilliant things
on the earth finally fade away" (p. 1193; vol. IX, pp. 586–87).
Juliette's desire and fulfillment were substitutes, rhetorical
vicars, of Sade's own. The installation of the third-person
narration at the end of the novel is the sole available means
for the author to produce the text, to come forth. Of course,
it is a return of the repressed: the phallic discourse is absent
for so many hundreds of pages, except the occasional footnotes
with the implied rhetorical author. But it is also the necessary
closure, or, perhaps the orgasmic death and rebirth in text, for
this author who cannot go on eternally like his heroine. It is
the necessary closure for this pornography for pornography,
after all, is etymologically not phallic writing or discourse, but
choric writing, the writing of the oldest profession.

NOTES

1 Marcelin Pleynet, "Sade, des chiffres, des lettres, du renferme-
   ment," *Tel Quel* 86 (1980), p. 28.
2 Jean-Jacques Rousseau, *La Nouvelle Héloïse*, in *Oeuvres complètes*
   (Paris: Gallimard [Pléiade, 1970–79], vol. II, p. 4.
3 The Marquis de Sade, *The 120 Days of Sodom and Other Writings*,
   trans. Austryn Wainhouse and Richard Seaver (New York:
   Grove Press, 1966), pp. 97–116. For the French text, see The
   Marquis de Sade, "Idée sur les romans," in *Oeuvres complètes*
   (Paris: Cercle du Livre Précieux, 1966), vol. X, pp. 3–22. I shall
   give the references to this work in the body of the text with the
   English page number followed by the French.
4 Angela Carter, *The Sadeian Woman and the Ideology of Pornography*
   (New York: Pantheon, 1978), p. 18.
5 Writing "fictions," each of these has challenged generic and
   canonic norms. Each has also written on Sade: Pierre Klossowski,
   Sade mon prochain (Paris: Seuil, 1947); Georges Bataille, *La*

Littérature et le mal, in *Oeuvres complètes* (Paris: Gallimard, 1970–88), vol. IX, pp. 239–58; Maurice Blanchot, *Lautréamont et Sade* (Paris: Minuit, 1963). At another remove, see Jane Gallop, *Intersections* (Lincoln: University of Nebraska Press, 1981). Clément Rosset criticizes Bataille, Klossowski, and Blanchot for trying to introduce intellectual and philosophical coherence into a text (Clément Rosset, "L'écriture violente," *Nouvelle Revue Française* 320, 1980, p. 64).

6 One critic expresses the thought as follows: "In many ways, Sade belongs more to the twentieth century than to the eighteenth, for it is this century which, starting with the research of Apollinaire and Maurice Heine and culminating in the 1950s and 1960s with the criticism of Beauvoir, Paulhan, Blanchot, Klossowski, and Bataille, has brought his texts and significance to light." Jacob Stockinger, "Homosexuality and the French Enlightenment," in *Homosexualities and French Literature,* ed. George Stambolian and Elaine Marks (Ithaca: Cornell University Press, 1979), pp. 175–76.

7 Sigmund Freud, *Three Essays on the Theory of Sexuality,* in *The Standard Edition of the Works of Sigmund Freud,* ed. James Strachey, 24 vols. (London: The Hogarth Press, 1953–74), vol. VII, p. 157.

8 Jacques Derrida, *Of Grammatology,* trans. Gayatri Chakravorty Spivak (Baltimore: The Johns Hopkins University Press, 1976), p. 112.

9 Roland Barthes, *Sade, Fourier, Loyola* (Paris: Seuil, 1971).

10 The Marquis de Sade, *Juliette,* trans. Austryn Wainhouse (New York: Grove Press, 1968), p. 1192. All references to *Juliette* will be to this edition and will be indicated by page number in the text. Since the translation is often less than faithful, and given the necessity of a more exact quote for the purposes of literary study, I shall include the original version in the notes when necessary. The references will be to the Marquis de Sade, *L'Histoire de Juliette, sa sœur, ou les prospérités du vice,* in *Oeuvres complètes,* vols. VIII–IX. When the translation is fairly accurate I shall just list the French reference after the English in the body of the text; here it is vol. IX, p. 585.

11 *OC,* vol. IX, p. 587: "et cette femme, unique en son genre, morte sans avoir écrit les derniers événements de sa vie, enlève absolument à tout écrivain la possibilité de la montrer au public. Ceux qui voudraient l'entreprendre ne le feraient qu'en nous offrant leurs rêveries pour des réalités, ce qui serait d'une étonnante différence aux yeux des gens de goût,

et particulièrement de ceux qui ont pris quelque intérêt à la lecture de cet ouvrage."

12 *La Nouvelle Héloïse*, p. 37.

13 See, for example, the introduction and first chapter of Mikhail Bakhtin, *Rabelais and His World*, trans. Hélène Iswolsky (Cambridge, MA: MIT Press, 1965), pp. 1–144, where Bakhtin discusses the Menippean satire as the basis for the carnivalesque novel and the liberating effect of laughter in such novels; see also Mikhail Bakhtine, *Esthétique et théorie du roman*, trans. Daria Olivier (Paris: Gallimard, 1978).

14 See Crébillon Fils, *Le Sopha* (Paris: Desjonquères, 1984). The novel appeared originally in 1742.

15 Denis Diderot, *Les Bijoux indiscrets*, in *Oeuvres romanesques*, ed. Henri Bénac (Paris: Classiques Garnier, 1962), p. 9. See *The Republic*, 359E–360A, for the story of Gyges' ring.

16 Diderot, *Les Bijoux indiscrets*, pp. 194–96.

17 Bakhtin calls this space the "sentimental pathetic *in camera*" (*Esthétique et théorie du roman*, p. 209).

18 Choderlos de Laclos, *Les Liaisons dangereuses* (Paris: Classiques Garnier, 1961), p. 27 (Letter 10).

19 Rosset ("L'écriture violente," p. 61) sees Sade's writing as violent because it is violating or raping the real. One way it accomplishes this violation is by filling every possible space with writing, the novelistic equivalent of *foutre*.

20 In "Gender and narrative possibility" (this volume), Nancy Miller sees *Juliette* as participating in the tradition of the *Bildungsroman*. She believes that Juliette's self-development is "a reversal of the valorization assigned to the cultural and literary conventions encoding femaleness, the positively marked status of daughter, wife, mother" (p. 214). But, as I have already tried to show within the framework of the horizon of literary history, Sade's text is not one subject to simple reversal. Moreover, the concept of *Bildungsroman* is tied to a morality: the *Bildung* always occurs within a moral code.

In "Another look at the Sadean heroine" (*Essays in French Literature* 13, 1976, pp. 28–43), David Williams stresses the opposition between male and female, though not in the structuralist-semiotic mode that Miller uses. Williams (p. 30) seems to feel that the "price of survival for Juliette involves a sacrifice of those very qualities that Justine retains to the bitter end. By becoming one with the predatory world around her, however, her femininity has been cauterized, and a loss of human identity has taken place."

In her article on Sade, "Ambivalence in the gynogram" (*Women and Literature* 7:1, 1979, pp. 24–37), Beatrice Fink also stresses the bivalent logic of sexuality. For Fink (p. 25) "Gynocentrism in Sadean fiction is understandable in terms of adherence to novelistic tradition of the period on the part of a writer who was prone to using conventions and clichés in his literary formats. The basic explanation, however, lies in the manifest necessity of having inferiors in a never-ending process of domination. Women, in other words, are indispensable targets of refutation and victimization within the confines of phallocratic politics."

The articles of these three critics are certainly illuminating, but in distinction to the bivalent logic of sexuality they propose, I would like to propose a more complex system in which a less oppositional sexuality is the sign of the space of Sade's writing. As I will show below, the opposition in *Juliette* is not one of male versus female, but rather one of heterosexually defined viability and space (male and female) versus everything else. To reduce Sade to a bivalent sexuality of power and dominance, and to make him thereby the champion (or enemy) of women, is, I think, to use a rhetorical gesture similar to that of Bataille or Klossowski, who, in their phallocentric universes, invent the Sade of liberation.

21 *OC*, vol. VIII, p. 404: "Aucune flétrissure juridique, aucun mépris public, aucune diffamation n'empêchera d'être reçu dans la Société."

22 *OC*, vol. IX, pp. 434–5: "– Eh bien! poursuivit Durand, si jamais Raimonde périt d'une manière tragique, et dont tu ne puisses soupçonner la cause, n'en accuse que moi. J'exige maintenant que tu laisses un écrit dans les mains de cette fille, qui l'autorise à me dénoncer comme ton assassin, si jamais tu péris toi-même d'une manière malheureuse, pendant notre liaison.

– Non, je ne veux point de ces précautions; je me livre à toi . . ."

23 The English here is particularly aberrant, since it is not the cunt but the person that is still warm: "Je la branlai; elle était encore chaude; armée d'un godémiche, je la foutis" (*OC*, vol. IX, p. 429). Maurice Grévisse, *Le Bon Usage* (Gembloux, Belgium: Editions Duculot, 1969, p. 653), says that *foutre* is a defective verb which lacks a *passé simple* and for which the imperfect subjunctive is rarely found. Significantly this grammatical impossibility occurs in Sade in a situation where a woman is fucking a corpse, a double "impossibility" in the world governed by "good usage."

Is the verb defective because a completely perfective verb, for the first person, could only exist *post mortem*?

24 For Jacques Derrida, "white mythology" is both the constant fiction that metaphysics tells itself about presence and its search for presence and the tropes of light, purity, and whiteness it uses to move a text toward this goal. See Jacques Derrida, "White mythology," in *Margins of Philosophy*, trans. Alan Bass (Chicago: University of Chicago Press, 1982), pp. 207–71.

25 Seventy-five years later, Flaubert's *Madame Bovary* was to scandalize for many of the same reasons.

26 The word *foutre* can be translated as "to fuck" and as "cum." I am maintaining this joining of action and result by using the French word in the text.

27 Plato, *Timæus* 52b.

28 "il me socratise" (*OC*, vol. ix, p. 447). Other instances of this singular verb that introjects the Platonic space into Juliette's *cul* can be found at p. 95; vol. viii, p. 100, p. 290; vol. viii, p. 279, and p. 1007; vol. ix, p. 407.

29 "La nature n'a donc point de voix; celle qui tonne en nous n'est donc plus que celle du préjugé, qu'avec un peu de force nous pouvons absorber pour toujours" (*OC*, vol. ix, p. 184).

30 As has often been stated, Sade's text refuses every aspect of procreation. Carter (*The Sadeian Woman*, p. 109) remarks to what extent the mythology of procreation is refused as well: "The womb is an imaginative locale ... it lies in an area of psychic metaphysiology suggesting such an anterior primacy of the womb ... Sade's invention of Juliette is an emphatic denial of this emphatic rhetoric."

31 We should recall that Emile Benveniste calls the third person a "non-person." When Juliette becomes this third person, her text and validity have come to an end (Emile Benveniste, *Problèmes de linguistique générale*, Paris: Gallimard [TEL], 1966, vol. i, p. 228).

CHAPTER 12

Fantasizing Juliette

Chantal Thomas
(Translated by David B. Allison, Mark S. Roberts, and Allen S. Weiss)

A dormitory is not a brothel. You must know how to sleep on a regular schedule. Exhaustion has nothing to do with it. The system will wake you up anyway. Everyone's dreams end at precisely the same hour. That's not much of a sense of community – not even if you consider the last fifteen minutes, when everybody is caught up in the diverse metamorphoses of the morning alarm. The most gifted, the most philosophically crafty among them dream that they hear a bell; the more imaginative (because least self-assured) dream of Descartes as a tea-kettle forgotten on the stove. Every time I try to read, it shrieks in my ears. In fact, it almost scalds me, the damned thing. A sad scenario for hard-pressed dreamers. But what follows is even worse: Bordeaux literary studies. A year of being closed up in grey surroundings. The dull and overcast presentiment of catastrophe, always looming and ever-present. A dead port. But to fight it is to succumb to it. Better to feign being bothered by some inner suffering. A mechanical but no less flexible strategy worked out under a dull grey skirt. Oval calves symmetrically divided lengthwise by the fine seams of flesh-colored stockings. (Like sexology, cosmetic surgery becomes more perfect every day.) All these are bitter victories, however, when confronted by the inevitable corruption of the flesh, the steadfast resistance of the perversions – in short, by anything that perfects us by making us worse.

The elegance of the administrative office. Madness is just a respite, the opposite of abandon or of a wrong move. The woman stops. She opens her compact and looks at herself in the mirror. She traces the labyrinth of her wrinkles with the point of a knife. This inveterate coquette, and great businesswoman besides, henceforth seems to prefer the play of a knife to that of a powder-puff. It must be said that this is an appropriate substitution. Why not go out and take a walk? The windows in the shoestores are, after all, deep and alluring. But it's not worth getting up for that. Stop the flow. The sleepy girls get dressed, hardly aware of themselves. It's been a long time since the ships have actually set sail. Literature. Emerging from such sublimated depths, such wretched origins. There is a tacit understanding on this point. Even to ask the question amounts to excluding yourself from the answer. The authors' names on the reading list ring in their ears like colonels' orders, like measured steps, secret executions. Several suicides followed – the romantics.

Whatever the reasons, and it goes without saying, if you keep to what's said it's always possible to do literature. The teacher exposes his gums while speaking. The young girls vomit. Nothing had prepared them for such crudeness of enunciation. Some of them no longer choose to return to that spectacle and so they continue to see, behind nauseated, closed eyes, a very blue and smooth sea torn by the blood of wounded fish. After evening studies, they return to the dormitory – exhausted by the hopeless task of reconstituting dead languages. Verbs open up a weary path, after all, one which quickly leads to discouragement. One suspects the most animated conversations to be quietly repeated in some ultimate and silent effort of memorization. They write their diaries before going to sleep – a polite insistence on the part of the physiological functions.

R. saw us, M. and I, when we were walking together during recess. I like R. very much – especially the disproportion between her heavy breasts and her thin arms. There is an engaging kind of awkwardness that moves me to tears. I think of Rousseau in the Parisian Salons. She also has a very pretty notebook, with a black, shiny cover, strangely supple under the pressure of her fingers. The white of the pages has a soft luminosity, and even at a distance it emits a perfect light. A friend brought it back from Venice for her. Professor T. hates me – unless she is just hateful in general. In any case, I'm not complaining. No letter from S. The day had been longer than usual; when I opened the door of the study hall (returning from a brief excursion to the toilet), the metal doorknob left a cold, hard impression in the palm of my hand. It produced a cruel shiver in me and I felt a deep pain. Sitting down again to work on my Xenophon translation, it seemed to me that, in a kind of vertigo, all the lines began to swirl in a circle, whose center was legible to me. If only I had followed the lecture . . .

Twist of Death. The sun split from the outset.

Debauch yourself with the work of death. Speak and let your words translate you.

She doesn't surrender to sleep. The eyelids burnt with yellow light. The nape of the neck crushed. She drools. The page itself swells up with moist pustules. This book is unhealthy. You would need a torture by fire to dry up the malignant humors. I'm talking about *Les Crimes d'amour*.

My friend said that the theater occasionally presents equally frightful scenes, but that it's less dangerous than a chance reading of these very same grave horrors. They sleep in the same dormitory, but all they have in common is the air they breathe. Reclusive girls bound together by nothing more than the daily fatigue of awakening and, occasionally, perhaps, the prospect of a dazzling insight. *Libido sciendi*. Absolute Sin. Furtive practice. Space closes in upon a day completely broken up by the work schedule. A day pacified by the senseless boredom of merely being there. But there was some release. That the celebration was austere should not mislead us. You must realize that the young souls did love one another, which, in addition, permitted them to show off a bit. This is why, alas, they could sleep so peacefully. Flush, with her cheeks on fire, she is attentive – to those inaccessible bodies, so white and rhetorically smooth. Idolatry and collapse. Large blue eyes filled with the most tender interest and with the form of the Graces. Blond, brunette, hair black as jet descending below their thighs. She had a thin, narrow tongue and the most beautiful blush – her breath couldn't be sweeter – skin so white, so soft, so fresh, an ass so precisely and artistically formed, of the most exact roundness. Infatuated with exactitude, surprised that the field of geometry can be so invaded by voluptuousness, she reads, and is devastated by the words. The wildest readings – spread out upon the most coherent narratives and the strictest punctuation – are finished, and again taken up, randomly, all in a spasmodic rhythm. Pleasure is separated from each passage as the form of torture is prefigured on the victim's body. An infallible and unconquerable knowledge which originates in the mystery and clarity of complicitous forms. This can't be limited to the false reciprocity between sado-masochism and its techniques, or to an infinitely mobile play of differentiations, subject to pregiven rules. The definition of an ass is as perfectly open as that of a circle. What is important is not to let oneself be deluded by the premises. No one has the despotic right to submit me to what he says or thinks. She doesn't believe what she reads. Words aren't verified on the level of verisimilitude, but rather, upon the unknown regions of her body. That is what cuts off the breath, the heave of this massive, solitary, and disproportion-ate respiration by which she sleeps and dreams. The torture reserved for her is doubtless insomnia. It burns her eyelids with a match, allowing her neither rest nor sleep, nor even to close her eyes. There is no longer any compensation behind the curtain of her eyelids, no possible satisfaction. At 10:30 they shut off the lights – a violence strictly governed according to the tranquil irresponsibility of a divine arbiter. Beyond this is a resistance disseminated only in some few scattered lights. Small circles of light projected on the pages to which the readers' eyes are expectantly riveted, their faces effaced by the night. And the letters seem drawn out from this same murky blackness from which they are formed. This precarious and so assuredly abandoned attempt at reading gives the same impression of confidence and risk that is experienced while driving at night. Driven into an open grave. A double row of naked girls, frigid, almost plant-like, who can't be made to die, not because of the resistance they pose, but because of the incredible lethargy they lend to this task.

Their imperceptible deaths annul murder itself, swallowed up in the void of an immobility without place for memory or imagination. They sleep in the scent of their hair, within the sureness and density of their images. They possess the only real force. Sleep, finally, carries it away.

This is repeated every night.

She reads to the extent that she invents. The dictionary is there to correct the most notable distractions.

Lure: a term from falconry. A piece of red leather in the form of a bird used to bring the bird of prey back when he doesn't immediately return to the wrist.

Libertine: what is said of a bird of prey which deviates and doesn't return. A point in the sky. The libertine would recognize himself by virtue of his knack for spiriting himself away.

And the libertine woman? It's certainly possible grammatically. But yet . . . Is she, too, defined by a deviation without return? In the end, no doubt, neither takes a piece of red leather for a bird.

At the height of her friendship with Clairwil, Juliette tells her: "My atheism has reached its limits." But in any case this isn't enough. Libertinage is affirmed within the intransitivity of a restless demand, within the paradox of an exhortation to pleasure without respite. Sadean libertinage is a philosophy of intransigence. Its joy is terrorist.

A repetition that no way adds up. A mania for numbers founded on the mystical problematic of all or nothing.

A production which in no way entails reproduction. This propagation of libertinage works essentially against the very "laws of propagation."

A fire, a flood, a scourge.

An expenditure without reserve.

An untenable discourse, which is ordained only to be annulled, which is constructed only in anticipation of its own abolition.

Discharge/blasphemy.

The final point of orgasm, the climax of the orgy, is punctuated by the indefiniteness of an ellipsis. By suspending the masculine libertine discourse we pose the question of the libertine woman. This is also the case if the illegible figure of these three points (what punctuates writing, by definition, is not readable) is not merely to be reconstructed according to the triangulation of the female sex.

One is caught between the end of the libertine discourse, its gaping openness – its rent fabric – and the unspeakable idea of imposing the following torture upon the mother: "'Spread your legs, mother, and let me sew you up, so that you don't give me any more brothers and sisters' (Mme de Saint-Ange gives Eugénie a large needle threaded with a thick red waxed thread; Eugénie sews)." We see here the similar but inverted connection which ties hysterical delusion to women's work. We believe that torture and hysteria both originate in "daydreams," so common even among healthy people. After all, women's work offers many occasions to produce these daydreams.

From here on, their unlaced and asinine purposes, until now so well policed, so strictly articulated – invoking the ethic of sealed lips – do not side so much with libertine pleasure as with the victims' screams. Neither the pervert nor the hysteric can work in peace (hoping for family happiness or for the realization of her morbid adolescent fantasies.) And Eugénie delights and screams like a lunatic in spending the afternoon sewing up her mother's cunt.

The narratrice.

In an ostensible fashion. Sadean libertinage depicts a space where only *some* women speak.

Duclos, the narratrice of the month, in a very elegant and revealing state of undress, lots of rouge and diamonds – baits. A narrative setting in which only the actress is at risk. The spectators are inflamed by it – they become fragments detached from the totality of those perversions known as hell. They hear nothing of what is being said.

At this point, the narratrice goes silent. The scene is described in purely visual terms, without the tone or beauty of her voice.

A voicelessness brought on by the transparency of concepts – the ecstasy of The Word. By suppressing vocal singularity, this silence allows for the free deployment of discourse. Silence is but a prelude to unleashing the orgy. Such silence is opposed to the libertine's reduction of what is foreign to his universe and exists only to serve crime, even in the absence of discourse about the snow covering the external world or the cotton in the throats of the tortured. A voice passed over in silence to augment the meaning of libertinage – a meaning both plural and homogeneous (homosexual.)

The female libertine is a forgotten oblation to her vocal organ, a silence not caused by suffocation, but by something hidden or screened.

The libertine can't have an *other* voice.

As a woman, I think the same way, and I insist that if I were a man I would only fuck up the ass. The libertine's goodwill is boundless. It is renounced only at the moment of physiological lucidity (and humility). At these moments it becomes difficult to *unconditionally* affirm the imperative of fucking up the ass – except by means of developing a certain fantasia of the clitoris. (Thus, Volmar buggered with her own burning clitoris.)

Paradoxically, the libertine exists only within total acquiescence in a discourse which unfolds without the least subjective intervention, a sound-track which is automatically triggered by a flick of the hand. It functions better when it utilizes every lost voice, within the mad certainty of a purely logical energy.

The female libertine is a good schoolgirl who learns with pleasure and enthusiastically repeats lessons which she doesn't really understand, except for the frenzy they produce. Her head was spinning: proof enough that she had entered into the vertigo of libertinage, and that she could therefore, in turn, convey its meaning.

Her lesson, her chant, is of unlimited variations, of untiring digressions, upon the theme: Let's go, everybody, fuck and be fucked (up the ass, assuredly).

The virtuous victim, already silenced and virtually dead, can't help but hear – beyond "good advice" with its noble denotations but insulting connotations – brutal rejection with all its hostility. But crime is deaf. It is heedless to any injunction whatsoever, to the extent that its performance is caught up in a radical but limited polysemy. Libertine humor implies constant control over a play of words, ultimately acquired at the victim's expense. This is why the libertine, with all impunity, suffers no shortage of discourse. To listen to the victim is to be put into the position of being *overcome* by language, of no longer *knowing* the pleasure of losing one's head.

It is known that the height of drunkenness coincides with a kind of cold clarity, like the grey dawn, where Volmar, in this state of drunkenness, even more beautiful than Venus herself . . . When day breaks she is satisfied. Her sobriety both reawakens the darkness of crime and sustains a dream, one haunted by the sort of exclusion which is fundamental to libertinage. The relief of arrested movement.

Neither sister nor mother.

In an existence systematically woven by crime – like the total realization of perversion – dreams can be inscribed only within a rent, a fault, a neurotic shudder.

I thought I saw a frightful figure, embracing my house, my things, in flames; amidst this conflagration, a young creature held out her arms, trying to save me, and she herself perished in the flames. Justine: the repressed part of Juliette, whom she doesn't understand. We find this same gesture of the outstretched hand, the helpless demand, in one of Sade's dreams.

"Why are you down on the ground, moaning?" she asked me. "Come and join me. No more suffering, sorrow, or trouble in my immense domain. Be brave enough to follow me there." With these words, I prostrated myself at her feet and said to her, "Oh Mother! . . ." And the sobs stifled my voice. My tears covered her outstretched hands; she also wept.

But female libertines don't touch outstretched hands. First of all, because they only permit bodily contact for the direct, immediate, and localized pleasure they derive from it. Second, because they acknowledge no physical bonds and no sympathetic feelings for the flesh of another being. Whence the notion of eroticism as a combinatory play based on holes and wholes. But desire does not pass from hand to hand. To belong to the caste of libertines requires a double transgression, namely, to be excluded from the community of man and – a condition more twisted and impassioned – to be excluded from the rites of women.

Lesbians, orgiasts, villains.

In the Sadean universe only a woman can express all the pride and devotion with which she serves her passion: I love women. Libertines admit and encourage this, as an element of libertinage, as proof of corruption, and as demonstration of a philosophic mind. This must not be read as a declaration of lesbianism, or even of homosexuality. Granted, the female libertine may say that she prefers only women, or even more radically, that she hates men: Juliette – "I care very little for men; rather, it's with two charming women that I satisfy my desires. We would sometimes be joined by two of their friends for all kinds of extravagances." Clairwil – "I love to avenge my sex for the horrors men have made it undergo, when those villains come out on top." Nonetheless, she never denies herself the pleasure of using and enjoying men. In this way she acts in conformity with the male libertine, whose use of women is equally balanced between a somewhat nuanced distaste and complete horror. The system of libertinage is ruled by its division into two different kinds of homosexuality, symmetrically defined by means of the simple deployment of the masculine figure. (I know nothing more unjust than the law of mixing sexes to produce pure voluptuousness.) This dividing line is somewhat confused due to the principle of indifference according to which *everything* that concerns lust is valuable. Surely, this is the source of the pleasure in surreal juxtapositions, even of joining with the other sex. On this point the female libertines embody a peerless philosophy, and employ the penis with perfect ease. Male libertines, on the other hand, are incapable of the same detachment in regard to what they don't have. If these evil males are always hard, a cunt is enough to soften them up. But the female libertine goes forth hidden – white on white – and knows the master's secrets, even when they withdraw.

It is precisely to distance herself from this state of affairs that she speaks the libertine's language with such formal ease and freedom. She doesn't give a fuck about what she says – being a well-endowed student whose aptitudes her teachers find ravishing. Libertines acknowledge her the privilege of excessive cruelty, which they see as stemming from a greater sensitivity (hardly a libertine characteristic), and not from any fundamental duplicity (an essentially libertine quality which signals a constant danger to the very existence of libertine society – itself founded on a logical aporia). Being *absent* from the discourse that she sustains, she is only defined in terms of her interlocutor. Whence this madness, this transport of rationality, towards what allows such endless flight. The female libertine assumes the impossible economy of a discourse founded on loss. She is led to realize the very letter of libertinage by her extreme dispossession within the space of a society which ignores her. In just such a way the Society of the Friends of Crime, to which Clairwil introduced Juliette, is dominated by women.

I asked Noirceuil if he was going to join my girlfriend's club. "So long as men were in the majority," he replied, "I would be perfectly willing. But I gave up this idea ever since the club fell into the hands of a sex whose authority displeases me. Saint-Fond followed my example."

They simply turned away. Women's authority may be unpleasant, but it is in no way menacing, since in the strict sense it rests on *nothing*. This nothing, which so splendidly propels them into the domain of libertinage, nonetheless deprives them of a resting place, of any lover's identity.

The relations between female libertines are multiple and passionate, complete and inconsistent. They are bound together within a protected space – by the same token, an uncertain space – sheltered by the laws of libertinage. They follow a broken rhythm. Sadean women are united by violent shocks and baroque contortions, at the very heart of the inconceivable. They silently regard themselves and fuck. Under the protection of libertine discourse – which develops mechanically out of the given rhetoric – they offer themselves up to the pleasures of their mouths, lips, and tongues, all animated and mingled. By the expedient of a language used only as a password, they unite their bodies and venture their professional libertine caresses upon unknown regions. They find their speech in their deepest kisses. Lovers' speech, a mute tongue – all this is inscribed within the prohibitions of libertine discourse where everything is possible except love. Libertine pluralism, limitless in its diversity of tastes, does not extend to a taste for love, nor to a passion for Unity. It runs up against the contradiction of a reading which can only belong to singularity, but which must nonetheless be able to repeat itself infinitely.

Every cessation of the destruction of subjects stems from a lack of apathy, from the temptation to love against which the libertine must constantly keep guard.

"Do you really love her, Juliette?"

"I don't love anything, Saint-Fond, it's just a matter of caprice."

Short of a hidden declaration, and hidden behind the certainty of judgment, Juliette keeps the reality of her inner agitation – the excitement to which she hasn't given voice – to herself. (I loved Palmire. To give her up to that cannibal cost me dearly, but how could I refuse?) The formula "I love women" holds only as a deviation from libertinage, in that it indefensibly maintains the uniqueness of women. The attraction which draws one female libertine to another must not valorize the feminine: that would only give rise to another system. They join together according to the principle of a radical separation from "other" women, and they break from a standard homosexuality, whose persistence, nonetheless, informs their gestures with that radiance of pleasure and sensuality which overcomes them. My friend was as nude as I – we examined each other in silence for several minutes. Clairwil burned with excitement in seeing the beauty with which nature endowed me. But I wasn't satisfied simply admiring her beauty. There had to be a transfer of images, a return to that boundless enigma beyond all truth. They looked at each other and saw Beauty. Skin like fine sand. Blinded by the white beach, they closed their eyes. Then they opened them wide, companions in blindness.

I adore you without loving you, and I'll betray you since I do love you. In exchange for any resting place whatsoever, they inhabit a sacrificial, essentially *traitorous* space. Within the libertine logic of rigorous equivalence they indicate their preferences by a negative trait. The object is designated by its very suppression, according to a play of elective betrayals marking the impassioned exploits which ultimately destroy them – to speak and to take pleasure in betrayal.

Across the exemplary figure of the female Sadean libertine – under the pretext of a completely gratuitous choice (a fantasy valued only for the pleasure it brings us) – what we end up with is the following:

– the genius of this empty wisdom which has us meet and embrace one another (within a lost communication) without nostalgia or project, in that overwhelming moment of rediscovery.

– the theater of a discourse wherein we blithely perform – proudly ignorant of its own mastery but not of its practice – leaving to others the illusion of recognition, and holding us to the unfounded right of mutual betrayal.

– the desire to laugh which seizes us when we see ourselves thus develop a most convincing behavior, guided by a deficient speech which alters us according to the rhythm of our intoxication. For a well-conceived atheism must not deprive us of childish profanities otherwise it would be no less repugnant than religion itself.

Don't forget that when we die of laughter, we do so totally. Never alone, but always as an accomplice to murder, participating in an absence, and in the burden of a suicide lovingly deferred from one encounter to another. But perhaps nobody has sufficient psychic energy to kill himself if he hasn't first killed what he identifies with.

I slip the poison hidden between my fingers into the dish I serve Clairwil. A close-up of Juliette's fingers reveals an effusion of renounced tenderness. The brilliance of the rings, stones and slender nails captivates us and delivers us over to the deadly glitter of her extremely white fingers veined with invisible poison. Juliette: Digitalis. Purple digitalis alters the rate of heartbeat, reducing it to the white void of death. Her own servants, who detested her, thanked me gratefully for having freed them of such a horrible mistress, and took it upon themselves to secretly carry her to the sea as soon as night fell. (Liquidation if ever there was any.) A secret sea, obscure in its own transparency, in the somber depth traced by the interminable fall of a body.

The space she inhabits is immense. I turned toward you with no need of orienting myself. Your hair floats above your head, a halo of brown algae. As you emerge, it will incise a relief of fine plumes upon your skin. In the Gold Museum I saw the ponchos and plumes worn by Inca kings. Aerial relics, remains of imperialist pluckings, which did not serve as gifts, but which may with the passage of time fill museums. The Museum of Feathers. A nice name for a library. I prefer to think of your soft white skull under those red tresses, and it's not true that they lie in wait for me and threaten me like snakes of fire. I'm obstinately literal. I'm not the madwoman you think I am – though everyone says that. But you dive again and I shall wait for you, lulled to sleep under the waves, foam, and your own will. You enter this store to buy me a gift. I order a mint diabolo, and I continue to watch you behind the window, through the bubbles, and that's how I came to notice that your eyes are green. I never would have noticed this if I had bought a newspaper. I no longer need to read them to avoid sexual commerce (or how a woman comes to have spirit). It doesn't matter anyway, since I have exhausted the library. Let's go out into the street, the Via della Donna – I say a name at random, it's her, and it's in Florence. I know exactly what I want, and you choose it. They are multicolored and set in a white porcelain basket: I adore the red one. You offer it to me, this porphyry egg – oval, volcanic and smooth

– into the hollow of my palm. What coolness. Give me your vagina; you swoon; it's purple.

One day she receives a letter, cut up, too small for its envelope. She thinks: it's a death announcement with the black band, the ring of mourning, cut off. The empty space between the envelope and the card seems to hide something suppressed. Was this the effect of an unknown considerateness, or simply the pleasure of cutting paper? She doesn't read the card, and only keeps thinking of this somber border's absence.

Select Bibliography

The present bibliography is a selection of the major books, collective works, and articles on D. A. F. Sade in English and in French. The most recent and complete annotated bibliography on Sade was published in 1986 by Colette Verger Michael, *The Marquis de Sade, the Man, His Works, and His Critics* (New York: Garland). It includes all material published on Sade up to 1983. Other important bibliographies include E. Pierre Chanover, *The Marquis de Sade: A Bibliography* (Metuchen: Scarecrow Press, 1973); Françoise Laugaa-Traut, *Lectures de Sade* (Paris: A. Colin, 1973); Françoise Rosart's bibliography, published in *Obliques* 12–13 (1977); Michel Delon, "Dix ans d'études sadiennes (1968–1978)" in *Dix-Huitième Siècle* (1979); and Giorgio Cerruti, "Il Marchese di Sade: la sua recente fortuna egli ultimi studi critici (1958–1968)" in *Studi francesi* (1969). The reader will also find useful the bibliography found in Gilbert Lély, *D. A. F. de Sade*, 16 vols. (Paris: Cercle du Livre Précieux, 1966–7). Those readers interested in a chronology of Sade's life in English should refer especially to G. Lély's biography, *The Marquis de Sade* (New York: Grove, 1970), as well as to the Grove Press edition of *Justine, Philosophy in the Bedroom, and Other Writings* (1965). French sources include Lély's *Vie du Marquis de Sade* (Paris: Gallimard, 1952–7); Jean-Jacques Pauvert's *Sade vivant*, vols. I–III (Paris: Laffont, 1986–90); and Maurice Lever's *Donatien Alphonse François, Marquis de Sade* (Paris: Fayard, 1991), among others. The last has now been translated by Arthur Goldhammer as *Sade: A Biography* (New York: Farrar, Straus and Giroux, 1993.)

EDITIONS OF SADE'S WRITINGS

Oeuvres complètes, Paris: Cercle du Livre Précieux, 1966. This edition contains, as prefatory articles, most of the major studies on Sade published through 1965.

Oeuvres complètes, Paris: Pauvert, 1986. This reprint of the complete works excludes the prefatory essays mentioned above.

Oeuvres, vol. 1, ed. M. Delon, Paris: Gallimard, Pléiade, 1990.

Correspondance inédite du Marquis de Sade, de ses proches et de ses familiers, ed. P. Bourdin. Paris: Librairie de France, 1929; republished by Slatkine, 1971.

Lettres et mélanges littéraires écrits à Vincennes et à la Bastille, ed. G. Daumas and G. Lély. Paris: Borderie, 1980.

Juliette, trans. Austryn Wainhouse. New York: Grove Press, 1968.

Justine, Philosophy in the Bedroom, and Other Writings, trans. Austryn Wainhouse and Richard Seaver. New York: Grove Press, 1965.

The 120 Days of Sodom and Other Writings, trans. Austryn Wainhouse and Richard Seaver. New York: Grove Press, 1966.

COLLECTIVE WORKS

Europe 12–13, 1972.

Libération, 23 May 1986. A dossier on Pauvert's republication of the *Oeuvres complètes*, containing texts and interviews by Thibault de Sade, Jean-Pierre Thibaudat, Annie Le Brun, Alain Garric, Antoine de Gaudemar, Gérard Meudal, André Pieyre de Mandiargues, Octavio Paz, Chantal Thomas, Noëlle Châtelet, Jean Deprun, Philippe Roger, Pierre Naville.

Magazine Littéraire 284, January 1991. A dossier entitled "Sade écrivain," with articles by Jean-Jacques Brochier, Jean-Louis Debauve, Michel Delon, Pascal Dibie, Henri Lafon, Annie Le Brun, Pascal Pia, Philippe Roger, Philippe Sollers, Wald Lasowski.

Le Marquis de Sade. (Colloque du Centre Aixois d'Etudes et de Recherches sur le XVIIIe siècle.) Paris: Armand Colin, 1968. Articles by Henri Coulet, Jean Biou, Jean-Marie Goulemont, Jean Molino, Jean-Jacques Brochier, Jean Deprun, Jean Tulard, Claude Duchet, Jean Fabre, Jacques Cain, Pierre Naville.

Obliques 12–13, ed. Michel Camus. Paris: Borderie, 1977. Texts and reprints by Michel Camus, Pierre Guyotat, Marcel Moreau, Françoise Buisson, Philippe Roger, Marcel Hénaff, Jacques Henric, Jean-Pierre Faye, Alain Robbe-Grillet, Noëlle Châtelet, Lucette Finas, Bernard Sichère, Gérard Durozoi, Georges Daumas, Gilbert Lély, Maurice Heine, Guillaume Apollinaire, Jean Benoit, André Breton, Jean-Jacques Brochier, Jean-François Reverzy, Jean A. Cherasse, François Barrat, Georges Bataille, Maurice Blanchot, Philippe Sollers, Roland

Barthes, Hubert Damisch, René de Solier, Octavio Paz, Pierre
Klossowski, Jean Paulhan, Julius Evola, André Masson, Jean
Deprun, Eugen Duehren.

Sade, écrire la crise (Colloque de Cérisy), ed. Michel Camus and
Philippe Roger. Paris: Belfond, 1983. Articles by Lucette
Finas, Jacques Proust, Chantal Thomas, Noëlle Châtelet,
Andreas Pfersmann, Michel Delon, Jean-Marie Goulemot,
Jean-Claude Bonnet, Philippe Roger, Beatrice Fink, Pierre
Frantz, Béatrice Didier, Jean Ehrard, Michel Camus, Jean
Gillibert, Jean-Pierre Faye.

Tel Quel 28, 1967. Articles by Pierre Klossowski, Roland Barthes,
Philippe Sollers, Hubert Damisch, Michel Tort.

Yale French Studies 35, 1965. Articles by Georges May, Mark J. Temmer,
Jacques Guicharnaud, Raymond Giraud, Henri Pastoureau,
Pierre Klossowski, Jeremy Mitchell, J. H. Matthews, Joseph
H. McMahon, Michel Beaujour.

The Divine Sade, ed. Deepak N. Sawhney (Warwick: PLI-*Warwick
Journal of Philosophy*, 1994). Articles by Deepak N. Sawhney,
Stephen Pfohl, Annie Le Brun, Lucienne Frappier-Mazur,
Philippe Sollers, Margaret Crosland, Catherine Cusset, David
Allison, Kathy Acker.

SECONDARY SOURCES

BOOKS

Barthes, Roland. *Sade, Fourier, Loyola*. Paris: Le Seuil, 1971. English
translation: *Sade, Fourier, Loyola*, trans. Richard Miller. New
York: Hill and Wang, 1976.

Bataille, Georges. *L'Erotisme*. Paris: Editions de Minuit, 1957.
English translation: Mary Dalwood, *Eroticism*. San Francisco:
City Lights, 1986.

Blanchot, Maurice. *La Littérature et le mal*. Paris: Gallimard, 1957.
English translation: *Literature and Evil*, trans. Alastair Hamilton.
New York: Urizen, 1973.

Sade et Restif de la Bretonne. (1st edn. 1969) Brussels: Complexe, 1986.

Carter, Angela. *The Sadeian Woman: An Exercise in Cultural History*.
London: Virago, 1979. (Republished as *The Sadeian Woman and
the Ideology of Pornography*. New York: Pantheon, 1979.)

DeJean, Joan. *Literary Fortifications: Rousseau, Laclos, Sade*. Princeton:
Princeton University Press, 1984.

Deleuze, Gilles. *Présentation de Sacher-Masoch*. Paris: Editions de
Minuit, 1967.

Didier, Béatrice. *Sade: Une Ecriture du désir*. Paris: Denoël/Gonthier, 1976.

Favre, Pierre. *Sade utopiste: Sexualité, pouvoir et état dans le roman "Aline et Valcour"*. Paris: Presses Universitaires de France, 1967.

Gallop, Jane. *Intersections: A Reading of Sade with Bataille, Blanchot, and Klossowski*. Lincoln: University of Nebraska Press, 1981.

Gorer, Geoffrey. *The Life and Ideas of the Marquis de Sade*. New York: W. W. Norton & Co., 1962.

Hayman, Ronald. *De Sade, A Critical Biography*. New York: Crowell, 1978.

Heine, Maurice. *Le Marquis de Sade*. Paris: Gallimard, 1950.

Hénaff, Marcel. *Sade: L'invention du corps libertin*. Paris: Presses Universitaires de France, 1978.

Klossowski, Pierre. *Sade mon prochain*. Paris: Seuil, 1947. English translation: *Sade My Neighbor*, trans. Alphonso Lingis, Evanston: Northwestern University Press, 1991.

Laugaa-Traut, Françoise. *Lectures de Sade*. Paris: A. Colin, 1973.

Le Brun, Annie. *Les châteaux de la subversion*. Paris: Pauvert, 1986.

Soudain un bloc d'abîme, Sade. Paris: Pauvert, 1986.

Sade, aller et détours. Paris: Plon, 1989.

Lély, Gilbert. *Vie du Marquis de Sade*. Paris: Gallimard, 1952–7. Reprinted in Sade, *Oeuvres complètes*. Paris: Cercle du Livre Précieux, vols. I and II, 1962–6. Partial English translation: *The Marquis de Sade*, trans. Alec Brown. New York: Grove Press, 1970.

Lever, Maurice. *Donatien Alphonse François, Marquis de Sade*. Paris: Fayard, 1991. English translation: *Sade: A Biography*, trans. Arthur Goldhammer, New York: Farrar, Straus and Giroux, 1993.

(ed). *Bibliothèque Sade*, Vol. I, *Papiers de famille; le règne du père (1721–1760)*. Paris: Fayard, 1993.

Paulhan, Jean. *Le Marquis de Sade et sa complice, ou Les Revanches de la pudeur*. Brussels: Complexe, 1987.

Pauvert, Jean-Jacques. *Sade vivant*. Vol. I: *Une innocence sauvage 1740–1777*; Vol. II: *Tout ce qu'on peut concevoir dans ce genre-là. . .*; Vol. III: *Cet écrivain à jamais célèbre*. Paris: Laffont, 1986–90.

Roger, Philippe. *Sade: La philosophie dans le pressoir*. Paris: Grasset, 1976.

Thomas, Chantal. *Sade, l'œil de la lettre*. Paris: Payot, 1978.

Sade. Paris: Seuil, 1994.

ARTICLES

Blanchot, Maurice. "La raison de Sade," in *Lautréamont et Sade*. Paris: Gallimard, 1969. English translation: "Sade," trans. Richard

Seaver and Austryn Wainhouse, in The Marquis de Sade, *Justine, Philosophy in the Bedroom, and Other Writings*. New York, Grove Press, 1965, pp. 37–72.

de Beauvoir, Simone. "Faut-il brûler Sade?" (1955) Paris: Gallimard, 1972. English translation: "Must we burn Sade?", trans. Annette Michelson, in the Marquis de Sade, *The 120 Days of Sodom and Other Writings*. New York: Grove Press, 1966, pp. 3–64.

Foucault, Michel. "Préface à la transgression," in *Critique*, 195–6 (1963), pp. 751–70. English translation: "A preface to transgression," by D. Bouchard and S. Simon, in *Language, Counter Memory, Practice*, ed. Daniel Bouchard. Cornell University Press, 1977, pp. 29–52.

Harari, Josué. "Sade's discourse on method: rudiments for a theory of fantasy," *Modern Language Notes* 10, (1984), pp. 1057–71.

"D'une raison à l'autre: Le dispositif Sade," *Studies on Voltaire and the Eighteenth Century* 230 (1985), pp. 273–82.

Klossowski, Pierre. "Nature as Destructive Principle," trans. Joseph H. McMahon, in the Marquis de Sade, *The 120 Days of Sodom and Other Writings*. New York: Grove Press, 1966, pp. 65–86.

"Sade et Fourier," in *Les derniers travaux de Gulliver suivi de Sade et Fourier*. Montpellier: Fata Morgana, 1974. English translation: "The phantasms of perversion: Sade and Fourier," trans. Paul Foss and Paul Patton, in *Phantasms and Simulacra: The Drawings of Pierre Klossowski*, a special issue of *Art & Text* 18 (1985), ed. Paul Foss, Paul Taylor, and Allen S. Weiss, pp. 22–34.

Lacan, Jacques. "Kant avec Sade," in *Ecrits II*. Paris: Seuil, 1971, pp. 119–48. English translation: "Kant with Sade," trans. and annotated by James B. Swenson, Jr., *October* 51 (1989), pp. 55–75 (annotations pp. 76–104).

Miller, Nancy. "Justine, or the vicious circle," *Studies in Eighteenth Century Culture* 5 (1976), pp. 215–228.

Paulhan, Jean. "The Marquis de Sade and his accomplice," trans. Richard Seaver and Austryn Wainhouse, in The Marquis de Sade, *Justine, Philosophy in the Bedroom, and Other Writings*. New York, Grove Press, 1965, pp. 3–36.

Weiss, Allen S., "A new history of the passions," *October* 49. 1989, pp. 102–12. Reprinted in Allen S. Weiss, *The Aesthetics of Excess* (Albany: State University of New York Press, 1989), pp. 43–53.

Index

Cambridge Studies in French

General editor: Malcolm Bowie (*All Souls College, Oxford*)
Editorial Board: R. Howard Bloch (*University of California, Berkeley*),
Terence Cave (*St John's College, Oxford*), Ross Chambers (*University of
Michigan*), Antoine Compagnon (*Columbia University*), Peter France
(*University of Edinburgh*), Christie McDonald (*Harvard University*),
Toril Moi (*Duke University*), Naomi Schor (*Harvard University*)

Also in the series (* denotes titles now out of print)